LIBRA

LIBRA

Learning and Inquiry-Based Reuse Adoption

Sidney C. Bailin
Knowledge Evolution, Inc.

Mark A. Simos
Synquiry Technologies, Ltd.

Larry Levine
Change Management Consulting

Richard Creps
Lockheed Martin Corporation

IEEE Computer Society, *Sponsor*

The Institute of Electrical and Electronics Engineers, Inc., New York

This book and other books may be purchased at a discount
from the publisher when ordered in bulk quantities. Contact:

IEEE Press Marketing
Attn: Special Sales
445 Hoes Lane, P.O. Box 1331
Piscataway, NJ 08855-1331
Fax: +1 732 981 9334

For more information about IEEE Press products, visit the
IEEE Online Catalog & Store: http://www.ieee.org/ieeestore.

Printed in the United States of America.

10   9   8   7   6   5   4   3   2   1

ISBN 0-7803-6009-5
IEEE Order No. PP5859

Library of Congress Cataloging-in-Publication Data

Libra: learning and inquiry-based reuse adoption / Sidney C. Bailin... [et al.].
       p. cm.
    ISBN 0-7803-6009-5
    1. Computer software—Reusability.   I. Bailin, Sidney C.

QA76.76.R47 L53 2000
005.1—dc21

                                                        00-033487

CONTENTS

PREFACE

If software reuse is such a good idea, why does it not occur more often? With all the work over the past 20 years in software reusability—modularity, information hiding, object orientation, domain modeling, component-based development—and all the work on cost–benefit models, why is software reuse still more an idea than a reality? In this book we offer some answers and recommendations, drawing on ideas about learning organizations and knowledge-creating companies.

The book began life as a document funded by the Defense Advanced Research Projects Agency (DARPA) as part of its program in Software Technology for Adaptable, Reliable Software (STARS). The STARS program pursued a tripartite strategy comprising software reuse, process-driven development, and software development environments. As part of the reuse initiative, in 1995 the authors were chartered to write a reuse planning guidebook. Not typically for such tasks, we were allowed considerable latitude in deciding the best approach. We decided a new approach was needed, one that would augment the guidance already available by focusing on issues such as beliefs about reuse, organizational dynamics, and receptivity and resistance.

The authors brought varied backgrounds to the project. First and foremost we drew on our own and others' experiences in promoting reuse as developers in contractor and commercial software organizations, in contract research and development, and as external consultants. We had the benefit of a coauthor (Larry Levine) with considerable experience in organizational development, organizational learning, and change management. Exploring and unifying these viewpoints, we came to see software reuse as one aspect of the broader problem of organizational learning and knowledge creation in a software shop. This insight led us to rethink many assumptions about reuse adoption and its breakdowns, and the beliefs and practices of reuse advocates.

The resulting approach—Learning and Inquiry-Based Reuse Adoption, or LIBRA—was a radical departure from top-down, broad-based approaches. Initial response from our colleagues was encouraging. Readers said the document helped to surface difficult issues that had troubled them for some time, which they had assumed were specific to their situation. In our subsequent research and consulting, we applied and field-tested various versions of LIBRA. While it is not a formal, scientifically validated methodology, our recent work has reinforced its pragmatic value.

In revising the guidebook for commercial publication we have expanded, updated, and reorganized all the material. We focused the emphasis to complement rather than overlap other approaches. We view the book as a basis for experimentation, and a first step in a dialogue within and between the software reuse and organizational learning communities.

We see our contribution as threefold:

- As *theory*, it advances a new view of software reuse as a form of organizational learning.

- The example *content* of the book illustrates this view. It captures the authors' distillation of the experience of the software engineering community—filtered through our subjective perspective. This is both a key value and a limitation of the book. We owe the validity of our insights to the wisdom of the reuse community as a whole, and we apologize in advance for any failure to attribute specific ideas to the appropriate individuals. At the same time, any distortions, inaccuracies, or omissions are the responsibility of the authors.

- Finally, the book offers a repertoire of *techniques* so that readers can generate data for their own organizations. Although we provide guidance and suggestions for readers who want to try the techniques, we do not represent LIBRA as an established and scientifically validated methodology.

Sidney C. Bailin
Knowledge Evolution, Inc.

Mark A. Simos
Synquiry Technologies, Ltd.

Larry Levine
Change Management Consulting

Richard Creps
Lockheed Martin Corporation

ACKNOWLEDGMENTS

We thank Linda Brown and John Foreman of the STARS program, who sponsored the initial LIBRA work as well as earlier work that led to development of the concepts. We express our appreciation to colleagues who have contributed to or constructively critiqued the work in progress, especially Mike Webb of Lockheed Martin, Margaret Davis of Boeing, and Bruce Anderson of IBM. Finally, we thank the members of the working group at the 7th Workshop on Institutionalizing Software Reuse (WISR7) that formed the first pilot for these techniques: Ernesto Guerrieri, Wing Lam, Sadie Legard, Kathryn Yglesias, and Barbara Zimmer. On the production side, thanks to Paul H. Butler who developed the book's art work and graphics and to all the staff at IEEE Press for their enthusiasm in making the book a reality.

Sidney C. Bailin
Knowledge Evolution, Inc.

Mark A. Simos
Synquiry Technologies, Ltd.

Larry Levine
Change Management Consulting

Richard Creps
Lockheed Martin Corporation

LIST OF FIGURES

CHAPTER 1

INTRODUCTION

We begin by

- Summarizing what this book is about: key features of the LIBRA approach and the problems it aims to address.
- Describing the intended audience of the book and the benefits each type of reader should gain.
- Explaining the unusual style and structure of the book, and offering some tips for how to read and use it.

1.1 WHAT THIS BOOK IS ABOUT

1.1.1 The Problem

Software reuse is a multidisciplinary field concerned with the "art of not reinventing the wheel" in software development.

Progress in introducing reuse as a comprehensive practice within software organizations has been disappointing in many respects. Reuse advocates who have seen their efforts frustrated have long acknowledged the influence of organizational and cultural factors and the resistance of individual engineers as primary barriers to adoption of reuse practices. Though these well-known factors of culture, belief, and attitude are often used as explanations for the failure of reuse initiatives, they fall outside the scope of most systematic reuse planning processes. Lacking systematic ways to address issues of receptivity and resistance, reuse advocates too often fall into a mode of persuasion and exhortation, preaching the reuse gospel to recalcitrant and skeptical engineers and managers. In our experience, this style of interaction is self-defeating, fails to persuade most people to change their practices or their beliefs, and may even incite more resistance on the part of the unbelievers.

"

1.1.2   LIBRA: A Qualitatively Different Approach

In response to these problems, we have developed a new and different approach, which we call *Learning and Inquiry-Based Reuse Adoption*, or *LIBRA*. The central insight of this approach is that systematic reuse is one aspect of mature organizational learning in a software organization.

To transform an organization into one that exhibits such qualities, processes need to be established that allow software development knowledge to be more effectively shared, exchanged, refined—in short, reused—within the organization. In any given organization, attempts to introduce these processes and their associated interactions are met with a unique mix of receptivity and resistance that stems from people's beliefs, values, and concerns about knowledge sharing. Reuse can be both propelled and stalled by strong beliefs of software developers, managers, and users—beliefs about software, about organizations, and about people. Typically, conflicts in beliefs among people in an organization lead to a vicious cycle of advocacy and resistance.

To break this cycle, a different approach is needed: one based on *inquiry*, rather than advocating, preaching, or proselytizing the virtues and advantages of reuse as an abstract thing. Unlike the argumentative style of championing the reuse cause, inquiry requires an effort to model another's belief or perspective without judging it, or immediately comparing it to one's own, or trying to change it.

Inquiry, we believe, plays an essential role in reuse assessment and planning. You start by asking questions: What past history at that company has left people skeptical of such initiatives? How threatened do people feel that if they "spill the beans" and share their knowledge freely, their value to the company might be compromised? Maybe they'd even lose their job?

Besides deriving the necessary data for assessment, inquiry is often more effective than advocacy in producing real and lasting change in an organization. The importance of inquiry increases the more the desired change concerns beliefs and values rather than a simple transfer of information.

Inquiry is an integral part of the core interactions by which reuse happens on a day-to-day level in a software shop. Reuse happens when people have conversations to support learning and to codify knowledge—what we call *knowledge creation*—in addition to production goals. Other planning techniques can suggest who should hold the conversations and what their content should be: but inquiry is essential to the success of the conversations. Assessment, adoption, and sustained reuse are all linked through the common theme of inquiry.

1.1.3   LIBRA Tools and Techniques

As the name implies, LIBRA is an approach to reuse assessment, adoption, and practice in which learning and inquiry are key integrating principles. LIBRA starts from a view of systematic reuse as a form of organizational learning. The approach requires a close look at the culture and belief patterns of key individuals, the organization, and the proponents of reuse. This perspective allows us to address many real-world problems encountered in introducing reuse—problems not accounted for by strictly technical approaches, nor by approaches that emphasize the business case, nor by models that view reuse as a technology to be transferred.

To support these principles, we have selected, adapted, and integrated several conceptual tools. Some techniques were borrowed from the organizational learning field, some adapted from other sources, some newly minted. The tools stem from a common, learning-oriented view of software reuse. Each tool helps to improve skills for inquiry, reflection, and dialogue about software reuse opportunities. They are integrated into a tailorable, structured self-assessment framework that can be extended to include other techniques as well.

There are four major LIBRA tools, described in detail in Chapter 4:

- *Dramatic scenarios* are used to describe individual and organizational interactions. Scenarios help us see people not only in light of their structural roles within the organization, but also in terms of their beliefs, values, and personal interests as stakeholders. Dramatic scenarios help reuse change agents to develop the required observation and reflection skills to be able to read such situations clearly.

  Chapter 5 contains a hypothetical case study in the form of a dramatic scenario. The chapter includes an extended analysis of the case study, identifying both productive and problematic interactions among the characters. Although dramatic scenarios have proven useful in general change management contexts, they have seldom been applied to software reuse assessment. They were first piloted in a software context at the Seventh Workshop on Institutionalizing Reuse (WISR7) in 1995 [Lato96]. In developing the Chapter 5 scenario (and other similar ones) we gained substantial new knowledge about the process (both dos and don'ts). In this book we include guidance reflecting these experiences.

- *System diagrams* are used to illustrate patterns observed within scenarios. They depict a series of interactions (and perhaps forces that prevent interactions) linked together into a system that has persistence (it continues over time) and resistance (it cannot easily be changed). Resistance can be good or bad: sustainability or robustness for patterns we want to remain in place, stubbornness for patterns we want to change. We provide examples of interaction patterns at both the micro level (e.g., dramatized or idealized conversations) and at the macro level (larger strategic pictures of business settings, market forces, organizational structure).

  System diagrams are an established technique in other fields such as psychology and organizational development. Our use of them is particularly modeled on [Seng90], which vividly describes the workings of a *learning organization*.

- *Belief maps* describe relationships between diverse beliefs that individuals hold on a common topic. An individual belief can be thought of as an underlying theory someone uses in evaluating proposed plans or guiding personal actions. Beliefs exist within a network of supporting and conflicting beliefs. Belief mapping involves seeing beliefs in relation to each other. Achieving the ability to see your own beliefs within the map and understand their relationships with other beliefs is a significant reflective step.

  Our use of belief maps borrows from ideas in cultural anthropology and ethnography.

- *Inquiry techniques*: The Ladder of Inquiry is a framework for assessing the level of inquiry within conversations. It provides a way to keep conversations focused on areas of interest while cooling down interactions. People can then reflect and listen better, and discussion of *undiscussables* can take place. Inquiry techniques such as the ladder are essential for deriving the full value of the scenarios, system diagrams, and belief maps.

  The Ladder of Inquiry is an adaptation of the Ladder of Inference, introduced by Chris Argyris in his work on learning organizations [Argy92].

Together, scenarios, system diagrams, belief maps, and the Ladder of Inquiry can be used as an integrated, flexible toolkit for identifying important beliefs and interaction patterns, understanding how they may inhibit or enable reuse in your organization, and exploiting that understanding to improve reuse.

1.2   WHO SHOULD READ THIS BOOK

The book has a very practical focus. It is primarily targeted toward *reuse proponents*, that is, engineers, managers or technology advisers who are familiar with software development realities, are generally aware of major issues in reuse adoption, and are looking for practical strategies to help their companies (or clients) transition toward more systematic reuse. We offer advice and tips for introducing reuse into an organization gracefully and with lasting impact, by overcoming or avoiding the many forms of resistance that a proponent may encounter.

The book is very consciously and explicitly ***not*** intended to persuade readers about the benefits of systematic reuse. We omit much available data about the economic and other benefits of reuse. Our omission of such data does not imply that the data do not exist. Rather, the point of the book is to explore why reuse efforts sometimes fail after all such material has been presented (and even believed).

If you are a reuse proponent, after reading this book you should be able to:

- Recognize patterns of belief and behavior that serve as motivators or barriers to reuse adoption in your organization.

- Elicit and understand the evidence or experiences underlying those beliefs.

- Recognize your own beliefs within this repertoire of patterns and reflect on how those beliefs affect you in your role as a reuse proponent.
- Apply this understanding to create new interactions that foster, and in fact exemplify, reuse.

The book is applicable to a broad range of organizational settings. Proponents typically work (or consult) with an organization that acquires, develops, and/or maintains software-intensive systems as a critical or core process of its business operations. The setting could be a product development company, a services company where employee knowledge is the key asset, a government software acquisition organization, a government contractor with development or maintenance contracts, or a large bank or manufacturing company that develops and uses custom applications to support in-house operations. The approach can be applied in concert with virtually any technical software development method, including product-line architecture-based methods, web development, and knowledge management. It applies whenever software technology is driving fundamental change in business strategies or processes.

Software engineers and managers new to the reuse field, interested as potential advocates or because they are making reuse technology purchase decisions, will gain a perspective that allows them to assess the claims and beliefs of reuse proponents. Those concerned with more general software engineering management (managers, supervisors, and consultants) will gain a better understanding of how reuse dovetails, overlaps, and contrasts with other organizational change and productivity approaches.

Even reuse skeptics should find this book useful. It will help them to articulate the basis for their skepticism. The principle of inquiry should allow reuse skeptics to make their case more effectively to reuse proponents. It is quite possible that for their organization and context, their skepticism is justified.

This book does not presume in-depth knowledge of software development, organizational learning, or the history of software reuse; neither does it provide a thorough introduction to any of these fields. The discussion focuses on organizational concepts and experiences, not on the nuts and bolts of software development. Some exposure to the language and concepts of software reuse will be helpful, but is not essential. Some examples will be difficult to follow in detail without a software background. This is partly because we wanted the dialogues to be representative of the actual conversations that take place in a software shop. But since technical details are not the substance of the method or the unique contribution, we do not provide references for many technical terms or acronyms, and readers can skim such sections without missing the most important points.

We provide some references to the organizational learning field, but the book is not intended as an introduction to this area for software developers, any more than it is a primer about software engineering management for the non-software-oriented reader. Techniques we have borrowed or adapted can be used with minimal preparation. We give credit where appropriate to sources for these ideas and techniques, but do not present the ideas in depth beyond what is needed for their practical use in LIBRA.

1.3 HOW TO READ THIS BOOK

This book offers reuse proponents a fresh perspective on factors underlying a number of well-known breakdowns and barriers in reuse. It may help reveal tacit assumptions in their own approach and ways in which these can lead to counterproductive efforts. We hope it will also provide guidance in developing and implementing strategies that allow reuse to flourish.

Toward this end, we intend the book to be read and used as a practical field guide. It will be most effective if read, then actively used. We recommend that you treat the tools as starting points for constructing your own descriptions of current and desired behaviors, and identifying meaningful next steps to take. The dialogues, scenarios, and example models reflect the authors' personal experiences; the specific example scenarios and interpretations should not be treated as an integral and inseparable part of the assessment techniques. They are intended only as seeds or catalysts to help you create and capture the knowledge most relevant and accurate for your own organization.

The style in which this book is written is unusual for a nonfiction book about a technical subject. Much of the content of the book is presented in the form of fictionalized dramatic dialogues or scenarios. It is important to understand the intent behind each chapter and the motivation for this unusual format. Here is a roadmap:

- Chapter 1 (this chapter) provides an overview of the LIBRA approach, describes the book's intended audience and objectives, and outlines how to use the book.

- Chapter 2 provides historical background for our approach. In effect it presents the problem: where the reuse field is today, how it got there, and some of the breakdowns in reuse advocates' strategies. This chapter is presented as a dialogue between multiple characters with varying backgrounds, set at a reuse conference; the dialogue form allows us to present a variety of perspectives about the reuse field.

  We encourage you to read Chapter 2 regardless of whether you are already familiar with the history of software reuse. If you are familiar with the field, use the chapter as an opportunity to model your own beliefs and to recognize how these might influence your interaction style or your expectations about change.

- Chapter 3 continues the dialogue to describe the conceptual foundations of LIBRA. Characters in the dialogue discuss the core LIBRA concepts: software development as knowledge creation, the central role of beliefs, and the role of inquiry in reuse assessment, adoption, and practice.

- Chapter 4 explains the core LIBRA *tools:* a repertoire of techniques for applying the LIBRA concepts conveyed in Chapter 3. Some of the tools borrow heavily from techniques of organizational learning consultants. However, the LIBRA tools are our own adaptation and do not necessarily conform to any other theory of organizational learning.

- Chapter 5 presents a fictional case study and a set of commentaries. This chapter is a play within a play: the scenario is developed by the fictional conference attendees as a LIBRA practice session. The case study and commentary offer insight into a variety of adoption barriers, and how they can be identified, analyzed, and overcome. While it illustrates the use of the LIBRA tools, it is itself a tool: you can use the scenario and commentary as part of your own internal assessment effort.

- In Chapter 6, we move from assessment to adoption. While the LIBRA approach to assessment is built around the reading or creating of a scenario and its collaborative analysis, reuse adoption in LIBRA is founded on the idea of reuse-promoting interactions. We create the neologism "reuseful" to describe such interactions. The chapter offers perspectives on interaction patterns characteristic of reuseful organizations. In assessment, the conversations are *about* reuse in the organization; in adoption, inquiry skills are integrated into the business of software development—a bottom-up organizational change strategy.

- Chapter 7 provides guidance for how to use the tools (e.g., how to develop and use your own dramatic scenarios) and how to integrate and use them in concert.

- Chapter 8, a brief conclusion to the book, summarizes the LIBRA approach, examines its potential impact, and suggests areas for further work.

- The References and Recommended Reading sections include all references cited in the book, as well as other resources we recommend if you want to learn more about LIBRA-related topics.

Exercise

We close this introductory chapter by suggesting an exercise to clarify your own roles, beliefs, and perspectives. Making this knowledge more explicit should give you a firmer foundation for appreciating the material and for experimenting introspectively with the LIBRA techniques.

We encourage you to ponder the following questions (and perhaps others more specific to your situation) before proceeding to the next chapter. You may find it valuable to revisit them at times while reading the book (e.g., at the end of each chapter or every time you gain an important new insight).

- Take a moment to describe yourself in terms of our assumptions about our readers. How would you characterize your beliefs and values about reuse (as you understand it)? Are you a reuse proponent? A skeptic? Neither? Both?

- How would you characterize your organization and your role or position within the organization? Are you a decision maker or in the trenches? Do you have a sense that your personal initiative could lead to more systematic exploration of reuse opportunities within the organization?

- If you are a reuse proponent: Can you recall an interaction you had with someone in the organization who did not know the reuse "lingo"? With someone whose beliefs appeared to present a barrier to reuse within the organization? Were these interactions successful, in your opinion? Why or why not?

- If you are new to reuse or consider yourself a skeptic: What are some of the claims you have heard that most incite your resistance? What experiences have you had that strongly shaped your opinions about the feasibility of systematic reuse?

CHAPTER 2

PERSPECTIVES
ON THE PROBLEM

We now present the *problem:* where the reuse field is today, how it got there, and some of the breakdowns in reuse advocates' strategies for fostering the transition to more systematic reuse.

To liven things up, the chapter is presented as a fictional multicharacter dialogue, set at a fictional reuse conference.

As you read the dialogue, place yourself within the matrix of beliefs that are voiced, and think through the consequences such beliefs would have on strategies for introducing reuse.

2.1 THE SCENE

At the December 1998 Annual Conference on Software Reuse held in New Orleans, participants have just attended a panel entitled: "Whither Reuse: A 30-Year Perspective After the 1968 NATO Conference." Several prominent figures in the reuse field spoke on the panel, several of them with an air of pessimism. Now everyone is at dinner. At the table a large party is assembled, ranging from graduate students quite new to the reuse field to old-timers who have been involved for many years.

2.2 THE CAST OF CHARACTERS

Rudy: A graduate student who has come to the conference with little background in reuse. He has some experience as a programmer, but mostly has done HTML and VisualBasic hacking.

Hans: A software developer, interested in Java, dynamic languages, and generative approaches to reuse, such as Aspect-Oriented Programming.

Figure 2-1   We describe the problem through a dialogue between reuse advocates.

Cassandra: University professor and well-known guru in the object-oriented field.

Paula: A reuse advocate in a large commercial software product environment. She is moving more and more into the framework of organizational learning and knowledge management. She has brought Jack to the conference to expose other colleagues to someone with in-depth expertise in organizational learning.

Jack: A consultant and trainer with a strong background in organizational development and change management. He has had some experience working with software organizations from a management consulting perspective.

2.3   THE INITIAL CONFLICT: TECHNICAL VERSUS MANAGEMENT SOLUTIONS

Hans: I'm perplexed. I came to this conference expecting to find like-minded spirits: people who believe that Java, mobile code, and aspect-oriented programming finally provide us the technology to make reusable components a reality. But all you people are dwelling on is this soft stuff—general management issues about adopting new technology.

Paula: Most of us have learned from experience that the nontechnical issues are the real stumbling blocks. There are always more technical issues to be solved, but even with current technology we could reuse far more than we do. Why don't we? We've seen a succession of silver-bullet technologies come and go, each touted as the key to higher productivity in software development. With each one, the promises were eventually deflated and the nontechnical issues cropped up again.

Hans: But introducing technology is the cleanest way of fostering organizational change. People start using a tool because it's there; then it starts encouraging them to think in new and different ways. When these come in conflict with the host organization, there may be some initial struggle, but in the end the technology always wins. At the end of the day, people would rather have a tool than some set of fuzzy and intrusive guidelines.

Rudy: What's most exciting is the advent of the Web, and widespread component interconnection infrastructures like CORBA. We can finally begin to do what the reuse visionaries have been touting all these years. The new technology offers a whole different type of reusable component, comparatively fine-grained and adaptable to diverse contexts. It is even possible to link components dynamically at run time, so that the decision to reuse can occur much later in the life cycle. What used to be a feature of research languages is now emerging as the computing paradigm of choice for the Web.

Paula: But surely the nontechnical issues deserve some scrutiny. Face it: the reuse community comprises two factions, the technical and management sides. Each questions whether the concerns of the other are keys to reuse. That goes for you too, Hans. I've heard the technical discussions about *design for reuse*, but I can never pin down how this is anything more than applying someone's favorite method of software engineering. Object-oriented techniques are fine for writing good OO programs. But that's not the same as reuse!

2.3.1   Origins of the Reuse Field

Jack: Speaking as an outsider: How did these factions emerge?

Paula: Reuse as a field goes back to 1968, when Doug McIlroy issued his call for a software components industry. By the time I joined the stream, in the early 1980s, the two factions were starting to emerge.

Cassandra: There were some technical heavyweights working on knowledge-based approaches: program generators, meta-generators, application-specific languages, transformation systems.

Hans: Many people thought that Ada would be the answer, with a comprehensive set of domain-specific packages. People worried about how many parameters made for a good reusable component, how to document reusable code, and what should be in a standard header. It seemed like all you needed for reusable code was careful documentation of the original context and impeccable program design skills.

Paula: But reuse didn't magically happen. So there was a gradual shift from technical issues to procedural stuff, like staffing a reuse library group, and certification standards. People acknowledged that something was broken at the highest levels of system acquisition practice: economic, business, legal, and data rights issues.

Hans: But then a reuse wave hit, with a rapid acceleration of technology. Whereas Ada had always appealed to a specialized community, the object-oriented revolution got many people talking and thinking about reuse.

Cassandra: The patterns community offered a loose, knowledge-gathering, design-level form of reuse that was easily grasped and transferred. Concern with frameworks, hot spots, and object-oriented architectures all started making people aware that reuse across multiple systems wouldn't be free. The spectacle of massive C++ libraries built with OO but with no systematic reuse processes in place disillusioned some people about OO; but it convinced others that maybe there was something to the reuse story that wasn't just good OO design.

Hans: The component-based software industry put a new twist on things. Suddenly component meant something more than "module" and even something more than a "managed asset" in a corporate-wide reuse repository. It meant code that could be brokered in a wide-open software marketplace of component providers, integrators, infrastructure providers, et cetera.

Paula: But the hype caught up with us. It became clear that institutionalizing reuse was a strategic business decision that must be motivated with a business case. Reuse advocates started working on how to build the right business case. We realized that technology alone would sell it only to other technologists. But if a clear cost–benefit case could be made for reuse and the perceived risk were sufficiently low, management might decide to initiate it.

Jack: So is that where the debate stands?

2.3.2 Reuse as Technology Transfer

Paula: No, we got smarter still. We acknowledged that even a compelling business case for a reuse initiative might be rejected.

Cassandra: Then we started looking at the technology transfer issues. There is a vast base of theory and practical knowledge about technology transfer and innovation diffusion.

Jack: So reuse is basically technology transfer?

Cassandra: OO definitely requires technology transfer. Let's face it: in most organizations today, reuse is happening in tandem with the shift to OO.

Figure 2-2   Jack questions the terms of the debate.

Paula: I beg to differ. Many people migrated to OO in hopes of making gains in reuse, only to be disappointed. Reuse is as elusive as ever.

Jack: One conflict I'm hearing in your discussion is the starting belief that reuse is a technology in the first place. Some of you seem to believe that, and frame the problem in those terms. But I just don't see how reuse is a technology. Reuse seems to me to be a set of organizational practices, a particular pattern of learning or knowledge-creating interactions that happen in a stable and persistent way in an organization. Making that kind of shift is simply not a technology transfer problem. Or rather, that frame doesn't capture most of what's interesting, unique, or challenging about that shift.

Paula: I'd go a step further. Part of what makes technology transfer hard is that it's a *push*. People feel the technology is being foisted on them from management, or some technology consultant who has the ear of management; they can't connect the technology with an urgent need they can perceive. But engineers in the trenches *can* perceive the need for reuse; they're the ones who are staying up until midnight trying to get systems put together under time pressure, when systematic support for reuse might make their job easier. I guess they can't see the connection between that need and the technology brought in to do the fix; or they don't believe it will really help.

Jack: So what I'd claim is that when you go in as a reuse advocate and push a particular technology, you might actually create *more resistance* to reuse adoption. You're literally working against yourself. And even if you apply all the clever insights the field has to offer about how to do technology transfer, you will still be digging a hole for yourself, because you've allowed the *goal* of reuse to get confused with the *means,* which happens to be, in a particular setting, a particular supporting technology.

Hans: So what do we do instead? If you take away the technology angle, what you're left with is advocating some wholesale restructuring of the organization, a kind of business process reengineering (BPR). Isn't that just as likely to incite resistance as the technology push?

2.3.3 Shifting the Emphasis to Knowledge Management

Jack: Part of what's going in here is the underlying *metaphors* we're using. Just think about what's conjured by "adoption," "transfer," or "technology insertion." I hate to be graphic here, but see how the imagery we use suggests putting something external into the environment of the organization? Whereas it seems to me that, with reuse, you're talking more about mining the knowledge that's already been created *in* the organization and drawing it out.

Hans: Or at least distributing it more effectively, laterally within that same organization. And possibly outside the organization as well—not proprietary knowledge, of course.

Paula: One disturbing trend I've seen is the very way we toss around the term "reuse." What bothers me is that the term loses all connection with the relevant practices, technologies, and processes in an organization. We talk about how we need to "do more reuse," "adopt reuse," "transition to reuse." Maybe it's just a linguistic peccadillo of mine, but I think the sloppiness of our language indicates some fundamental fuzziness in our thinking.

Reuse isn't something you "do." Nor can one "adopt reuse." Yet the reuse community allows and even encourages this way of speaking of reuse. I think it helps legitimize the social forms of our community. We all come together to talk about reuse. These forms might be threatened if we dissolved the monolithic label "reuse" back into constituent and possibly even conflicting elements. You could call this the *reification of reuse.*

Jack: Reification creates both a distancing and an objectification of the theme. This can encourage cooptation, that is, hanging ancillary and even conflicting agendas on the reuse bandwagon. The more the term "reuse" becomes an unexamined label within the community—a semaphore or a shorthand—the more people with fundamentally different belief systems and stakeholder interests can use the term blindly. They may not even realize how little they understand each other.

Figure 2-3   Paula laments the reification of reuse.

Rudy: So is reuse, by definition, always the pot of gold that the next technology shift will help us find? If we keep getting our hopes dashed, shouldn't we ask whether we're missing an essential part of the problem?

Paula: Look at it this way. No matter where a company's horizon of planning is, reuse advocates come along and say, "You're thinking too narrowly." In a way, they'll always be right and they'll always be wrong! You can always point to economies of scope that you could gain by thinking more long term, just like a programmer can always find a way to further parameterize a routine. But there are always practical limits to how much of this long-term thinking you can really do. Maybe we've fallen into a pattern of always asking organizations to do what they aren't yet capable of doing. Maybe that's our role!

Jack: When we looked at the technology side, we saw a continuing pattern of the reuse advocates attaching themselves to the latest technology as the answer to the reuse problem. Now, on the management side, we have found a similar recurring pattern. To advocate reuse in a company is to demand long-term, strategic, optimizing thinking that is beyond what they can currently tolerate doing.

You have success and impact by getting a few people to go along with the visionary plan. You sign on a couple of empire-building middle managers, a few starry-eyed technical idealists fresh out of Ph.D.

programs, a "don't bother me with the details" high-level champion who gets the big picture but doesn't see the barriers. You start a project, you get good results. Then the immediate results get picked up but not the continuing practice. Or the results vanish into the black hole of successful and forgotten projects. Or there is a backlash, and the organization snaps back to the old way of doing things.

Hans: I thought I was cynical! You paint a bleak picture for an outsider who just sauntered in here.

Paula: Yes, Jack, the way you describe it is very depressing! Have we been barking up the wrong tree all this time?

Rudy: What's depressing to me is that this picture cuts right through the argument about technology versus management. It's as if both sides of the fence have fallen into recurring patterns that ensure they will never actually succeed, or will define success away once it's attained.

Cassandra: Even the argument about technology-versus-management solutions to reuse looks like a form of denial.

Jack: Let's review where we've come with this conversation. First, we've told a story about the progression of thinking in the reuse field. That progression led to some insights about ineffective patterns into which reuse advocates have fallen. We've stumbled on the notion that the reuse drama involves *perennially asking of organizations more than they can give!* There is a self-defeating element in the way that the case for reuse is made. This is not just a matter of packaging: it is built into the rhetoric of the field.

That must be a scary thought for someone who's made a career in this field. But at the same time it offers some hope of shifting things. I have some ideas about how we can look at the whole problem in a different light to get out of the old ruts. Why don't we follow up on this at a Birds of a Feather session tomorrow?

CHAPTER 3

LIBRA CONCEPTUAL FOUNDATIONS

We now present the core LIBRA concepts. After reading this chapter you will have new ways of assessing organizational receptiveness and resistance to learning and knowledge creation.

3.1 THE SYMPOSIUM DIALOGUE CONTINUES

The morning after the preceding dialogue, Jack presents his introductory remarks at the Birds of a Feather session on "Reuse as Knowledge Creation." His message: thinking about reuse as a knowledge creation problem makes it easier to understand the competencies required for sustainable reuse and the challenges that arise in reuse adoption.

3.1.1 Reuse as Technology Transfer in Reverse

Jack: I am going to offer a new way of thinking about reuse—as a problem in organizational learning or knowledge creation. To make my case, I first want to review some of the theories about reuse that I've heard espoused by reuse advocates, either in terms of their own convictions or their reporting of others' views. We sat around the dinner table last night and heard quite a crisscross of opinions. I'll use these complementary views as an example of something I call *belief modeling,* which I'll talk about later, a way of articulating the mental models people use as they reason about situations, models that can be shared and tacit (hence almost invisible), or divergent and a source of miscommunication and conflict.

- **Reuse as a technical problem.** I'm imagining an archetypal reuse advocate, let's say a recent computer science graduate who takes on a real-world programming job and quickly sees how inefficient the software development process is. Armed with elegant approaches from his university training, he sees many opportunities for applying object-oriented techniques, component-based technology, generators, et cetera. He sees reuse as a technical problem. It's so blindingly obvious: of course he assumes that if he makes the technical case to others, the motivation and potential savings will be clear.

Strangely, he encounters resistance to adopting these fine schemes. The first loss of innocence may come in trying to introduce reuse within the organization at a nontrivial scale. Nontechnical issues begin to surface, such as short-sighted managers and a "get the job out the door as quickly as possible" mentality. Attention to these nontechnical issues is grudging at first; they are annoyances that obscure the central, technical merits of reuse.

- **Reuse as an economic problem.** Gradually our hero realizes that reuse requires an up-front investment, someone has to make that investment, and this someone has project-specific accountability that provides no budget for such an investment. Making the case for reuse thus involves an economic argument that the company will save money by building a set of reusable *assets*. This newfound wisdom leads to its own form of naïveté: the notion that if a clear cost–benefit case can be presented for reuse, rational management (a phrase some might call oxymoronic!) will initiate it.

- **Reuse as a technology transfer problem.** Experience shows that even these rational business cases are not always persuasive, and when they are, and initiatives are undertaken, they may not succeed. There are other factors to be considered. So our advocate begins to draw on the theory of transferring new technology to explain the barriers and resistance to reuse.

Framing reuse adoption as a technology transfer problem makes sense to the extent that reuse involves acquiring or developing a specific technology or set of technologies (e.g., object-oriented development methods, a software repository infrastructure, application generation techniques). But I'm going to argue that these are merely means to an end, or rather, they can be taken as supporting evidence of commitment to reuse.

Furthermore, reuse as technology transfer applies a fundamentally flawed and unhelpful metaphor for reuse: the metaphor of some external material that must be "transferred," "inserted into," or "adopted by" an organization. This diverts focus from the software assets and knowledge developed within the organization itself, technology that the organization could transfer more effectively both internally and externally.

Thus it might be more accurate to think of reuse as *technology transfer in reverse*. The significant transfer in systematic reuse is from the inside out, that is, from the organization to the surrounding environment, rather than from the outside in. Reuse captures and more effectively disseminates technology (or more generally, the competencies, expertise, knowledge) that emerges *within* an organization. It's about the celebration and systematization of local software culture: making technology that has been buried and hidden *within* an organization more widely visible throughout, as well as outside, that organization.

Any questions or comments so far?

Hans: I find this notion that reuse is all about legacy technology very disquieting. I mean, all the reasons I thought I was involved in reuse as a discipline revolve around advanced technology: generative techniques as an alternative to strict OO, the whole notion of component-based architectures, et cetera. If we don't have new software engineering techniques to share in order to make reuse a reality, what kind of contribution are we making?

Rudy: Yes, according to this definition of reuse I could reuse old COBOL code and be doing systematic reuse! I mean, not all local software culture is good software culture, right?

Paula: But I see Jack's point. Not all good software culture is local software culture, either. We're not saying those are bad technologies to introduce; just that when you do you'll face technology transfer issues but won't necessarily trigger the dynamics of reuse, no matter how much the technology you're introducing may seem to be about the activity of reuse.

Cassandra: So, let me see. If I introduce OO technology, you're saying the challenge of getting people to use a shared class library is not a systematic reuse problem?

Jack: Getting people to use a specific new library you've introduced is a technology transfer problem. Getting them to reuse libraries they create themselves, or to seek out class libraries they can reuse, is a *technology transfer in reverse* problem.

Paula: I get it. What makes it reuse is a certain movement of the knowledge with respect to the boundaries of the organization. Essentially, systematic reuse is a movement that must be initiated from *within* the organization; it may propagate laterally, or out of the organization. You may want supporting technology to help sustain that flow of information; and that technology may be brought in from outside, via traditional technology transfer. But that's not the same as the knowledge or technology that will flow via the reuse channel.

Jack: Right. Adoption of technology that supports or facilitates reuse is instrumental, but not central, to the change process. Reuse support tech-

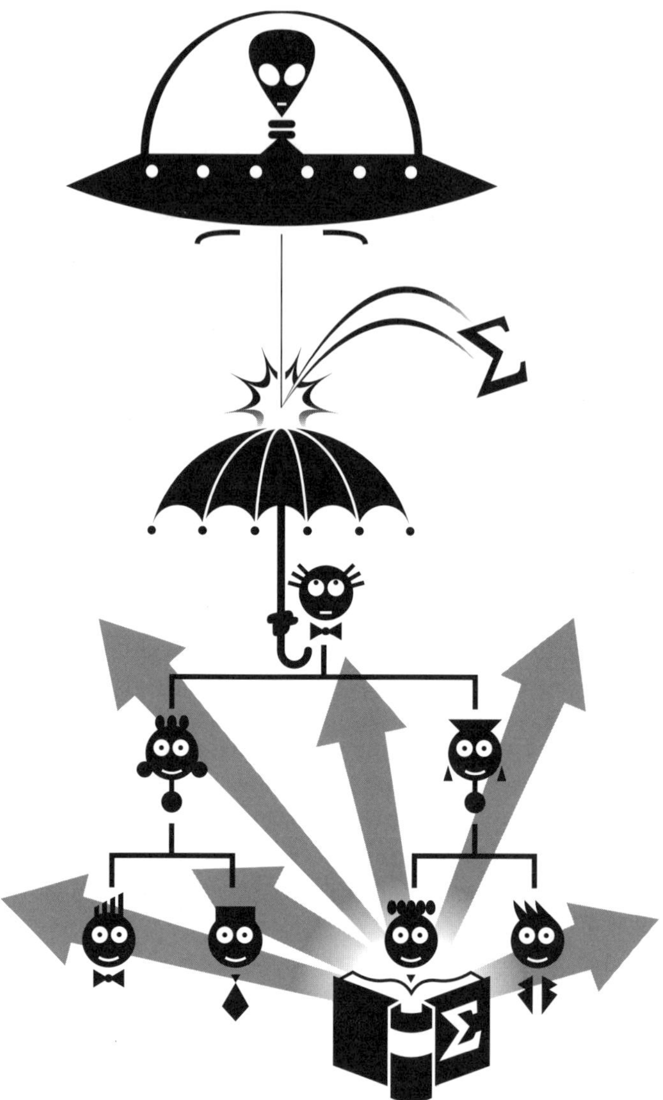

Figure 3-1   Reuse can be thought of as technology transfer in reverse.

nology makes it easier for people to share knowledge more effectively with each other. But the primary change is organizational, involving the transfer of knowledge and the establishment of new channels of communication within and across groups in the organization. As far as the problem of reusing poor local practice: if the process is truly systematic, then some way of vetting the quality of the material to be reused has to be in place. That's part of what makes it hard.

Paula: Surely, though, being open to reusing components from outside the organization is just as important an aspect of sustainable reuse practice. You make it sound as if reuse would thrive in a atmosphere rife with NIH—the "not invented here" syndrome. But in fact that attitude discourages reuse, not just of things from outside the organization, but of things from elsewhere in the organization. Since willingness to reuse assets is as important as the discipline of producing those assets, I would think reuse should include looking for components *outside* as well. Otherwise you might build the wrong assets.

Jack: Fair comments. But *the looking itself comes from within*. It might be more accurate to say that technology transfer issues are only part of the story of reuse, not the whole story. TT focuses only on transfer flowing in one direction, outside in, whereas reuse is about a balanced set of flows, into and out of the organization, laterally as well. There can be different factors of resistance and beliefs that affect different flows.

Paula: I see some advantages right off the bat. This approach places reuse proponents more in the position of facilitators than persuaders, allies for technical people in the trenches who may have had difficulty communicating their insights to their own managers. It can help reverse the power relationships that are typically perceived when reuse initiatives are started. Reuse is often presented to software developers in a way that leads them to believe it is just another management fad imposed from above, subject to abrupt and arbitrary changes. Instead, it can be presented as—no, it is—a way to legitimize and support the developers' knowledge. That approach invites commitment, buy-in, and ownership on the part of those whose involvement is crucial.

Rudy: So you're saying that this is all a fancy form of PR, using the rhetoric of empowerment to help sell reuse within the organization?

Paula: Ouch!

Jack: I think the spirit of Dilbert™ just visited us, and there's some truth in the sting. For example, this kind of argument could be used by managers to shift the responsibility for reuse down to the trenches, as a grassroots activity, and then ensure that the needed resources and management support are lacking. Saying the knowledge comes from within the organization, maybe even at the grassroots level, doesn't mean that all the required commitment comes from that sector.

3.1.2   Reuse as Knowledge Creation

Jack: This picture I've given of technology transfer in reverse is really just a way to get us thinking in a different way about reuse. What kind of process is it? What do we know about it? My theory is that the problem is most usefully thought of as *organizational learning taking place within a software firm.*

In a learning organization, learning activities are explicitly supported and managed alongside direct production activities. (Plain BPR won't get you there; in a learning organization, learning is viewed as equal in importance to direct production.) Emphasis on making results of learning explicit and codified is central to systematic reuse: *reuse is systematic learning about software development processes and products, and codification of that learning in explicit, shared forms that are made accessible to the organization.* Systematic reuse is thus one natural outcome of a software organization that is becoming more of a learning organization.

Rudy: What's the difference between a learning organization and a knowledge-creating organization? I've heard you use both terms as if they're interchangeable.

Jack: The definitions aren't strict. But you could draw a distinction in degree. Where a learning organization might still treat learning activities as mere process improvement activities (perhaps very important ones), a *knowledge-creating* organization [Nona91, Nona95] would consider systematic learning as strategic. It's a more radical version of a learning organization; a knowledge-creating organization, as I use the term, recognizes creation of new knowledge as an integral part of every work process and makes the capture of such knowledge central to its mission and business model.

Of course, we're accustomed to thinking of certain organizations as producing and consuming knowledge: R&D groups or university settings, for example. But in most business settings, the generation of new knowledge within the work process has traditionally been viewed as a by-product of the core processes of providing a service, fulfilling a contract, or developing and marketing a product. The idea that knowledge creation is central to the daily activities of all or most departments and individuals in the workplace is quite new. Escalating business pressures are forcing organizations to rely more on producing new knowledge, applying it systematically, and expanding their capacity through learning.

When I talk about software reuse as knowledge creation I don't just mean the fact that you can reuse more than code; or that unless you capture surrounding contextual knowledge you can't reuse even code the right way. I mean more: *for reuse to work, people must interact in ways that support knowledge creation.* Three concepts are useful to recognize how these common interactions create knowledge:

- **Knowledge is more than information.** Most interactions are not just exchanges of information; they involve creation of new knowledge. This often happens so automatically or at such a fine-grained level that we do not recognize the knowledge-creating aspects of the interactions. For example, in the software field we often overlook or discount the kind of knowledge created when people in a software group recognize that they are designing similar interfaces for different products, or that a customer proposal has close similarity to one that was bid two years earlier.

- **Knowledge is socially situated.** New knowledge is created when people interact. That is, knowledge creation is not merely a matter of identifying and debriefing isolated experts within the organization. Knowledge resides within sustained networks of interactions. This is a lesson learned in software company acquisitions, where software systems treated as tangible (and transferable) assets prove to be highly dependent on the web of informal knowledge held by the development or maintenance team.

- **Knowledge is often invisible.** The most important things we know are often those things we know so well that we don't know we know them (i.e., "second-nature" knowledge). This problem is central to systematic reuse: the attempt to reuse an artifact created for one system context reveals hidden contextual dependencies that were not noted by the original developers. Progress occurs when this invisible knowledge gets raised to awareness.

Rudy: How would this apply in a software development environment?

Jack: The position could be stated in the following way:

> "This company (division/group) knows a lot about building—oh, say handheld devices. Up until now management has counted on informal ways of transferring this knowledge from developer to developer. If we provide supporting infrastructure to make this knowledge transfer a legitimate and valued part of everyone's job, we will be better able to capitalize on this corporate expertise.
>
> We may even be able to market this expertise externally in ways that are not yet evident to us. Right now we think of ourselves as primarily a product (or service, or contract)-driven business. If we make our *knowledge* a core part of our business identity, we will be better able to grow new services out of existing products and new products out of existing services, and to use our experience as leverage for new contracts."

3.1.3   Reuse as a Belief System

Hans: Suppose we were willing to accept this basic premise: that when we try to encourage reuse, we're really trying to encourage knowledge sharing among software engineers; and that this is a hard task in any company, but particularly among software engineers, who tend to be the skeptical, "I'll do it myself" kind of people. How does this insight help us make reuse happen any more effectively than we're doing it right now? What exactly does this buy us?

Jack: The short answer is that you get a better understanding of why people don't want to do it! And maybe some insights into how you can bring about conditions under which they are more receptive to reuse as a knowledge-creating activity.

To get at what I mean, let me ask another question. When you are trying to persuade people about the advantages of reuse, do you often run into the same recurring attitudes and points of skepticism?

Hans: Sure, software engineers and managers tend to have strongly held ideas about the viability of reuse. Some of these ideas are based on technical ideas (e.g., how hard it is to code a reusable component in a given programming language); some are based on ideas about organizations and management (e.g., project managers will never be willing to pay for the extra effort it takes to make a module reusable beyond their project's scope).

Jack: Some ideas can be considered *beliefs* ("how I think the world/this organization is, whether I like it or not") and some reflect *values* ("how I think the world ought to be"). Values in turn can reflect perceived stakeholder *interests* ("what outcome I think would benefit me the most"). Beliefs, values, and interests may overlap and diverge in all kinds of subtle ways. When you talk about fostering knowledge creation, you are talking about changes at these fundamental levels. And that is very, very hard.

Paula: Perhaps this is a reason so many reuse proponents fall into persuasion mode as they attempt to be good reuse change agents—attempting to persuade short-sighted managers, argue with skeptical engineers, or temper the certainty of devotees of various methods claiming to solve the reuse problem.

Cassandra: Of course, maybe we like being the voices crying in the wilderness. Maybe part of being a member of the reuse community involves a commitment to resist any method's claim to solve the reuse problem. Because if the problem were solved, our community would go away.

3.1.4   Reuse Adoption as Shifts in Beliefs

Jack: Once you accept that the change you are trying to create is toward a knowledge-creating enterprise, it becomes easier to understand some of the resistance that advocates run into. You are not just dealing with a body of knowledge that must be transferred. You are dealing with belief systems. For people to be willing to change their work practices, they must first or simultaneously change their belief systems.

Reuse proponents generally assume that much of the work of reuse adoption lies in *conveying information* to people about hidden costs of development without reuse and the benefits of systematic reuse. But software engineers and managers have strongly held ideas about the viability of reuse. This being the case, to motivate people within organizations to adopt reuse-based practices, we must do more than present them with new information. Systematic reuse requires organizational changes that challenge people to shift deeply held beliefs and values.

Paula: This sounds familiar. The importance of beliefs in reuse adoption is by no means a new idea. The transition to reuse is often described as a paradigm shift or a change of mind-set implying a shift in beliefs. Reuse literature is full of anecdotal mention of beliefs that create barriers to reuse adoption. For example, the oft-cited NIH syndrome.

But there have been few empirical studies done to examine the beliefs held by engineers or managers that create motivators or barriers to reuse. There's been even less examination of the possible legitimacy of those beliefs; and still fewer guidelines to aid reuse proponents in shifting beliefs.

Jack: And there's another twist: the belief of the reuse advocates themselves—a complex set of assumptions, not only about reuse, but about organizational change, programmers' beliefs, their validity, and how those beliefs change. The advocates' folklore is tacitly reflected in the reuse success stories, economic arguments, and "myths to be refuted" offered as source material for persuading people about the benefits of reuse. These beliefs have not been critically examined, but they dramatically affect the quality of the interactions between reuse proponents and other people in their organizations.

3.1.5   Inquiry Versus Advocacy

Paula: Suppose we accept all this. Reuse is technology transfer is reverse, reuse is knowledge creation; knowledge creation depends on beliefs; and people's belief systems are hard to change. On some level we've always known we're trying to change people's attitudes and beliefs. As I said, systematic reuse is often spoken of as a shift of mind-set, beliefs, and values, a change in the way software is developed. In doing so, we frame the task in a way that invites resistance and creates unnecessary obstacles. So what should we do, as reuse advocates?

Jack: My work is founded on the idea that the most effective means of organizational transformation is not to entertain a fixed agenda for how beliefs should change, but to foster situations that help reveal implicit beliefs and make them more discussable and open to examination. This opens options for people to choose the best course of action and their best future.

To encourage desired shifts in underlying beliefs, advocacy—persuasion and argument—is usually less successful than creating conditions where people can engage in *dialogue*: reflecting on their own situation and beliefs, openly articulating the reasoning behind their positions, and entertaining different perspectives. These conditions facilitate and encourage a shift of beliefs but still leave people free to change or not change as they see fit.

Our most deeply held patterns of belief are sometimes nearly invisible to us. They are so much a part of our view of the world that we may not make a distinction between "what I believe but don't know for sure" and "the way the world is." Such beliefs are often *undiscussable*, especially if they touch on issues that are sources of anxiety and uncertainty—*harsh realities*—for the individual or the organization. Dialogue creates a situation in which tacitly held beliefs become explicit, hence at least potentially amenable to examination and choice.

I use the term *inquiry* to denote a broad set of skills that help to elicit dialogue. One way of suggesting the difference between an inquiry and an advocacy mode of interaction is that in inquiry, participants do not try to change the beliefs of other participants, but rather focus on building a shared model of the diversity of their beliefs. In other words, *rather than merely agreeing to disagree, participants endeavor to agree about what they disagree about and how they disagree.*

Inquiry can be thought of as an individual competency that helps to sustain a group competency of dialogue. Dialogue is great if all participants are practicing it. It can break down or be disrupted if even one participant jumps back into advocacy. There are also different levels of inquiry skills. Besides the ability to participate in dialogue, inquiry facilitation skills can help *move* a situation from advocacy to dialogue.

Hans: Let me get this straight. To change people's beliefs about reuse, we should inquire about their beliefs regarding reuse, and then their beliefs will magically change? Sounds *just* a little touchy-feely to me.

Jack: No one can make anyone else shift beliefs. Managers can attempt to enforce behavior changes, but they cannot force changes to the underlying beliefs that motivate behavior. Attempts to do so may be self-defeating (by creating resistance and strengthening beliefs counter to the desired change). Ironically, many vociferous reuse advocates may actually work against their intentions, increasing resistance by the way they interact with people unconvinced about the benefits of reuse. I'm convinced that the mode of persuasion, a natural rhetorical mode to slip into when dealing with irrational and recalcitrant beliefs, is by and large counterproductive to the goals of reuse.

But I don't expect you just to believe me about this!

3.1.6   Inquiry-Based Assessment

Paula: What are the implications? As a reuse change agent I should create situations that allow people to articulate their beliefs about reuse, without (at least directly) trying to change them. What do you call this? Planning? Climate survey? Focus group?

Jack: I'd consider it a form of assessment. That can be a loaded word, implying a lot of judgment—even audit—which isn't the intent. Living with the word for now, what we want is an assessment process that directly addresses reuse-related beliefs and values, and the interaction patterns that they support. Beliefs about reuse are understood to be beliefs about knowledge sharing.

Hans: And what benefit will we derive from this kind of assessment that we wouldn't gain via more traditional means?

Jack: Inquiry provides data about the barriers to reuse adoption in the organization. The process also helps reuse advocates examine their own beliefs and interaction patterns to see where they may be counterproductive. Finally, giving people a forum to articulate and reflect on their beliefs is a positive step toward their examining and possibly shifting beliefs (when this is justified by circumstances). At the very least, this approach avoids the risk of increasing resistance to change.

3.1.7   Assessment That Does Not Create Resistance

Rudy: Are you saying that all this just provides some improved diagnostic tools? Once you've assessed the state, how can you make the change any more effectively?

Jack: Let's start more modestly. Suppose you accept my contention that many of the actions you take as reuse advocates may work *against* your aims by increasing resistance. Then, along with the obvious goal of assessment—getting a better handle on what we're up against—we'd like to know that our activities do no harm—that is, they do not increase resistance, and maybe they even increase receptivity. I think I can make that claim about the techniques I suggest.

Inquiry reveals core beliefs already in place. These are based on several types of evidence:

- Past history and how it has been interpreted (we believe what we have seen)
- Stakeholder analysis (we believe what we need to believe in order to get our jobs done)
- Temperament, training, and inclination (software engineers have certain beliefs, managers have other beliefs; or maybe people with certain beliefs gravitate toward these professions and roles)
- The organizational culture that is established and maintained through interactions both formal and informal

Reuse advocates may think of the required message as a shift from a bundle of typical beliefs to the reuse faith, but in fact there is a great diversity of beliefs and configurations of beliefs on the part of individuals and groups, which provides a basis for both receptivity and reasonable resistance to reuse. We need a way of finding out what is living in the organization before we attempt to intervene.

We also need to challenge our own beliefs as advocates to see where we may be applying failed or inappropriate models to new situations. For example, much of the reuse literature arose in government contracting environments. Rapidly changing business structures, economic trends, and technologies may be changing many of the ground rules assumed in this previous research. We need to be able to deconstruct and reconstruct our own belief patterns.

Finally, helping people articulate their beliefs explicitly is a key to making a shift of those beliefs possible. We create situations in which shared and implicit beliefs get made explicit, perhaps by presenting a scenario that violates a certain belief, hearing the words, "It wouldn't happen like that here," and eliciting "because…"? Where there are polarized or conflicting beliefs, we create a scenario that makes different predicted outcomes visibly divergent, and then facilitate a discussion around the different anticipated outcomes. In both cases, you avoid the sense of a belief push from outside the organization by making the articulation of belief both an activity and an expression of the organization.

One of the most important tasks of reuse assessment, as a first step in reuse planning, is to identify these points of receptivity and resistance, particularly as they are manifested in patterns of behavior and beliefs. We can discover these patterns and beliefs through inquiry.

Figure 3-2   Cassandra questions the relevance of Jack's ideas.

3.1.8   Inquiry as Integral to Reuse Practice

Cassandra: Look, I'm as great a fan of inquiry and learning organizations as anyone. But I have to admit that right now this just sounds like general organizational change theory at work. I mean, any change agent could benefit from taking an inquiry-based approach. Isn't this a slick form of rhetoric—to persuade by not persuading—that could be used in any kind of change management? Why is it particularly relevant to reuse?

Hans: I have a related question. Are these techniques actually ways of making reuse happen, or just ways to assess how easy or hard it will be?

Paula: Let me take a crack at that. Reuse means taking a component originally used in one context and reusing it in a new context. Approaches to reuse vary in the degree to which this transfer process is conscious and designed. In ad hoc reuse, the transfer takes place naïvely and is prone to all sorts of breakdowns because implicit contextual information embedded in the original software is carried over to the new situation, usually with inappropriate side effects.

What competencies must working engineers have for sustainable reuse? How can we reuse more effectively? The answer can't lie in just being a dutiful reuse citizen who reuses components uncritically from some central library because management has established a reuse quota or an incentive program. Nor can the answer be that if the rest of the process, design *for* reuse, were only methodologically pure, the reuser would have no grounds for fear or caution. Even with planned, systematic reuse there will *always* be attempted reuse situations that break assumptions made in the code.

To know how to use and how not to use a component intended for reuse, one exercises a discipline of contextual inquiry to understand the original context, and hidden assumptions of that context. *When I wish to reuse a piece of software, I must engage in inquiry with the original context of that software. No other form of reuse will be robust.*

It's really the essence of reuse. We have artifacts that are inflexible and brittle. We have the idea of using the material in a context that goes beyond its original scope. We have the need to assess whether the material will be relevant in the new context, to assess how it needs to change, and to make the change in a way that preserves the integrity of the element.

Jack: Right. The connection of inquiry to reuse is fundamental, far beyond assessment. And yet emphasizing inquiry during assessment is one way to start building those capacities in the organization. I'd predict that if you try to implement a reuse program without developing these capacities, you will get a number of predictable types of breakdown: people not reusing what they could reuse because of assumptions, people trying to reuse what they can't reuse. You will get "jumping through hoops" reuse or "going through the motions" reuse. You will get attempts at rigid, generic standards. Inquiry-based assessment provides opportunities for people to practice skills necessary to build both *for* and *with* reuse.

Hans: This is starting to make sense to me because I can now relate it to what I actually do when I believe I am developing with good reuse instincts. Inquiry means digging down below the surface, below what is explicitly understood as context (e.g., what is written in an official interface specification and code documentation), down to the implicit assumptions that were embedded into the code as a result of the situation in which it was created. One must look at that original context and the new context into which one would place the component, and look for potential differences that might not at first meet the eye.

Jack: Right. Good reusers have well-developed abilities to do this kind of inquiry. They will more consistently find mistakes by noticing significant differences in the two contexts; alternatively, they may see more opportunities for action precisely because they can also discern the *commonalities* between two diverse contexts.

Paula: There are more systematic approaches to reuse besides the ad hoc scenarios we discussed earlier. In each case, the ability to practice inquiry on the original source of the material to be reused is a crucial step. In managed reuse this step is performed once by a reusable asset *creator*

Figure 3-3   Hans sees the light.

rather than over and over again by would-be asset *utilizers*. In domain engineering, unlike incremental reuse, which involves adapting one example at a time, reuse is made more predictable by gathering, analyzing, and comparing a set of examples for the domain. Inquiry lies at the heart of design *for* reuse as well as design *with* reuse.

Rudy: I must confess a bit of skepticism. Are you saying that reuse is largely an attitude of openness? We could make programmers better reusers if we just taught them to be better inquirers?

Hans: Are you saying you don't need technical solutions to real software problems to make reuse a reality?

Paula: Are you claiming you don't need comprehensive reuse plans, and buy-in from upper management? You can make reuse happen through this inquiry guerrilla warfare? It sounds a little mystical to me! Worse, it seems to play into the "grassroots" version of reuse that we had to work to overcome in communicating the need for an economic business case. An individual programmer practicing inquiry in deciding whether to reuse a legacy component will not substantially change the way software is developed.

Jack: I don't claim inquiry techniques are *sufficient* for systematic reuse, just *necessary*. These other aspects are important; but you could have them in place and still have a reuse effort fail for a host of reasons that

Figure 3-4   Rudy leads the opposition.

might go unexamined without an assessment process that at least puts them on the map.

In fact, without that assessment process it's hard to measure what successful reuse could mean. If reuse is knowledge creation, many conventional measures of reuse are of limited value.

For example, maybe a lot of code is being shared but not in a knowledge-creating way. If the code was not created with some inquiry in the process, it is probably laden with undocumented contextual assumptions of all kinds; it's probably more complex than it needs to be; in fact, reusing that code might be a mistake.

Now suppose I'm the engineer deciding whether to reuse this code. Perhaps inquiry convinces me of the facts above; and then I don't reuse. Inquiry has done its job. I've made the right *decision* about reusing—that is, I've decided not to. I'd call this systematic reuse: I asked the question; I found candidate material to try to reuse; I made a cost–benefit decision. Still, no measurable reuse occurred.

Conversely, suppose I go ahead and reuse the piece of code and wind up with breakdowns because of it. I got my (measurable) reuse quota but it didn't help. I got burned, system quality has suffered, and I will be less willing to try reuse the next time. If you ask people to go through the motions of reuse, you wind up measuring conformance to the letter and not the spirit of reuse.

So attempting to measure the surface phenomena of reuse really misses the point. Reuse involves trusting that the engineer who created that component knew what she was doing, that management won't fire you once they've picked your brain, that you can get paid by value instead of by hourly labor and still prosper. These are not trivial things to request of people. It may be disingenuous to ask this of your engineers, as a manager, if the reality of the circumstances doesn't address the obvious concerns.

3.2 THE EXPERIMENT

Hans: I must admit this is all intriguing. But I'm skeptical. I don't know how I could validate for myself whether any of this holds water, although much of it rings true. Even if the theory is right, I have a hard time accepting that situations could actually unfold much differently simply from practicing this different approach. I've been in too many political battles to believe that the entrenched interests that resist reuse in most business situations are going to be appeased by the art of holding conversations more politely. It sounds a bit like David and Goliath, to be brutally frank.

Jack: I have a proposition for us. Why don't we try it? Let me introduce you to some tools that will make this approach we've been talking about a bit more concrete and practical. Some will be tools for analysis and understanding, some will be tools for actually holding conversations in a different way. Let's create a believable scenario for ourselves about a typical reuse adoption situation and apply the tools to that scenario and see what insights we gain. Will the tools help us better understand the dynamic of what unfolded? Can we imagine that the people in the scenario might have gained different results if they were using the tools themselves? Where could an interaction based on inquiry as opposed to advocacy have made a demonstrable difference? Admittedly, this will be nothing more than a thought experiment, but it will have the concreteness of a specific situation. What do you say?

Paula: Sounds worth a try. How about tomorrow morning?

CHAPTER 4

CORE LIBRA TOOLS AND TECHNIQUES

Before proceeding to the experiment the group is going to perform in Chapter 5, we need to describe in more detail the LIBRA approach and its tools.

We focus here on a repertoire of techniques that form the core of a new kind of reuse assessment. These tools can help you identify reuse adoption barriers early in the process.

4.1 THE LIBRA APPROACH TO ASSESSMENT AND ADOPTION

A defining insight of LIBRA is that *systematic software reuse is a key practice of a knowledge-creating software organization.* Framing software reuse as an aspect of organizational learning and knowledge creation helps explain the frustrations experienced by reuse advocates and suggests more effective assessment and adoption strategies. Let us consider why this is so.

Most approaches to reuse adoption in software organizations follow a common pattern:

- The initial impetus toward reuse results from the efforts of reuse advocates (e.g., technologists) to *persuade* decision makers (e.g., managers) to invest in reuse.

- To decide what reuse actions are appropriate, an assessment is performed. This involves characterizing the organization via checklists of criteria that can be linked to recommended actions. Whether performed by an external agent or applied internally, this form of assessment is often viewed as evaluative in nature—that is, as an *audit*.

- Further planning for reuse adoption involves a top-down, structured approach that maps out an overall plan for institutional change by *mandate*.

- When planning leads to a specific project, the transfer of reuse concepts takes place through *training*.

These four approaches—advocacy by persuasion, assessment by audit, change by mandate, education by training—occur at different steps in the adoption process but are closely interwoven. They reflect values and approaches to organization change and technology transfer (much broader in scope than the reuse field). They fail to surface and address many hidden barriers to change, while not revealing and exploiting potential motivating forces for change. They can actually increase certain dynamics of resistance.

In contrast, the LIBRA self-assessment process helps identify motivators and barriers to reuse within the organization, while avoiding the creation of new barriers from technology push or advocacy. The LIBRA approach is

- **Informal:** does not require a big learning curve
- **Small scale:** can be initiated with a single meeting of a few people
- **Incremental:** can be grown in small steps, with clear value delivered at each step
- **"Populist":** at least in principle, can be initiated by motivated people at any level within an organization, not just upper-level decision makers
- **Empowering:** helps people to identify activities they can directly initiate— small local initiatives that would likely be missed in large-scale, top-down reuse planning
- **Self-assessment based:** motivated, performed, owned, and tailored by and for the individuals and organizations involved rather than by an outside auditing organization using preestablished criteria

Inquiry skills are critical to this approach. Since reuse involves belief, not just information, people will adopt more systematic reuse practices only if they make shifts in their underlying patterns of beliefs. Beliefs (we believe) are not shifted through advocacy and persuasion as effectively as through dialogue and inquiry. Thus the LIBRA approach to reuse assessment is based on a set of techniques designed to let people within organizations form small, structured *inquiry sessions* to gather information about points of reuse receptiveness and resistance.

These sessions are structured in ways that encourage interactions with an appropriate balance of inquiry and advocacy. They are the building blocks of an incremental approach, an alternative or complement to large-scale planning that requires significant investment. Sessions integrate planning, assessment, training, and adoption. Initial conversations about reuse can flow seamlessly into assessment, planning, and education. Direct practice of the interaction skills essential for sustained reuse will increase the organization's readiness for reuse.

4.1.1 Reuse as New Interactions

Through LIBRA's incremental, decentralized approach to reuse self-assessment and adoption, new kinds of interaction can occur, which increase a software organization's capability for learning and knowledge creation. These new conversations not only engender and sustain reuse, but also offer a form of continual, ongoing self-assessment; that is, they can generate and continually update knowledge about the organization's potential motivators, receptivity, and barriers to reuse. The interactions may reveal new opportunities for reuse over time and may introduce new concepts and practices to participants.

An example of a new interaction might be a group of engineers, working on similar subsystems on multiple projects, who are given a chance to get together and compare notes on their respective approaches. The people brought together in these situations might only rarely have the chance to interact as part of ordinary workflow in their development environment. This is because, from a production standpoint, there are no work-related handoffs between these people; they may be working not only on different projects but in different parts of the organization. The reason for bringing them together is to support organizational learning.

The sections below explore the LIBRA tools and techniques. Sections 4.2–4.5 provide an overview of the four core LIBRA tools:

- Dramatic scenarios
- System diagrams
- Belief maps
- The Ladder of Inquiry

The relationships between the tools are illustrated in Figure 4-1. Section 4.6 closes the chapter by discussing how the tools can be used in concert. Consult the References and Recommended Reading sections at the end of the book for resources to learn more about the tools.

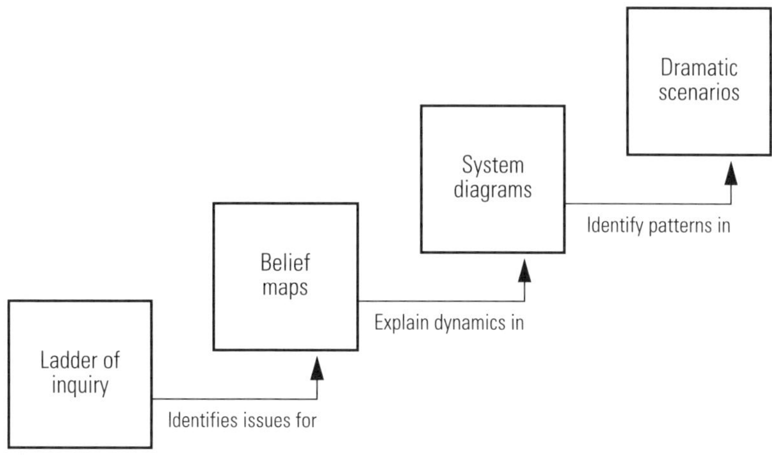

Figure 4-1   Core LIBRA tools.

4.2 DRAMATIC SCENARIOS

The primary assessment tool in LIBRA is the dramatic scenario. We use the term "dramatic scenario" (or "scenario" for convenience) to refer to a narrative description of events that focuses more on drama (conflict, tension, transformations) than on task descriptions or workflow analysis. A dramatic scenario includes descriptions of the organizational environment and broad business picture, as well as character profiles of the individuals appearing in the scenario.

LIBRA's dramatic scenarios should not be confused with the user scenarios that are often created as part of system requirements analysis. Both the purpose and the form are different, as will become clear through the examples we provide.

4.2.1 An Example Scenario: Competency Is Its Own Punishment

Consider the following scenario fragment:

A software engineer, Claudia, is given an intensive programming task in a specialized area—user interface development—within a handheld computer development project. After successful completion of the task, Claudia gains a local reputation (within her group) as the handheld user interface "expert." As more related tasks of this kind come up, they are directed her way; with each task, her expertise grows, and the proportion of her time dedicated to this domain also increases.

Eventually, as the learning curve levels off, the tasks become less and less interesting, more and more routine for Claudia. She asks her manager, Tom, for other work, but in the meantime user interfaces for portable devices have become critically important in several high-profile projects. Claudia starts feeling "pigeonholed" and requests a trainee so that she can begin to transfer her expertise in portable device user interfaces and move on to something else. Tom answers, "We can't spare your time training someone right now—you're on the critical path. And we're understaffed as it is."

4.2.2 Elements of Scenarios

- **Context.** An organizational setting is established for the scenario. Ideally, the business environment and other elements of the context shared by the characters in the scenario are presented explicitly.

- **Characters.** Each character in the scenario is described via a character profile that details as much as is relevant about the person's past experience, life and career situation, values and attitudes toward work, colleagues, and so on.

- **Story.** The main body of the scenario describes a sequence of events, interactions, and decisions. The story can be told in a variety of alternating forms, including narrative, dialogue and script, or even sample artifacts (e-mail message text, corporate memos, etc.).

- **Key events.** As a starting basis for analysis and interpretation of the scenario, the story can be annotated to identify key events that warrant focused discussion and commentary.

4.2.3   Why Use Scenarios?

The LIBRA scenario approach is adapted to the purpose of reuse assessment. Reuse is not an explicitly supported process in most development environments. If you ask direct questions such as: "How much reuse happens in your organization?" or "Do you have metrics in place for levels of reuse?" you may be asking for descriptions of practices that exist but are not codified in policies. If the processes are already codified, people may know how to answer these questions; if not, they may not even understand the question.

Formal process models are a good way to codify processes that we want to institutionalize, manage, and make repeatable. However, they frequently incur unnecessary overhead when used to describe interactions that we may want to change. Broken or nonoptimal processes often have missing or conflicting information, or information that is generated and then lost or ignored. To diagnose and fix such problems we need a simple language for describing what the problems look like. Dramatic scenarios allow people to identify patterns of interaction and link them to experiences in the organization, so that opportunities for systematic reuse can be recognized and understood in concrete, practical terms.

4.2.4   Features of Scenarios

Some features that distinguish a scenario from a more formal process description include the following.

- **The scenario tells a story.** It need not be factual (i.e., not a case study); if factual, the specific organization and people need not be named. On the other hand, the story is narrated with respect to particular characters, not abstract roles. Much of the value of the scenario as a starting point for interpretation stems from this quality of concreteness. Because the scenario tells a story, it engages the listener's imagination without raising issues of historical correctness ("It didn't happen that way ..."). But the presence of specific data about the characters makes the description richer than an abstract process. It is easier for people to see themselves in the story, to relate the story to incidents in their own experience, and to see the possibilities for action in the story based on the characters' beliefs and choices.

- **The scenario's story has a beginning, a middle, and an end.** By contrast, a process model describes a set of interactions that are repeatable (an input–output flow). Since process models are used to describe workflow, the statement that "there is an established process in place" implies that the organization can repeatedly respond to inputs of the same type and produce similar outputs. This applies best to a conventional production environment, somewhat less to a software development environment where each system developed may present unique design issues, and even less well to knowledge-intensive activities.

The beginning and end of the scenario are somewhat arbitrary: they are the frame of the picture. There is an understanding that events have led up to the scenario and that other events will follow afterward. The frame of the scenario is determined by the scenario author(s) to emphasize certain events. A single scenario can be discussed in its entirety in a single meeting; it does not attempt to provide a complete, seamless description of a process.

- **The scenario often describes a situation with inherent instability.** Action or events in a scenario can be those that occur when ordinary business processes break down or are in transition. Where repetition does occur in a scenario it may imply a problem—for example, a kind of *stuck quality*.

  By contrast, formal process models are usually valid only if the situation is stable. They are meant to enforce stability (recent work on evolvable process models notwithstanding). In principle, process models could be used to describe change processes themselves. However, such processes are not usually very orderly or repeatable.

- **The scenario can collapse and expand time scale to support analytical purposes.** Scenarios can alternate between fine-grained descriptions of interactions (even scripts of conversations) and broad-brush narrative that covers large-scale events ("Over the next few years Claudia worked on several more projects..."). The scenario can help make the rhythm of unfolding events more discernible (e.g., an acceleration of momentum, hurry-up-and-wait dynamics).

  This flexibility can provide insight into the interactions between processes in short and long time scales. For example, a scenario can describe how apparently stuck situations erode and finally change. Scenarios can describe the role of learning in an organization. Iterations through a knowledge-intensive process change the state of the situation—the participants learn more, or the overall business situation shifts. Yet this learning, since it is not a tangible output, cannot be easily expressed in conventional process models.

4.3 SYSTEM DIAGRAMS

System diagrams are pictures describing human interaction patterns in organizations. They include positions, actions, and impacts on other players. Most often they are used to show a breakdown or vicious cycle of self-defeating actions. They can also be used to show effective patterns of action that are adaptive to change and self-correcting.

Working from the scenario *Competency Is Its Own Punishment*, we present two examples of system diagrams that interpret the interactions (Figures 4-2 and 4-3). The diagram shows the cause–effect connection between events in the scenario: successful completion of the project task leads to increased perception of Claudia's expertise, which leads in turn to more related work being assigned, and eventually to a decrease in Claudia's satisfaction with her position.

A few points to note about the system diagram notation:

- System diagrams are informal. They are most useful for initiating dialogue and discussion. Excessive formality would impose a learning curve that would reduce their usefulness. (System diagrams can also be treated as rigorous mathematical models, but these applications are beyond the scope of this book.)

- The diagrams show *patterns* of events, trends, and interactions over time. They are not designed to show the flow of input and output data in a network of processes.

- The diagrams become most interesting when they include structures like flip-flops, cycles, and feedback loops (positive and negative). The diagrams are sometimes annotated with seesaws and snowballs to make these structures more evident.

As a starting point, Figure 4-2 shows one type of reinforcement cycle at work. This cycle is a *positive reinforcement* of the perception, by managers and colleagues, of Claudia as an expert. The more assignments in the domain Claudia re-

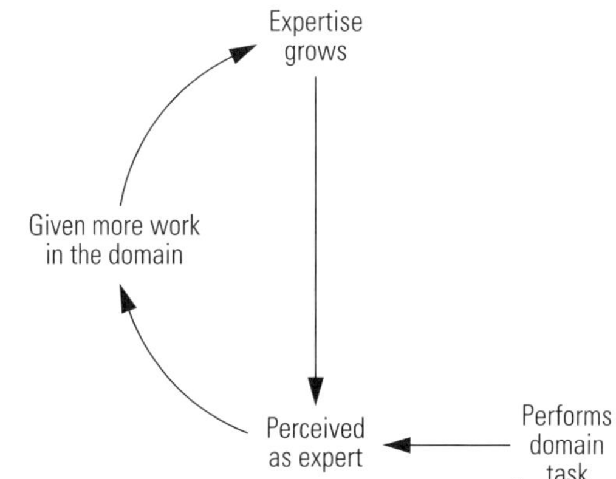

Figure 4-2   System diagram with positive reinforcement loop.

ceives, the more her expertise increases and the more work of this kind she is assigned.

One of the insights encouraged by system diagrams is that every action has a
reaction; in particular, positive feedback loops within one time window may evoke
counterbalancing forces within a larger time window. In the next diagram, we see
the effects of "too much of a good thing": after a while, what was a chance to learn
and gain new skills becomes routine and even boring. Claudia is ready to move on
to other things. Unfortunately, in this scenario, management came to depend on her
skills in this one area and began to box her into the resident expert role. Another
natural response to gaining expertise is the wish to codify that expertise or pass it on
to others. Again, the climate of the organization may be such that "no one can be
spared right now" to take on this apprentice task. This is illustrated by two new
loops in the diagram in Figure 4-3.

Negative feedback loops (vicious cycles) are one way in which situations get
stuck. System diagrams help make the dynamics behind such situations more visible in several ways:

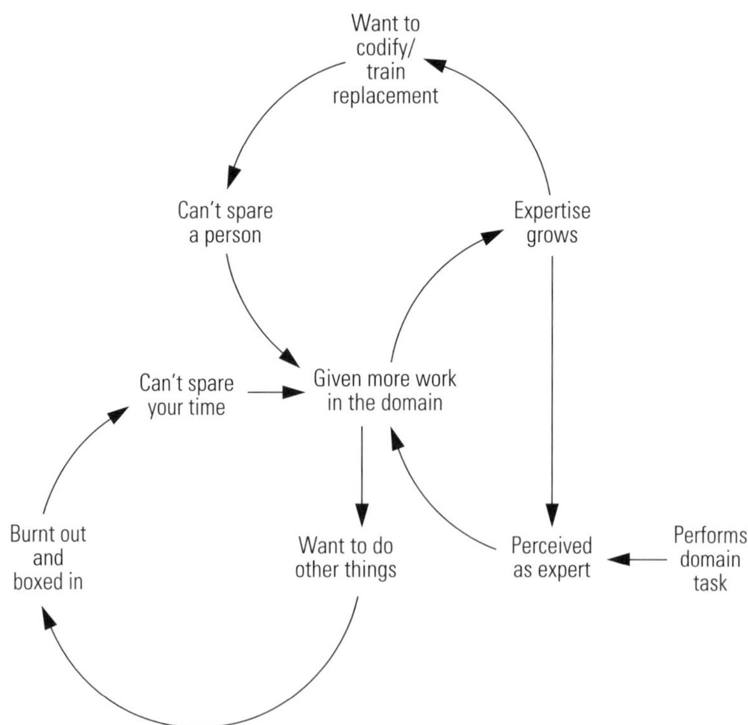

Figure 4-3   System diagram with negative feedback loops.

- They show patterns of interactions that may be invisible to any one player. Each of us tends to view our interactions with others from our own perspective. Through the process of building a system diagram, we can see how our perspective interlocks with the perspectives of others. The exercise can be even more valuable if done with people we otherwise would not interact with.

- They can telescope interactions that take place over long periods of time into patterns that we can comprehend as a whole. In this example, Tom, the manager who frustrates Claudia's repeated requests for new types of assignment, may see only the time crunch of the next critical project, and fail to look far enough ahead to realize that Claudia may quit.

- They can reveal how actions and strategies may work at cross-purposes to their apparent intent, in part through the shifts in scope, perspective, and time frame explained above. In the example scenario, Tom's policy was based on the perceived critical importance of continued access to Claudia's expertise. However, if pushed too far, the policy may produce just the opposite result: it may cost the company access to Claudia's expertise.

- They make it easier to recognize recurring patterns in different contexts. To continue with the example scenario, suppose Claudia announces that she is quitting. She is willing to stay on long enough to train a replacement. It might be all too typical in such a situation for Tom to use Claudia's remaining time on that last high-priority project task—thus perpetuating the same cycle that led to her resignation in the first place. (Claudia probably will then be brought back as a consultant!) If Tom saw this pattern enough times, he might begin to learn that his short-term strategy is counterproductive in the long term.

4.3.1 System Diagrams Suggest Corrective Actions

So far, we have described system diagrams as an assessment or diagnostic tool. However, if used as a basis for reflection and generating insight, they can reveal possible strategies to get situations unstuck, or to bring inherently unstable and chaotic situations back toward healthy equilibrium. The interpretation of a system diagram may reveal an effective course of action or leverage point that is counter-intuitive.

In the example scenario (highly simplified for the sake of illustration) a number of alternative strategies could be suggested. Following are some examples of possible next steps that would change the dynamics of the situation:

- Institute an apprentice/mentor program that brings new hires together with experienced developers.

- Create co-mentoring plans where developers with complementary expertise exchange information.

- If the employee is already leaving, allocate time and resources to debrief the employee.

- If the expertise is of strategic, proprietary value to the company, consider giving the expert a budget to codify the knowledge in some form (a training document, or a formal domain model). Offer as an incentive the chance for the expert to move into a new area once she has shown the expertise to be transferable.

- If the expertise is of strategic but nonproprietary value to the company, consider giving the expert opportunities for microentrepreneurship by selling the expertise outside the organization through consulting.

Each of these strategies places different demands on the individuals' and organization's capacity for change. One option involves transferring knowledge from one person to a new person (passing the torch). Another involves codifying the knowledge so that it becomes a corporate asset, not dependent on individual personnel. The last option might require a shift in the business model of the firm. All these options may require a substantive shift in management's behavior: to allocate resources to learning activities when production goals appear to be paramount.

4.3.2 System Diagrams and Scenarios

There may appear to be considerable overlap between system diagrams and scenarios. For example, both help to uncover blind spots of local or short-term thinking. Although the techniques are complementary, they are quite distinct. Scenarios are built from concrete data (either real or hypothetical). The character profiles, for example, are an essential component of scenarios, while they are generally absent from system diagrams.

One could model an entire scenario using system diagrams, but this is not the strength of the technique. System diagrams are most useful in interpreting the key events of scenarios. Learning occurs when a scenario is interpreted through system diagrams, or conversely, when a known diagram's pattern is recognized within a scenario.

4.3.3 System Diagrams as Archetypal Patterns

A dramatic scenario tells a story, which includes *archetypal* interaction patterns that can be represented by system diagrams. The system diagrams are important because the insight gained from inspecting an archetypal pattern may provide impetus to change the pattern. The impact of this analysis may be all the more powerful, the more the pattern conflicts with the current assumptions of the participants.

How does one recognize the scenes or situations that are most usefully described through system diagrams? What lends a given set of interactions an archetypal quality?

- **Structure.** The pattern of interactions has a clear form, topology, or other formal property, such as symmetry, that creates a signature recognizable in a variety of situations.

- **Coherence.** The pattern has cohesion and independence. It can be isolated from the surrounding interactions so that it becomes the focus.

- **Resonance.** The pattern resonates with observers. They recognize it as a recurring pattern from their own experience.

- **Reinforcement.** The pattern tends to intensify the energy of its constituent interactions. Through strong forces and counterforces, the pattern itself has an impact on interactions disproportionate to the importance of the interaction content (e.g., escalation of an argument about a minor issue).

- **Significance.** Observing the pattern in its diagrammatic form provides insight about the nature of the interactions. This meaning can be thought of as the moral of the story.

4.3.4   Self-Defeating and Self-Sealing System Dynamics

System diagrams are particularly powerful for visualizing *self-defeating* patterns: current behaviors that produce results contrary to the intended outcome. Working with system diagrams can help in eliciting or discovering such patterns.

Example

Reuse advocates setting up a component library may try to create incentives for reuse by rewarding engineers who place components in the library. The intent of the reward system is clearly to encourage design for reuse. But if the incentive program is not handled carefully—if incentives are set too low, or if the criteria emphasize the quantity of submissions instead of subsequent reuse—developers may submit lower quality components, or overcrowd the component base with close variants, and the use of existing components may be discouraged.

The natural course of action for a self-defeating pattern is adjustment or correction over time: persons engaging in self-defeating behavior can be confronted with the effects of this behavior, understand the self-defeating nature of the behavior, and correct it. But some self-defeating behavior is particularly difficult to change. These *self-sealing* patterns occur when there are strong mechanisms to dismiss or resist recognizing the connection between actions and results.

Example (*continued*)

Suppose the organizers of the repository see that only low-quality components are being submitted. We've suggested that the incentive system could have contributed to this result (the self-defeating pattern).

But suppose the reuse advocates have strong beliefs that result in both denial of this insight and its replacement with other theories. For example: "Low-quality components are being submitted because programmers don't know how to produce good software." Working from this theory, a natural reaction might be to tighten the qualification process for components, to allow only higher quality components, and to adjust the incentive structure to compensate only for accepted components.

Now the combination of insufficient incentives and lack of management support for reengineering components only strengthens the message to engineers that reuse is a low priority. In addition, there are now further irritants to the process of submitting a component. Motivation goes down, and the rate of submission goes down. Because of the restrictions imposed, however, the proportion of high-quality components goes up. The strategy is voted a success; and the lesson learned is that programmers must be held to strict standards of quality when they are creating reusable components.

Yet, fairly rapidly, the entire library effort fades away.

A self-sealing pattern combines beliefs with behaviors and interactions. The beliefs provide actors with an apparently self-consistent theory about why breakdowns are occurring, a theory that distracts attention from the self-defeating nature of the interaction. Options for action may remain hidden because they require shifts to pervasive, underlying beliefs held by players in the scenario. System diagrams do not represent these beliefs explicitly. To discover new options based on shifts of beliefs, a deeper level of analysis may be required. In LIBRA, we refer to this approach as *belief mapping*.

4.4 BELIEF MAPS

Belief mapping is the most exploratory part of LIBRA and the least thoroughly validated by experience in other fields. It is closely related to work in the learning organization field on *mental models*, maps of the reasoning behind people's behavior and decisions that are largely inaccessible to conscious reflection [Seng90]. Another body of work, focusing on deep-seated cultural and social norms within organizations (e.g., [Sche85, Sche93]), is highly applicable to beliefs specific to software engineering, reuse, and knowledge creation. Chris Argyris has proposed a theoretical framework that distinguishes between people's *espoused theories* (what they *say* are the reasons for what they do) and their *theories-in-use* (the beliefs out of which they operate, based on observations of their actions) [Argy92]. Our belief-mapping approach borrows from these ideas and integrates them with cognitive and interactional domain modeling, exemplified in the Organization Domain Modeling (ODM) method [ODM96].

Belief mapping is an important technique for the reuse inquirer. Typical technology transfer implies education in a vacuum; the assumption is that members of the adopting organization will be unfamiliar with the new technology. However, due to the close link between general reuse concepts and specific software practices, engineers often think they understand reuse from their own experience. This means that reuse adoption efforts are interpreted within an engineering culture that has its own beliefs about reuse—what works and what doesn't.

Mapping these beliefs is useful in several ways. At a minimum, it can help the reuse inquirer to better understand where the points of reuse receptiveness and resistance lie. In addition, it can help to sensitize the inquirer to the reasons for the existence of certain beliefs in a given setting. For example, previous experiences may have helped to confirm beliefs or expectations among the players. Or certain beliefs may help create a stronger sense of community within the organization. Or a belief may be a reaction to certain harsh realities in the environment. By inquiring about the evidence behind given beliefs, reuse inquirers can avoid falling unintentionally into argumentation or persuasion. If belief mapping is conducted collaboratively among the players, it may create opportunities for constructive dialogue.

4.4.1 Some Example Beliefs

Returning to the example scenario, it is possible to describe some underlying beliefs of the players. The main dynamic (the drama) lies in the tension between the beliefs of Claudia and Tom. Claudia's belief could be stated as follows:

"My value to this organization goes beyond the specific knowledge I have acquired in portable device user interfaces. I should be valued for my ability to rapidly acquire knowledge in new areas, to transfer knowledge from one area to another, and to create and codify new knowledge in a form that is transferable to others. Dealing with me this way is not only the best strategy for me to meet my individual objectives for career and technical growth, but is also the best overall strategy for the organization."

By contrast, Tom appears to be operating from a belief of this sort:

"Training people in new areas is expensive, while putting that expertise to work returns value for the company's investment. Once an employee has acquired adequate knowledge in a technical area of critical importance to the company, it is not in the company's best interest to dilute that person's focus onto other areas."

While drastically simplified, these representative belief statements highlight some important aspects of belief mapping:

- Individuals hold multiple, related beliefs, woven into a *personal belief map*. This personal belief map can include conflicting or even contradictory beliefs. The process of personal reflection or dialogue with others can bring such contradictory beliefs to attention. This can be a powerful experience that leads an individual to shift a belief without having been persuaded to adopt a different belief through debate or argument.

- Belief maps can show relations between the beliefs of multiple players. Often, the beliefs of different players in a scenario will conflict; moreover, the players may or may not be aware that they are operating out of different beliefs or assumptions. Such dissonance in beliefs typically engenders conflict in discussions. Making conflicting beliefs visible to each player without simultaneously trying to resolve or reconcile them can be a powerful inquiry technique.

- Organizations as a whole may also be thought of as embodying sets of beliefs. These are often tacitly shared by members and thus form part of the implicit culture of the organization. However, individual beliefs may be in conflict with the organization's beliefs.

To understand the dynamics of a given situation we need to know the beliefs from which each participant is operating. This illustrates a key value of dramatic scenarios, with their emphasis on fully drawn characters instead of the generic roles of process models. A complete scenario description includes up-front articulation of each player's core beliefs. During scenario interpretation and discussion, participants can test whether the scripted interactions ring true for the characters as described. They can explore what data in the interaction would hide or reveal the underlying beliefs. In assessing real organizational situations, on the other hand, we must reason backward from the data of people's actions, decisions, and stated positions; and we must do this reasoning when we are both involved as stakeholders and constrained by our own active beliefs and assumptions. Scenarios provide a way to practice these interpretive skills before attempting this difficult feat of reverse engineering.

4.4.2 Elements of Belief Maps

A belief map can be represented as a diagram such as Figure 4-4. Nodes in the diagram are short characterizations of beliefs. Various kinds of arc connect these nodes to represent relationships between beliefs.

Some other points to consider are as follows:

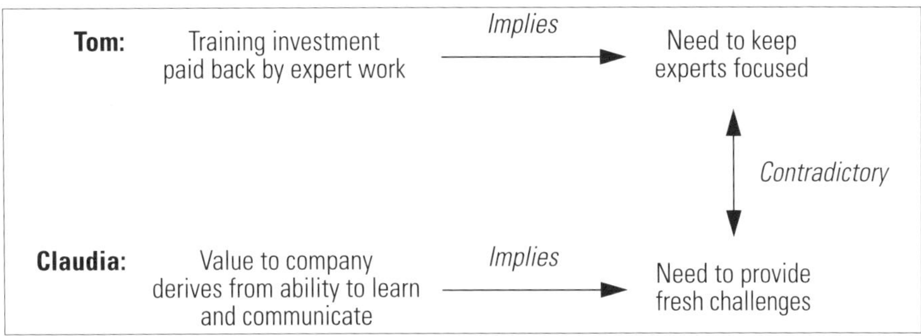

Figure 4-4   Belief maps can be represented as diagrams.

- An individual's beliefs can shift over time; similarly, the common beliefs that shape an organization's behavior can undergo broad shifts.

- A community is defined not only by the common beliefs of its members, but by controversies, schisms, or polarities that divide and structure the community.

- The contrast between beliefs can be illustrated effectively through a description of an individual's shift of belief over time, or through dramatic conflict between players operating on the basis of different beliefs.

4.4.3   Belief Clusters

Beliefs are most usefully thought of not in isolation but in terms of naturally occurring clusters of beliefs—sets of related, reinforcing beliefs, often with chains of inference among key beliefs. Key relationships within belief clusters include:

- **Inference.** On the basis of holding belief A, the person infers belief B.

- **Reinforcement.** Two beliefs seem to imply each other. Questioning either belief might call the other into question.

- **Conflict.** Two or more beliefs appear mutually exclusive. If one person holds both beliefs then usually one of the beliefs will be undiscussable or relatively hidden to that person. If the conflict occurs between people, it may signify an occasion for argument or competition.

When dealing with polarities of the latter kind, interactions based on advocacy and persuasion may only reinforce each position and diminish chances for dialogue. While these could be considered polarizing interactions, the polarities already exist as a conceptual substrate. The interaction simply serves to make the beliefs rigid and more difficult to influence. An inquiry-based approach must include techniques for anticipating and uncovering polarities in beliefs and bringing them into clearer, explicit relation.

4.4.4 Belief Communities

A software organization can be viewed as a network of interactions between individuals representing different *knowledge communities.* These communities have a complex relationship to the official structure of the organization. One knowledge community will typically span several different organizational groups (and may even cross external organizational boundaries). Conversely, a group that is homogeneous from the standpoint of business processes will often resolve into multiple interacting knowledge communities. In addition to seeing work processes as flows of activities and products among groups, we can discern learning or knowledge-creating interactions taking place within and across knowledge communities.

We can further refine the notion of a knowledge community by looking at the role of beliefs in the whole process. Beliefs exist within work groups and within knowledge communities; differences in belief systems are often a basis for community boundaries. Work communities, knowledge communities, and *belief communities* are interpenetrating, linked yet independent structures in any organizational setting.

In the technology field, this aspect can escape us because communities appear to be entirely defined in terms of knowledge. For example, the OO community can be said to have crystallized around certain technical beliefs: that OO is a superior strategy for software design; that OO languages should support run-time polymorphism, and so on. There is a knowledge community that shares information about these technical topics. But not everyone in that community will hold the same beliefs about the efficacy of the techniques. Some advocates of the techniques may be only marginally involved in the knowledge community. Beliefs are part of boundary formation, but they can also blur some boundaries.

Belief communities do not necessarily represent groups of people with homogeneous, identical beliefs. They may be defined and structured by established and ritualized polarities in belief. For example, in the history of the reuse community, the polarity between those emphasizing a technical and those advocating an organizational approach has been a defining principle. One might argue that these viewpoints resolve into distinct communities, but the factions have continued to identify as a single group (defined by conference events, literature, etc.). The dialogue around these issues has become a defining issue for the group.

This leads us to the notion of an *inquiry community,* a community temporarily created by an inquiry-based assessment or adoption process, a community that includes various constituencies from the other groupings. Inquiry groups include people exchanging knowledge or engaging with diverse beliefs through analysis and comparison of their sources and implications.

4.4.5   Beliefs About Reuse and About Organizations

As an example of belief clusters that reflect typical polarized stances within a community, let us explore some of the underlying beliefs of reuse technology advocates and skeptics. Beliefs about reuse interact with beliefs about change in organizations, and with beliefs about how knowledge is created. The belief polarity concerns the relative values of organizational change and organizational stability. That polarity interacts with an organization's reuse readiness in some subtle ways. It represents typical splits between the belief systems of reuse advocates and the people they would like to influence. In the following list, we show how beliefs on either side of the change/stability polarity can be used both to resist reuse and to support it.

Belief 1: Change is good; stability is…compulsive.

People in organizations who resist change are sticking to "the way we've always done things" even though a new way might be better. This kind of stability is compulsive, the gravity or weight of the past. It works against the adoption of new ideas and new technology.

Applying Belief 1 to support reuse:
The argument goes something like this: "Reuse is a new idea that needs to be supported by new technology. Resistance to reuse is therefore one form of resistance to change. Systematic reuse requires that we break down people's compulsive sticking to old practices." This frames the challenge of reuse adoption as an issue of technology transfer.

Applying Belief 1 to resist reuse:
The same belief, applied differently, can increase resistance to reuse. For example: "Reuse is the voice of conservatism, which says 'if it was good enough for one application it's good for the whole product line.' But the modern technology environment doesn't work that way; things change rapidly and the old reuse story of carefully planned support for variability just doesn't suit the current technical environment of furious-paced change. Those who support reuse are afraid of change and the messy, chaotic reality of fast-paced software development." This frames reuse as being largely about codification of best practice: that is, technology transfer in reverse.

Belief 2: Change is risky and…impulsive.

Change for its own sake is often not good. Changes often do not produce the intended effects. People in organizations who advocate change for its own sake may not be concerned about the organization at all. They are, rather, more concerned with their own career and power within the organization, since being an agent of change usually increases one's influence. Even if the motives are not so devious, the impetus to change is often an impulsive reaction to the latest management fad.

Applying Belief 2 to resist reuse:

If a reuse program is identified with change, it can be written off as "organizational change opportunism."

Applying Belief 2 to support reuse:

We could argue as follows: Although systematic reuse will generally involve new organizational structures and procedures, the knowledge that is propagated can be the *best practice* of the organization (ideally, reengineered for reuse). In this view, reuse is not about adopting technology from outside, but rather about propagating the organization's own technology base more broadly within (and possibly outside) the organization: technology transfer in reverse. This could be considered a conservative approach; engineers who resist reuse are those trapped in the cowboy programmer mentality according to which everything must be built from scratch.

If we view reuse as knowledge creation, we can find an intermediate stance that bridges these polarized beliefs. The polarity is generated from seeing reuse as either pushing innovation (in the form of a technology to be transferred into the organization) or pushing conservatism (in the form of existing or legacy technology to be transferred within and outside the organization).

Suppose we look at it this way: knowledge in particular domains is always growing, evolving, changing within organizations. To be knowledge creating, an organization must make strategic decisions about when to initiate knowledge creation cycles in particular domains.

Once such a cycle has resulted in public and explicit representations of knowledge, the organization can decide whether to shift or evolve that knowledge. We should neither cling to old techniques compulsively nor abandon them impulsively; similarly, we should neither institute nor avoid change for change's sake. Systematic reuse practices can help us to raise embedded knowledge to awareness, to validate it and make it strategic, sharable, and reusable. A person acting out of this belief will be able to converse effectively with people advocating either of the polarized beliefs. This makes it a useful belief for someone attempting to identify opportunities for reuse within their organization.

We will return to the subject of reuse advocacy as a belief system in and of itself after we have introduced the last of the core LIBRA tools.

4.5   THE LADDER OF INQUIRY

A fundamental assumption of LIBRA is that people cannot be coerced to shift their beliefs. Shifts in belief occur from within, when people conclude on their own that their prior beliefs no longer match their reality. The tools discussed so far—dramatic scenarios, system diagrams, and belief maps—can help people to describe and analyze their reality in a way that can lead to such shifts in belief. One of the key problems in using the tools for this purpose is that it can be very difficult to discover the beliefs that underlie the positions and interactions described in system diagrams. People usually do not articulate their beliefs freely; often they hide their beliefs or are not even consciously aware of them.

In the example scenario above, Claudia's belief would be characteristic of a knowledge-creating organization—if, that is, the belief were shared by her manager and the organization as a whole. How does change happen in such situations? How can shifts occur in the underlying belief structures?

Inquiry techniques can help increase people's receptiveness to shifts in beliefs. In this section, we introduce a tool, the *Ladder of Inquiry,* for diagnosing and enhancing the quality of inquiry.

4.5.1   Conversation, Discussion, and Dialogue

The focus of the tools up to this point has been on general *interactions,* exchanges of information, promises, requests, or assertions between people. We will use the term *conversation* to denote a specific verbal interaction between two or more people. Conversations are the easiest settings in which to recognize the dynamics of advocacy or inquiry. Depending on the dynamic or quality of a conversation, we refer to it as *discussion* (more advocacy) or *dialogue* (more inquiry) [Seng90].

Our usual picture of a conversation between people with different positions is a mechanical metaphor: positions collide with each other until one party successfully persuades the other to capitulate or shift position, or until a compromise is reached. This shift may be conceptual (we are convinced by the rational arguments of the other) or based on power and authority (one party ultimately has the power to decide). In this conversational dynamic, which we refer to as *discussion*, each participant's attention is focused on stating his position, and meeting disagreement with argument and persuasion. Because people are discussing issues that are important, they are highly involved and interested in the outcome. Because the outcome will result in winners and losers, the discussion can generate emotional heat. David Bohm cites the relationship of the word "discussion" to "percussion," literally "hitting against each other" [Bohm90]. In contrast, *dialogue* implies a willingness to explore the rationale, beliefs, and experiences underlying other people's positions.

4.5.2   The Ladder Metaphor

The Ladder of Inquiry (see Figure 4-5) provides a framework for understanding when conversing parties are stuck, competing, sparring, making discoveries, clarifying decisions, or misinterpreting each other's meaning and intent. It is adapted from Argyris's Ladder of Inference [Argy92]. The ladder metaphor illustrates a choice of movement in conversation, with one direction (down the ladder) leading

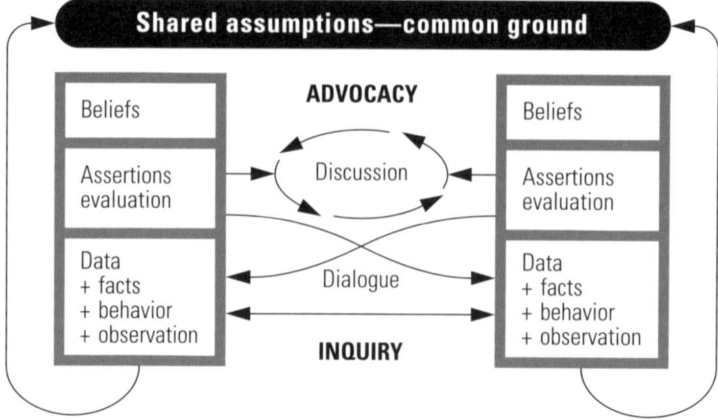

Figure 4-5   The Ladder of Inquiry.

toward collaborative discovery and the other (up the ladder) toward competitive debate. Both are needed, and distinguishing them clearly often makes both more effective.

The rungs of the ladder represent the qualities of listening, receptiveness, and resistance (from bottom to top). When conversations move up the ladder, assertions are defended by appealing to the beliefs that support them. This often leads to debate in which differing parties favor winning over discovering. Assertions and beliefs are pitted against one another in the form of advocacy or discussion. Moving down the ladder means using inquiry techniques to uncover the reasoning and assumptions (the data) behind a given assertion or position, opening more opportunities for dialogue. Moving up the ladder often leads to increased and more strident advocacy (leading eventually to some sort of process breakdown); moving down the ladder often involves interpretation of the underlying rationale behind positions.

There is one sense in which the ladder metaphor can create some confusion. In general, unless we are careful and disciplined in our conversations, the tendency is to move unconsciously *up* the ladder or to stay stuck at one level in an unproductive way. It takes self-restraint and personal discipline to intentionally move *down* the ladder. This means that gravity makes us fall up the ladder, while we must climb down by dint of personal effort. We leave the metaphor as it is because the notion of moving up the ladder corresponds to the physical sensations and intuitions we experience. To move *down* the ladder, we must generally damp *down* our immediate emotional reactions.

The ladder can be used as a diagnostic aid to assess how a given conversation is flowing. Are positions hardening? Are people able to inquire beneath the initial positions against which they are tempted to react? The ladder can also be used as a guide to monitoring one's own behavior in a conversation. The scenario analysis in Chapter 5 illustrates how the Ladder of Inquiry can be used to diagnose breakdowns in communications or characterize alternative paths that could have been followed.

In assessing or guiding conversations using the ladder, a few principles apply:

- The most productive conversations involve intentional moves on the ladder. That is, at certain times it is appropriate to move up the ladder and close on decisions and actions; at other times the ability to move down the ladder is critical to success.

- Staying at one level of the ladder may require as much discipline as shifting levels intentionally. Discussion can involve an inadvertent tendency to drift up the ladder.

- People get stuck at particular rungs of the ladder. To the extent that conversations stay at the surface level of conflicting positions, and do not move downward to discovery of underlying beliefs, conversations can break down, move in circles, oscillate back and forth between alternatives, or reach apparent resolutions that dissolve afterward.

4.6   INTEGRATING THE TOOLS

Finally, before continuing with our play within a play, here are some guidelines for using the LIBRA tools in concert. Chapter 7 provides more detailed guidance for applying LIBRA.

LIBRA is most effective when you can move from scenarios to system diagrams and from scenarios to belief maps in a process of reflection and interpretation. We do not expect scenarios to be appropriate for all organizations, or for all situations within a given organization. They play a central role in LIBRA, however, for several reasons:

- Scenarios provide a context in which to apply other inquiry techniques as part of interpretation and analysis.

- Scenarios transfer well from an individual's directed reading, to written commentary and discussion within a group, to interpretation in meetings.

Because fictional scenarios describe situations distinct from the real organizational setting, they give people a chance to practice inquiry skills on neutral ground. You can practice recognizing and diagramming a pattern in the scenario without having to struggle to recognize it in your current situation.

4.7 APPLYING THE TOOLS

The easiest way to use scenarios is to convene a group of people to read (usually prior to the meeting) and discuss an existing scenario, such as the one provided in Chapter 5. The scenario can be interpreted and analyzed by using a combination of free, unstructured dialogue and the other LIBRA tools. Here are some ways to use the tools in concert:

- Starting from the scenario, identify what appear to be significant or key events in the story. Try to transcribe the events in terms of a system diagram or belief map. If you succeed, you will have discovered a pattern.

- Start from a known set (or casebook) of system diagrams or belief maps that point to key issues encountered in reuse. Scan the scenario for instances in which one of these patterns seems active; then sketch a diagram to describe how the pattern is played out in the story.

- Use the Ladder of Inquiry to work from specific scenarios to the underlying belief maps of the characters involved.

It may seem strange to describe this as a form of assessment, since there is nothing in the process that directly involves compiling and validating data about the organization. A group of people could discuss a story about another hypothetical organization. This seems to have little to do with assessment in the conventional sense.

Nevertheless, LIBRA provides a powerful starting point for an organization's reuse self-assessment. Scenario interpretation provides a scaffold for the ensemble of LIBRA techniques. The very indirectness of the scenario in relation to the work practices and business environment of the organization can be an important benefit. Because the scenario does not refer to events and decisions that affect the participants as direct stakeholders, the interpretation can take place on neutral territory.

4.7.1   Relationship of the Ladder of Inquiry to Other Tools

Scenarios and system diagrams describe behaviors. Using these tools in an inquiry session can help the participants move from advocacy to inquiry (down the Ladder of Inquiry), even if the *content* includes interactions in which people move up the ladder. The goal is to change the *process* rather than directly change any position. The process changes shift the focus:

- From decisions ("We shall do this...") to recommendations ("We should do this..."), to possibilities ("We could do this...")

- From the search for a single outcome to the enumeration of possible outcomes and their relationships (e.g., from a *point* solution to a solution *space*)

- From positions to the beliefs and rationale underlying the positions

4.7.2   System Diagrams and Beliefs

A system diagram represents players' *actions* and *positions* in a given situation. We use the term "position" to mean decisions or stated preferences about actions and outcomes; thus a position could be stated in the form, "I intend to do X," or "I think we (the company, design team, etc.) should do X in this situation." In contrast, a belief is an assumption about how the world is, which is part of the reasoning behind actions and positions. The dynamics represented in system diagrams are thus fueled by the underlying beliefs of participants. Without a belief map, a system diagram by itself may not illustrate what keeps the dynamic persistent over time (the stability of desired behavior or the stuckness of undesired behavior). For example, a boom-and-bust cycle may persist at a company because managers believe they have no sensible option but to overstaff at peak times and lay off in lean times.

By combining system diagrams with belief maps we explain self-sealing interactions. By creating the explanations collaboratively, using inquiry to increase receptivity, participants may find themselves shifting some of the beliefs that sustain self-defeating and self-sealing patterns.

4.7.3   Beliefs and Alternative Scenarios

Belief maps can have a strong impact on scenario outcomes and system diagrams. We can gauge the extent to which a scenario or system diagram presumes certain beliefs by explicitly changing our assumptions about the characters and seeing what happens. For example, you can create alternative scenarios, replacing one character with another. Since the characters are not abstracted process roles but fully drawn descriptions, new characters can operate from different belief systems. In this way, you can iterate the use of scenarios, system diagrams, and belief maps to explore a given situation.

To illustrate this, let us return to the example scenario but replace Claudia with Howard, an engineer who is just a few years from retirement. Like Claudia, he has acquired expertise in an essential subsystem area of the organization's main product. Howard's operating belief may be along these lines:

> "My knowledge of this system area is my sole remaining source of job security here. The company could not get along without my expertise, because it would take a long time for anyone else to come up to speed on this part of the system."

This can lead to what might be termed the *knowledge hoarder* syndrome: an engineer tries to become and remain an indispensable source of information. This can be a problem, especially for a manager who values continual employee learning and knowledge sharing. In such a scenario, pressure to move Howard to a different technical area or to train a replacement is more likely to be initiated by the manager and resisted by Howard. The final outcome may be to "fire the deadwood." Such a situation is almost the mirror image of the "expert burnout" syndrome in the scenario with Claudia as protagonist.

On the other hand, if Howard's manager is operating out of a similar belief framework, there may be little open conflict in the situation. This could lead to an organizational climate that encourages guarding turf, strong divisional barriers, and complacency. Both individual engineers and the company as a whole may cling to competencies that are core ("that's what we do!") but are no longer strategic (no one cares any more) or competitive (others are doing it better).

Alternative scenarios suggest the importance of factors such as the following:

- The interaction of different players' beliefs (e.g., Claudia or Howard and their managers)

- The relation between players' beliefs and the beliefs and norms of the organization

- The viability of organizational beliefs in the current business environment (e.g., the strategic importance of portable device user interfaces)

4.7.4 Reuse Advocacy as a Belief System

The pattern of advocacy creating additional resistance can be seen as a system diagram playing out at a macro level in reuse adoption (Figure 4-6). It can also be seen as a macro-level unfolding of the Ladder of Inquiry.

The hardest thing for the advocate to understand and accept is that the way the message is presented can prevent its effective transfer, no matter how correct the content of the message is. This belief of the advocate is a necessary component of

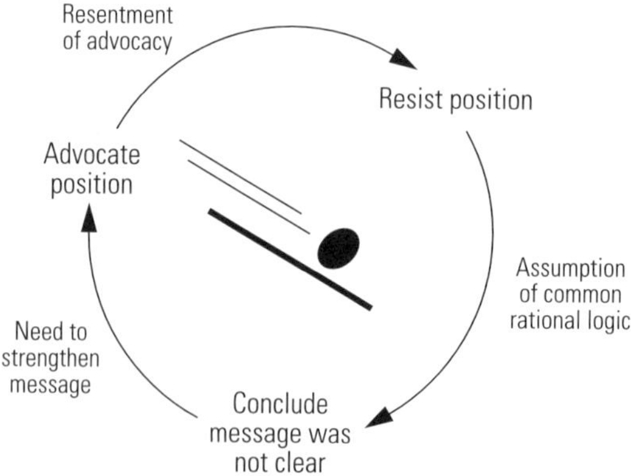

Figure 4-6   The advocacy–resistance cycle.

the pattern. Resistance created within the adopting community should be a counter-balancing force leading to reduction of advocacy efforts—if the advocate worked from a theory that recognized the resistance pattern as a phenomenon to be anticipated and overcome. Instead, most advocates are captivated by the rightness of their message; on some level, they also believe in the *theater of rationality:* my content is right, and my listeners must, in the end, make their decisions based on rational self-interest; if they really understood my message, they would be persuaded. Therefore, if they are not persuaded, they must not have understood the message; I need to adapt to this by restating the message in even stronger and more basic terms. The resistant listener then hears this as "You were too dumb to understand my message the first time," and this elicits even more resistance, particularly if the content *was* understood clearly the first time. The reinforcing cycle continues.

One might think this would lead to a breakdown and thus the pattern would not stay stable. Yet such patterns can become institutionalized and remain relatively stable. While individual situations may break down (e.g., a reuse initiative starts and fizzles), the researchers involved, if committed to the idea of reuse, may move on to a new situation. They often do not stay behind to live through the consequences of the initiative falling apart, and thus never need to challenge their assumptions about the effectiveness of their approach. The professionalization of reuse researcher as advocate creates strong incentives for holding the pattern in place.

Three rhetorical elements of advocacy contribute to this dynamic:

1. **The reification of reuse.** Over time, a vague and multifaceted concept (reuse) becomes a convenient placeholder. Using the term becomes a flag of membership in a particular community with certain shared values—values that can remain unexamined within the community, and are ritualized into a small repertoire of arguments made to those outside who need to be persuaded (project managers, engineers, CEOs, etc.). Reification is a strong way to encode a system of beliefs and leave them unexamined and unchallengeable.

2. **The mode of "exhortation."** In the reuse literature and on reuse panels, it is striking how moralistic the language is. Managers are too short-sighted in their goals. Engineers should consider the reusability of the code they are creating. People are paralyzed by the NIH syndrome: it is mere ego that prevents them from reusing something that was created elsewhere.

   Underneath the exhortation is a belief that people are already empowered to take action in accord with the advocated position. We exhort because we think our audience could be persuaded by the strength of our words, and if they were persuaded they could do what we suggest, and things would work better. If we thought the engineers were powerless to introduce reuse practice without buy-in from upper management, why would we harangue them?

3. Stereotyping of context. A final rhetorical element in the advocates' model of belief and communication is the implied generic story behind the arguments. Reuse is a complex phenomenon that can occur in widely diverse organizational situations for a variety of reasons. It is difficult to make a coherent shared story out of this diversity. Instead, a community of advocates adopts a central story (perhaps an implicit one) as the official story of how it could work and what goes wrong. The reuse community's central myth, or story, has been strongly shaped by the historical roots of the people involved in the community: the Ada, OO, government reuse, commercial 4GL, and academic researchers. It is important to name this story, make it articulate, understand how it became the tacit story, and, most importantly, reveal how the story may clash with the realities of the organizations in which reuse is attempted.

These are the mutually reinforcing elements of reuse advocacy. In describing them, we have shown a system diagram, a belief map, a scenario, and the Ladder of Inquiry, all working together to make the underlying patterns more visible and hence less powerful.

LIBRA suggests that reuse cannot be introduced in an organization by any single party making a unilateral shift of behavior. What is required is a change through an entire network of people acting in parallel. This implies that exhortation will not be effective. And indeed, exhortation does not get the message to the right sets of people and cannot effectively persuade any of them individually. The most important work is not transfer of a set of concepts, but rather creation of new interactions, new kinds of conversation.

4.7.5   Balancing Inquiry and Advocacy

Although a key premise of LIBRA is that inquiry is needed when a long history of advocacy has produced little change (or inhibited change), it is misleading to suggest that inquiry and advocacy are mutually exclusive alternatives. Reuse inquiry should not (and realistically, cannot) supplant or divorce itself from advocacy. Advocacy has an important role to play, even in the ideal reuse-oriented organization, and even in conversations guided by inquiry. In appropriate combination, inquiry and advocacy can increase the likelihood that a software-intensive organization will embrace, adopt, and incorporate reuse into its ways of working, both technical and managerial, in planning, and in software development tasks.

The dynamic that LIBRA warns against is better characterized as *unbalanced advocacy*. This applies both to the details of specific conversations and to the broad reuse adoption roadmap.

As a small example, suppose several stakeholders are discussing whether development of a proposed set of reusable software assets can be funded. In an undisciplined advocacy-style interaction, one stakeholder may take over and paint a rosy picture of the benefits of building the assets. Unless the process is specifically designed to elicit the potentially conflicting views, the advocacy position may be rail-roaded through. But this will almost never lead to success defined as utilization and evolution of the asset base. People might acquiesce to pressure in a task-oriented project; they cannot acquiesce to a general demand to "utilize assets" in the same way. There is no way to compel such usage, or to check that use of the assets was appropriate. Conducting such a meeting in a spirit of inquiry is the best way to en-sure that each stakeholder gets the chance to be an advocate for personal positions and interests. Only in this way is all the information available to make a rational de-cision.

To be an effective participant in an inquiry-based interaction, you have to know when it is appropriate to be an advocate. You have to know how to advocate in a way that does not foster greater resistance or compromise other people's ability to advocate. Conversely, you need to know how to hear others' advocacy as informa-tion, without interpreting it as an inappropriate attempt to control or manipulate. Good facilitators must excel at these skills, and must act in ways that encourage these behaviors and strengthen these skills in others. A key factor in sustaining inquiry-based reuse is to continually nurture a symbiotic, finely tuned balance be-tween inquiry and advocacy that spawns reuseful interactions that inspire individu-als and enrich organizations.

5

REUSE ADOPTION
SCENARIO AND ANALYSIS

Suppose that the attendees of the reuse conference Birds of a Feather session, armed with the tools Jack has introduced, meet the next morning to produce their own dramatic scenario, touching on issues drawn from their own experiences. They then proceed to analyze the scenario, using the LIBRA tools to identify problematic events in the drama and suggest alternative paths.

In this chapter we present our vision of their results. The scenario they produce identifies many of the key patterns and choices impacting reuse adoption (for better or worse), in a very specific, concrete form. The scenario gets to the heart of how stakeholders interact in a business environment, and what many of the real obstacles to reuse are.

Key interactions between characters—those indicating significant risks or choices being made—are flagged with a boldface number surrounded by angle brackets (e.g., <1>). For each of these key events in the scenario, we provide commentary (numbered accordingly) in Section 5.2 ("Scenario Analysis"). In these commentaries, we analyze and interpret the events, often by highlighting the underlying dynamics through system diagrams and by suggesting tools that can be used to steer such turning points towards a successful outcome.

5.1 THE SCENARIO

First, some context about the setting in which the story occurs.

5.1.1 The Organization

The case study concerns a division in a systems development firm that contracts with both commercial clients and the federal government. The division consists of approximately 400 staff. Reporting to the division head are the following people:

- **Business development manager:** responsible for cultivating sales and bringing in new customers.

- **Director of technology:** oversees research and development to keep the company at the leading edge.

- **Director of engineering:** oversees the methods, tools, and techniques that are applied to system development.

- **Line of business managers:** each is responsible for the production of systems for a specific class of customers. Project managers report to their respective line of business managers.

The case study focuses on one line of business (LoB) with a staff of about 80 employees. At any given time there are between three and ten active projects in this LoB, each headed by a project manager. The organization structure is shown in Figure 5-1.

Another important part of the organization is a corporate-wide software technology transfer group, responsible for bringing external tools and methods into the operating divisions.

5.1.2   The Players

The key characters in this study are the following (Figure 5-2):

- **Joe:** a senior software engineer
- **Mike:** a more junior engineer

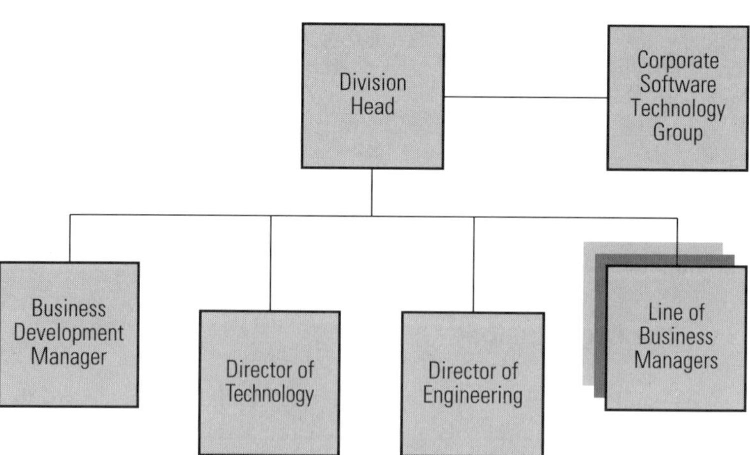

Figure 5-1   The case study focuses on one line of business in a division of a systems development firm.

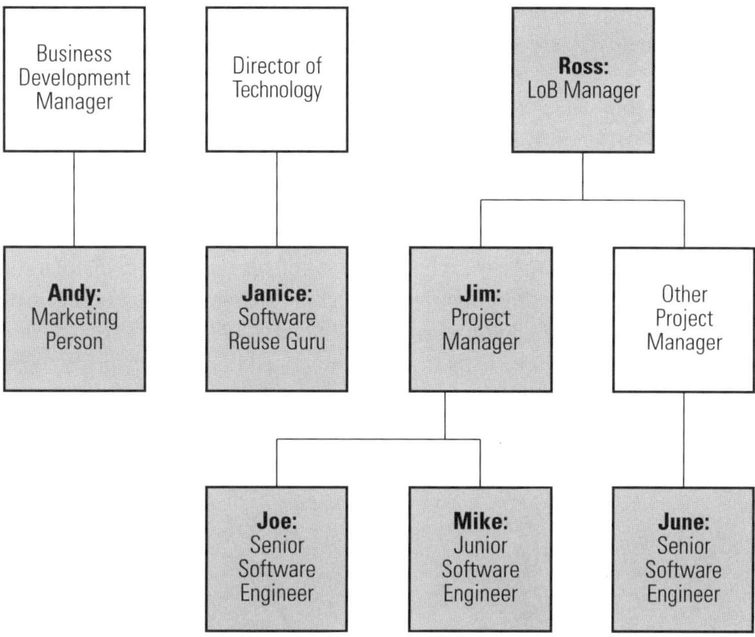

Figure 5-2   The characters in the case study span three levels of the organization.

- **Janice:** a software reuse guru reporting to the director of technology
- **Jim:** project manager to whom Joe and Mike report
- **Andy:** marketing person reporting to the business development manager
- **June:** a senior software engineer working on a different project in the same LoB
- **Ross:** the line of business manager.

Because much of our understanding of the case study will derive from an analysis of the characters' beliefs and motivations, we describe their goals, expectations, pleasures, and frustrations on the job in a series of brief profiles.

Joe

Joe, age 40, is a senior software engineer, a closet believer in reuse who is cynical because of his experience—he has seen the snake oil. His job, as he sees it, is to do excellent technical work on time and within budget, to provide good documentation, to teach more junior members and serve as a model for them, to give his opinions when asked by higher-ups, and to support the directions set by those above him. What he requires to do these things are, primarily, clear specifications, time uninterrupted by meetings, adequate hardware, and some contact with those who are still idealists and can keep him from becoming totally cynical.

Joe expects those above him in the corporate hierarchy to stay out of his way. He expects the customer to love everything he does. He expects his colleagues to be smart and honest; and he expects marketing people to talk straight and respect his art.

Joe is happy when the software works, when the problems that arise are those he anticipated, when he can say "I was right," and when his technical decisions stand the real-world test. He dislikes politics, fads, psychologizing, and customer arrogance. Joe is not quite up on new technologies and technical trends. He often dismisses them as "the same old thing." But he is open and is interested in reuse. He prides himself as a good reuser and designer of reusable code. He is semiconvinced that systematic reuse is better than the ad hoc variety. We see Joe at work in Figure 5-3.

Figure 5-3   Joe at his monitor.

Mike

Mike, age 27, is a relatively junior software engineer but he has valuable experience in a variety of application development contexts, as well as some academic grounding in cognitive aspects of software engineering (he recently obtained his master's degree in cognitive science). His job, as he sees it, is to complete his development assignments on schedule with reliable, understandable, and maintainable code. To do this, he needs clear and stable specifications, and a decent software development environment: efficient compilers, a rich set of design, programming, and debugging tools, and fast Internet access so that he can post technical queries and stay abreast of what the rest of the industry is doing.

Mike finds his current environment moderately useful, but limited because the tools are not fully integrated; he knows that a lot more is possible. He is also frustrated by the unstable infrastructure configuration, which frequently causes tools to disappear from where he expected to find them and, after much time wasted in searching, reappear on another system or in a different directory. A rather extreme incidence of this is shown in Figure 5-4.

Figure 5-4   Mike uses whatever tools he has.

Mike is a bridge builder: he enjoys informal technical talk with his peers, which he believes is the basis for growing a common development culture. He expects his colleagues to be open in sharing techniques, approaches, components, and experiences; he expects them to be willing to take the time to discuss design trade-offs and, through such exchanges, to build the common culture. He views this process as the essence of high-powered software development groups.

Mike dislikes isolationism in other developers ("I have my job and you have yours") and is frustrated when his colleagues and management respond with skepticism to his suggestions for productivity and quality enhancement. He is frustrated by the lack of an overall vision of excellence among the LoB's software staff, and he believes that a lot more would be possible if there were a will to achieve. Mike's motto (which he is careful not to voice to the wrong people) is "Work smart not hard."

Janice

Janice, age 38, is a technologist. Her job is to improve software quality and productivity in the division. She believes this can best be done by institutionalizing reuse (Figure 5-5). To accomplish this, she needs access to software engineers: a

Figure 5-5 Janice likes ideas.

reasonable commitment of their time as well as their cooperation. She would like, but does not have, her own small staff of software engineers dedicated to tool building, tool support, and infrastructure development.

Janice expects to encounter resistance to the changes she proposes, some of it due to inertia, some to lack of understanding. Despite this, she sees an overall willingness in both engineering and management to do whatever will enhance the company's competitiveness—if they can be convinced of this outcome.

Janice is thrilled when she sees process improvements take hold and spread through the division. She dislikes pessimism and stationary inertia, the tendency to do "what we have always done" in the belief that things cannot be any other way.

Janice has the ear of the director of technology, who had worked with her at another company and trusts her insights and judgments. She has been empowered to spend time working with LoB projects in an attempt to get products out the door "better, faster, cheaper." She has been given a small amount of additional funding to participate in reuse and software workshops, including writing and submitting her own papers.

Janice sees lots of opportunities for making real change happen, and this is what motivates her. Over the years, however, she has seen process improvement and technology efforts come and go, and she is getting a little tired of her division's tendency to shift direction radically upon the first indication of a problem. She is always saying to herself and others, "We can really make this happen if we just stick with it."

Jim

Jim, age 42, is a software project manager. His job is to ensure that products are developed and delivered on time and within budget (Figure 5-6). To do this, he needs several things: clear product requirements specifications, advice from his engineering staff about technical issues and alternative solutions, and timely information about the cost, schedule, and technical status of his project. In particular, he needs to know quickly about any problems appearing on the horizon.

Jim fosters an environment in which pride is shared by all when project challenges are met. He expects his staff to take ownership of their tasks, to be committed to getting the job done, and to be willing to change approach or shift direction if necessary for the benefit of the project. He manages a good mix of junior and senior software engineers, including some fine, trustworthy people; he also has some less than stellar performers whom he tries to pair up with his best people in a mentor–advisee relationship. Sometimes this works and sometimes it doesn't, but Jim has no illusions of ever having a team of only superstars: he is too firm a believer in Murphy's law.

From his project manager colleagues, Jim expects the same kind of burnout that he himself is experiencing, lots of pleasantries and mutual groaning exchanged among them but little substantive interaction. From management he expects, above all, an interest in customer satisfaction, and a grudging willingness to provide him necessary resources if he fights hard enough for them.

Figure 5-6   Jim goes by the charts.

Jim is happy if his customer is happy; he is unhappy when his customer is unhappy: it is really that simple. He always has that look on his face that says, "If it's not about my project, Go Away." He is overworked and underpaid—has been for a long time. Still, he usually gets the job done, customers like what he delivers, and he's still employed: nothing to sneeze at when all is said and done.

Andy

Andy, age 45, is a marketing person. He is a good-natured fellow who has retained remarkable enthusiasm for his many years of experience. His job, as he sees it, is to identify potential customer niches and specific sales opportunities, to cultivate a desire in potential customers for what the LoB has to offer and convince them that the LoB is the best possible source and to work with the LoB manager and project managers to enhance the marketability of their products.

To do this job, Andy needs market data, travel dollars, enough technical information to be credible, and access to engineers for backup presentations. He expects others to provide him with timely information about the LoB's products and potential compe-

Figure 5-7   Andy wants increased market share.

tition (Figure 5-7). He expects the LoB's engineers to help in marketing, and he needs funding from upper management to support the development of marketing materials.

Andy is happy when he sees the business base steadily expanding. He becomes unhappy when he feels he has to market a "bill of goods" that has low value. He has a graphic artist on staff to create marketing pamphlets and promotional literature, and an expense budget that he views as insufficient.

Andy gets much of his product information from periodic LoB planning meetings and many ad hoc meetings at all levels of the LoB. He has good contacts among the potential customer base, and he draws strategic insights from his conversations with these folks.

Andy does not fully understand the new software methodologies; however, he appreciates the basic principles enough to believe they have marketing potential. He finds working with bright engineers exciting and fulfilling, and takes satisfaction in being able to convey key ideas to customers who do not speak the technical language. Andy's guiding principle is: explain it to me simply, and I can give your idea a wide audience.

June

June, age 31, is a dyed-in-the-wool software engineer. She is skeptical about managers, who she feels do not know anything about software and always ask for more than is reasonable. She is skeptical about technology "hype," which she feels is a waste of time and energy.

Figure 5-8   June is skeptical.

June believes that organized reuse initiatives are intrusive and unnecessary: she feels that she already reuses plenty. But she will go along with such initiatives when colleagues she truly respects seem to believe in their worth.

June's guiding principle is to get the job done, whatever it takes. To accomplish this, she requires a fast workstation, a decent compiler, and a closed door. What she actually has is a not-so-fast workstation, a flaky network, and a CASE tool that she uses to draw design diagrams.

June's expectations from others are limited: from managers she expects hot air; from her peers she expects to hear a lot of war stories that tend to bore her. We see her doing what she likes best in Figure 5-8.

Ross

Ross, age 50, is the senior manager in this scenario. His main responsibility, as he sees it, is to ensure annual profitability in his line of business. To accomplish this he needs timely and accurate information, good advice from the director of technology, and good employee morale.

Ross places a premium on his employees' happiness, motivation, and desire to excel; he also expects sacrifice and long hours from them. He dislikes lack of "ownership" by his employees, apathy, low standards, and the attitude that this is just a job.

Figure 5-9   Ross means business.

Ross has at his disposal some excellent staff at various levels of the organization. He knows that his budget is inadequate for all the technology base and infrastructure needs that his people express. He knows that competition from other companies is getting stiffer, but is not sure how to address it: there is too much technology "hype" to understand (most recently, OO) and, indeed, too much management "hype" to understand (most recently BPR). As shown in Figure 5-9, his dilemma in this drama is the perennial question: Where to put the money?

5.1.3 The Story

5.1.3.1 *Act One: Stirrings.*

SCENE ONE: THE OPPORTUNITY.   Joe and Mike, software developers, are chatting about the current state of their project when Mike observes that there has to be

Figure 5-10   There has to be a better way.

a better way: he sees so much duplication of effort between projects, and it bothers him (Figure 5-10). Developers are continually creating similar system architectures and coding analogous components from scratch without seeing what could be borrowed from previous or concurrent projects, making the same mistakes, and learning the same lessons over and over.

Joe responds by agreeing in principle—but points out that he has seen this situation many times before, and he knows that the project managers will never buy into a plan for developing common components. Their jobs are complicated enough as it is.

Mike, ever on the lookout for ways to innovate, is not discouraged. He shows Joe a journal article about a new design-for-reuse technique and describes how he believes the technique can work in their organization.

Joe is open to trying, so he drafts a memo to Jim, their project manager, describing the opportunity and its potential benefits.

Jim knows about Janice, the methodologist, from a presentation she gave about reuse to a group of managers. He forwards the memo to her with an annotation-"It's probably a nonstarter, but let me know what you think."[1]

To Jim's surprise, Janice thinks it is a great idea. She sends e-mail to Joe and Mike (copying Andy, the marketer) to propose a meeting.

SCENE TWO: EXPLORATION.   At the meeting, Janice hands out some of her stock reuse literature (Figure 5-11). On the basis of what she has heard from Joe and

Figure 5-11   Janice describes her vision.

Mike about commonality between projects in their line of business, she conjectures that there may be an opportunity for domain engineering. She suggests that they begin to sign up others to support the idea.

Joe suggests that they try in particular to sign up project managers, since this group has been the source of resistance in the past.

Mike proposes that they talk to other software engineers, who will understand and appreciate the opportunity for reuse.

Janice's perspective is somewhat different: she has a strategic vision for reuse throughout the division.<2> She thinks that Andy, the marketer, should get involved as soon as possible to promulgate understanding of the competitive benefits of a reuse program—and that selected customers should also be brought into the huddle.

Janice's ideas make Joe nervous. He believes it is too early to bring Andy in, let alone customers.<3>

The three agree to talk the ideas around, and to hold a next meeting involving a larger group.

SCENE THREE: BROADENING THE BASE.   The three begin to hold one-on-one conversations about their ideas with prospective supporters. Joe approaches June, a colleague he has known for a long time (Figure 5-12). Since June works on a different project, Joe figures, signing her on will help spread support for the reuse program.

Figure 5-12   Joe recruits June.

June is skeptical, but she signs on because she sees the potential benefit and respects Joe's opinion.

Janice reports to Jim (Joe and Mike's project manager) on the initial meeting. She invites him to the next meeting, to represent marketing.

Jim agrees to come—he is surprised that the ideas are moving forward, and indicates that he sees no harm in them. However, he does not show up at the meeting.**<4>**

Janice also invites Andy from marketing. He does show up. Joe is not happy about this.**<5>**

At this second meeting, the group discusses possible experiments that could illustrate the benefits of reuse. They develop a plan to perform an experiment and, if it is successful, to use it as the basis for a pitch to management for increased support. The experiment involves adapting three existing software modules so they can be reused in multiple systems.

5.1.3.2   *Act Two: Beginning Changes*

SCENE ONE: AN EXPERIMENT.   To get the initial experiment going, the group enlists the support of other project managers. With Janice's influence and the help of the project managers, they obtain a small amount of R&D dollars to fund an ex-

Figure 5-13   Colleagues provide everything and the kitchen sink for the reuse team to generalize.

periment. The goal of the experiment is to develop a small number of components to be shared by several projects.

Technical meetings are now held, in which representatives from the different projects participate. The participants decide that their technical approach will be parameterization, and they begin hacking (Figure 5-13).

The resulting components are a modest generalization of the types of component previously developed in these projects. They appear to work, and the experiment is declared a success.

SCENE TWO: SUSSING THE BRASS.   The technical team are excited about their initial success and want to continue along those lines—perhaps developing additional common components.

Janice, as methodologist, urges a grander view of a division-wide (or at least line of business-wide) domain engineering program.<6> Janice and Andy meet with Ross, the line of business manager (Figure 5-14), and separately with the division head. Their goal is to judge the receptivity of these managers to the idea of a larger reuse program.

SCENE THREE: PLANNING THE PITCH.   Janice reports back to the technical folks that Ross is sufficiently receptive. She urges the group to prepare a pitch for a do-

Figure 5-14   Janice and Andy pitch to Ross.

main engineering initiative. She suggests that the principal argument in favor of the initiative be return on investment, emphasizing the savings in project development dollars and the consequent increase in competitiveness. They should request a management commitment to establishing a reuse-based product line initiative in the line of business, including a domain analysis and development of an architecture and asset base.

With all this excitement, the developers Joe, Mike, and June, are beginning to see themselves as being used by Janice and Andy.<7>

Jim, in the meantime, is beginning to feel bypassed. As Joe and Mike's project manager, he is nervous that the flurry of reuse-oriented activity will pull resources away from his project.<8>

Joe, Mike, June, Janice, and Andy all take part in preparing the pitch to Ross (Figure 5-15). They structure the presentation in terms of:

- The opportunity

- The return on investment (ROI)

- The risks

- The recommendation

They decide that the technical team will present the opportunity. Andy and Janice will cover ROI: Janice will present the Software Engineering Institute's cost

Figure 5-15   The reuse team prepares the pitch.

model for software reuse; Andy will speak about the ability to bid jobs more cheaply and thereby bring in more contracts. They try to anticipate Ross's objections. They identify possible risks, including the following:

- The waste of precious R&D dollars
- Tying up key engineering staff who are desperately needed on customer projects
- Compromising on "-ilities" in order to reuse an existing component

They develop responses for each of these issues. Joe, as the most seasoned engineer in the group, is tasked with responding to the last of these risks so that the proposal is technically credible.

SCENE FOUR: MANAGEMENT SIGNS ON.   As well prepared as they were, the presenters are hit with some questions they did not anticipate (Figure 5–16). Ross raises some expected concerns about Janice's ROI arguments, but surprises the presenters by saying that he does not understand how what they are proposing—this notion of reuse—is any different from what software engineers in the division are already doing.<9>

Ross asks them why object-oriented methods do not already solve the problem, as he had been led to believe when approving last year's OO R&D investment, in-

Figure 5-16   The reuse team pitches to management.

fluenced largely by the recent onslaught of OO literature targeted to management.**<10>**

He does not understand the idea of domain analysis at all.**<11>**

Finally, Ross suggests that if the ideas are so good, the team could get an R&D contract with the government to support the work.**<12>** Janice responds to this last point by recounting her nightmarish experiences in trying to use contract R&D for such purposes.

Ross finds merit in the proposal—even if he does not fully understand it— partly because of his long-standing respect for Joe. He does not commit to a full-fledged product line initiative as requested, but he approves funding for a pilot domain analysis project**<13>** and secures a commitment by two ongoing development projects to participate in the pilot.

5.1.3.3   *Act Three: New Conquests*

SCENE ONE: THE PILOT.   Although they put themselves fully into the presentation, Joe, Mike, and June, the developers, are still feeling put upon by Janice. They feel like her "technical guinea pigs."

Janice's approach is very tool and demonstration oriented, a consequence of her years of doing contract R&D. She has a reputation for pushing glitzy methods

Figure 5-17   The developers dispense with Janice's methodology.

and becomes more and more rhetorical with time. Her overall approach to technology transfer is based on push rather than pull, and this does not appeal to Joe, Mike, and June, who come from the trenches.**<14>**

In reaction, these three start taking shortcuts with the domain analysis method, as shown in Figure 5-17.**<15>**

It becomes more and more apparent that there is a distinction between a true pilot—an effort intended to enlighten the participants and lead the way toward change—and a "sandbox" project, which is insulated from real-world concerns. Certain factors pull this effort toward the sandbox category: there is no clear linkage to the final customers of the software; as a result, the line of business project managers begin to resist because they do not see it as being in their interests. They see their personnel resources diluted for the sake of the pilot project and the dog-and-pony shows that Andy arranges. In reaction, the project managers begin to retract their resources, calling technical personnel back to assist in handling project emergencies.

The pilot team reaches out to establish a link to one particular customer, and this liaison becomes the basis for most of the technical decisions. The other participating project bails out, justifying the action in terms of schedule: the results of the domain analysis were not ready in time for them to be used.**<16>**

Despite these difficulties, the pilot effort does produce a number of code assets, which are used by the remaining participating project. That project gives the pilot effort high marks for having saved it significant development cost. This assessment is met with some skepticism elsewhere in the line of business, however, because it did not consider the cost of the pilot itself. Furthermore, use of components developed through internal funding raised a host of ownership questions that the LoB's contracts people now have to negotiate with the project's customer.

SCENE TWO: SCALE-UP DIFFICULTIES.   The success of the pilot domain analysis, such as it was, turned out not to be transferable on a larger scale. Other project managers resisted adopting the asset base, for several reasons (Figure 5-18):

- They did not believe that the assets would meet their projects' needs, since these were not considered during the domain analysis.**<17>**

- They were concerned that they would not have influence over maintenance of the assets.**<17>**

Figure 5-18   Managers lose confidence in the so-called reusable assets.

- There was no clear statement of the context in which the assets were meant to be used (a consequence of methodological shortcuts taken during the pilot domain analysis).

Some of the projects tried to use a couple of the assets, but because the assumed context was not defined, the attempted uses were inappropriate and led to errors. This experience reduced the project managers' confidence in the assets.**<17>**

In the face of project manager resistance, the line of business manager did not go to bat for the asset base,**<18>** and the initial technology success failed to scale up.

SCENE THREE: ENTER THE GLADIATORS.   With the lack of demonstrable scale-up, the reputation of software reuse was waning within the line of business. The opposite, however, was true in the company at large. Urged on by recent government initiatives and mandates, and a slew of executive summaries about the benefits of reuse, the company's top management—just around this time—instructed the corporate software technology group to institute software reuse around the company.**<19>**

As we leave the scene, representatives from the corporate group are meeting with various members of our line of business, "introducing" them to the ideas of domain analysis, and taking notes about the experiences we have just described (Figure 5-19).

5.2 SCENARIO ANALYSIS

In the scenario, several key events were identified. These events are analyzed and interpreted in the commentaries below.

5.2.1   Event 1: Nonstarter

Jim's offhand comment—that the proposal from Joe and Mike is probably a nonstarter—raises questions about how reuse opportunities are identified and assessed. Frequently the motivation for such a remark is difficult to determine: Is it a knee-jerk defense against anything new? An implicit lack of trust in the judgment of Joe and Mike? An expression of pessimism about software process change in the company (or in general)? A belief that if the idea were any good they would already be doing it, or Jim would at least be hearing about it from his peers or management? A belief that some things that are "good in principle" can, in fact, be harmful if they interfere with the established working routines, schedules, and resource allocations?

As technology transfer "in reverse," reuse opportunities can be easy to miss. They can begin anywhere in a software development organization: they may grow

Figure 5-19   Corporate sends in the high-powered team.

from the bottom up, rather than as mandated initiatives or large-scale investments. Like the shoot of a plant, however, such bottom-up growth can be thwarted easily through neglect.

Belief maps can help in understanding what motivates a manager to sign on to, condone, tolerate, neglect, or discourage a reuse opportunity. Continuing the horticultural metaphor, does the manager view the "plant" as a source of nutrition for the organization's work, as a mere decoration, or as a weed? If he sees it as a decoration—nice but not essential; not of direct, quantifiable value—will he tolerate it because it might improve morale? At what cost? And is "toleration" an effective death sentence? Or does the manager see the proposal as neither nutrition, decoration, nor weed, but as a combination of features that has no chance of surviving—an evolutionarily unfit species?

Imagine that Jim had been gung-ho on the opportunity and Janice unenthusiastic. Then what would we wonder about Jim's motivation and underlying belief map? Does Jim see this as an unusual opportunity to satisfy his customers? Is he bending over backward on this occasion to keep Joe happy? Or maybe he doesn't like Janice and wants to send her on a fishing expedition.

Whatever Jim's motivations and beliefs are, his behavior regarding the opportunity permits rich interpretation. Grounding such interpretation by reflecting on underlying beliefs can help tease out early patterns that may later appear in a more fully developed form. Articulating beliefs and their reasons, then evaluating how well those reasons match the facts, can go a long way toward effective analysis of reuse opportunities.

5.2.2   Event 2: The Grand Vision

For someone who has bought into the ideas of software reuse—especially one who has recognized the nontechnical aspects of the problem—it is tempting to see reuse as a large-scale phenomenon, necessarily involving cultural change across the organization. The real challenges, after all, concern scale-up. Competent software developers have always practiced reuse in a private mode: they build their own function libraries; they adopt and refine their own processes to accomplish tasks of certain types. On occasion, they will share what they have with colleagues who seem receptive. The real problem is institutionalizing such practices. So, someone like Janice will argue, does not "systematic reuse" necessarily imply "organization-wide?"

The flip side of this issue is that the software engineers, who are already practicing private reuse (or even reuse on a project-wide scale), may see such grander notions as just so much hot air. They may believe that they are already doing what is necessary; or, like Joe and Mike, they may see an opportunity for improvement but their vision is still firmly rooted in the day-to-day realities of their assignments. They know that although private reuse already occurs, it is not trivial and requires substantial thought, experimentation, and skill. They know that the technical issues that arise are too specialized even to be expressed, let alone explained, to management. They will, therefore, view designs for organization-wide change with suspicion and skepticism.

There is justification for both these viewpoints. Underlying the grander view is the belief—justified by much empirical evidence in the industry—that private reuse

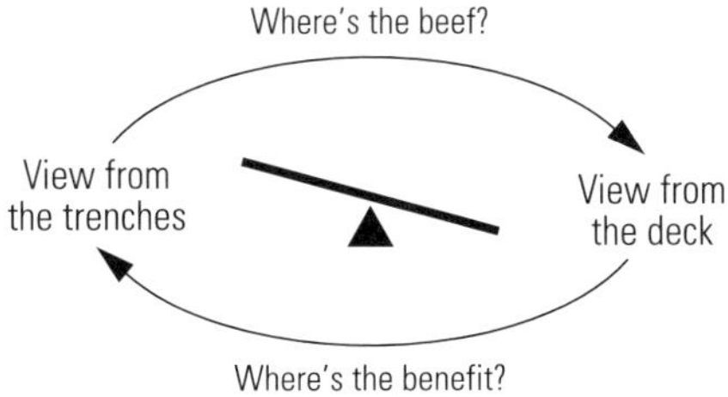

Figure 5-20   The view from the deck contrasts with the view from the trenches.

does not significantly impact the crisis of software engineering. Underlying the view from the trenches is the belief—justified by hard-earned experience—that reuse is difficult, that there is an art to creating reusable software, and that the process cannot scale up simply with a wave of the hand or a management endorsement of organization-wide reuse.

The fact that there is truth in both positions can lead to stalemates that frustrate reuse efforts at all levels. As shown in the system diagram in Figure 5-20, each side has an argument that—as long as it stays an argument—effectively defuses the other side's program. This defusing can be immediate and overt, resulting in aborted initiatives. Or, as in our scenario, it can be drawn out over the life of a reuse program and (intentionally or not) can reduce the program's effectiveness.

Alternatively, the tension in this conflict can be converted to fuel for learning that actually drives the reuse program. The knowledge creation grid (Figure 5-21), which identifies two dimensions of progress toward a knowledge-creating organization (private–public, implicit–explicit), provides a useful tool for accomplishing this conversion. The two positions, in the trenches and on the deck, are in fact advocating progress along different axes. The engineer in the trenches sees clearly (although he is unlikely to state it this way) the challenges in moving from tacit to explicit knowledge. For example: to define an interface that satisfies many different application contexts, the commonality in the applications must be articulated. This commonality may have been intuitively apparent for some time, but articulating it is not easy. Engineers like Joe and Mike recognize the difficulties, but also appreciate the benefits; hence they advocate focusing on progress along this path. The visionary on the deck, like Janice, understands the need for communication as part of reuse. Hence she directs her gaze along the private–public axis. The winning insight is that progress is needed along both axes. This observation can turn the unproductive conflict of our scenario into creative tension.

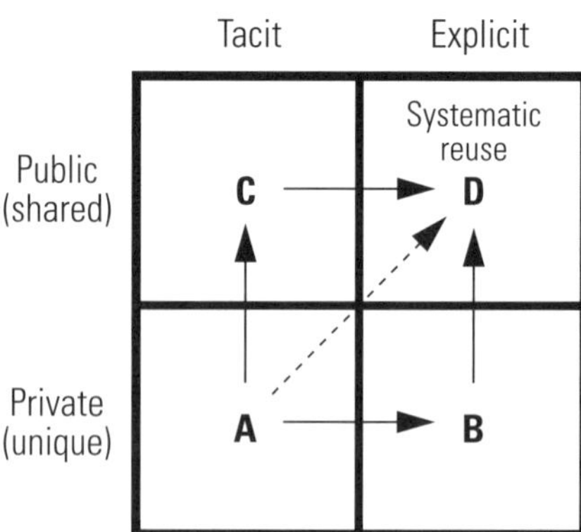

Figure 5-21   The knowledge creation grid clarifies the inherent tension between roles in the organization. (Adapted from conversations with S. Stuckey and R. McDermott.)

REFLECTION ON RESISTANCE:
"REUSE IS UNNECESSARY OVERHEAD"

The discrepancy between the view from the trenches and the view from the deck accounts for much of the resistance to reuse as a thing imposed from above. Consider, for example, the following scenario: a reuse advocate (who in our story could be Janice, Joe, or Mike) is urging other developers to package their output for dissemination and reuse. "This is not necessary," is one frequent response. Why is it not necessary? Perhaps because:

- "We're productive as is," or
- "We already practice reuse without the hype and trappings," or
- "There aren't that many opportunities to reuse."

Behind all these responses is a belief that what is being proposed (or imposed) is an "overhead" activity, which will not directly contribute to software development. Proceeding with a reuse initiative without addressing these beliefs runs the risk that developers will lose their sense of task ownership, and the overall alignment of the development team will break down.

5.2.3 Event 3: Bringing in Andy

Who does one involve in reuse planning, and how soon? At some point all stakeholders must be involved, at some level. But in the early stages there is a trade-off between the risks of exclusion (not involving those who hold an important stake in the outcome, or who can positively influence the process) and the risks of inclusion (involving too many varied points of view, goals, and assumptions, which may prevent the group from converging on a plan of action).

Janice sees institutionalized reuse as a major shift in the company's operating mode. She expects that the entire business model of the company might be affected, and she wants such issues to be considered explicitly from the beginning.

Janice's desire to invite Andy, the marketer, reflects her knowledge of the company's business reality: management will not invest in reuse if there is no clear return on the investment. The ROI can be assessed only by considering the impact of reuse on the company's customers. Since marketing is the liaison between developers and customers, Andy's presence is needed. It might even be possible to obtain direct funding from a customer to support the initiative; again, Andy is the person to assess this.

Mike and Joe may see Andy's presence as a potential diversion from the hard technical issues. They might fear that too much emphasis on the business questions might result in an overly simplistic plan: it may be sufficiently attractive that the nontechnical stakeholders will shake hands over it and then expect that the problem has been solved, thereby foisting unrealistic goals on the software developers.

Each participant is, at this point in the scenario, being driven by beliefs founded on his or her view of the harsh realities. The problem is that, like the seven blind men and the elephant, each participant has a restricted view of reality. In such situations, the beliefs themselves cannot be argued out to any real resolution. The facts underlying those beliefs must be articulated, and then used to construct a new model that encompasses both the technical and business perspectives.

5.2.4   Event 4: Manager's No-Show

The immediate question raised by Jim's absence from the meeting is: Why? We have already speculated on the reasons for his "nonstarter" comment; his "no-show" may simply be another iteration of this. But it may not be. There is an entire spectrum of possible explanations. Perhaps he really is resisting the initiative—passively, by not showing up—and maybe he does not even realize that this constitutes resistance. Perhaps he supports the initiative but only half-heartedly, and when other events require his attention he gives them priority. Perhaps, however, he strongly supports the effort since hearing Janice's response, but other matters that really do take priority prevented him from attending the meeting.

These are unknowns to the newly forming reuse team. Jim's absence indicates the possibility of a problem down the road. If that indication is accurate, understanding his guiding beliefs will become important for the success of the effort.

Asking Jim why he did not attend may provide answers, or it may not. Engaging him directly in an inquiry, in private, to draw out his reasons for not coming and not responding will be difficult but could be crucial to obtaining his future support of the project. Joe may be the person most well positioned to do this, but his skills at obtaining a nondefensive response from Jim are questionable. Generally, resistance is the indirect expression of some harsh reality. Can Joe elicit enough information from Jim to reveal the deeper meaning?

One approach that makes use of the Ladder of Inquiry is for Joe to articulate his own reasoning to Jim for why this project has potential for him, and also perhaps to reveal his own doubts. This will invite Jim to acknowledge his behavior and perhaps disclose some of the reasoning or "data" behind it.

Making a move of the type described above can be quite important at this point in the project. The cycle of broken promises often quickly becomes a vicious one that continually lowers everyone's expectations of each other. The more everyone accepts this lowering, the more difficult it becomes to see what is happening. Hence, the more difficult it becomes for Joe (or anyone) to inquire about Jim's nonattendance.

The system diagram in Figure 5-22 shows two self-reinforcing patterns of requests, promises, and follow-through on commitments. Especially at this formative point in a team's development, addressing failed commitments like the manager's no-show can set an important tone for how all conflicts are handled on the project. This is a critical moment in determining (1) how conflicts will be handled, (2) how to obtain support from management, and (3) what kind of support is actually needed.

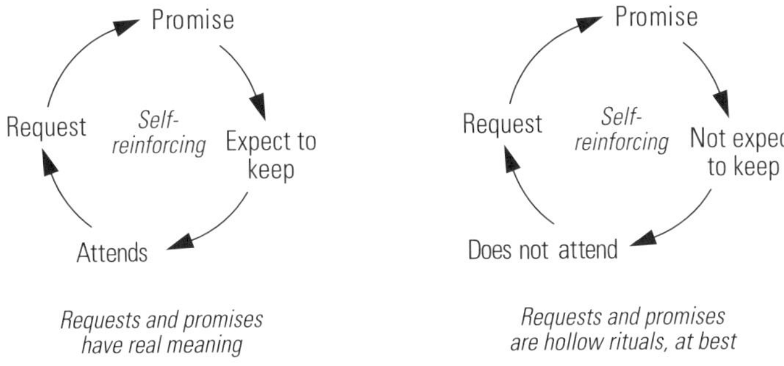

Figure 5-22   Self-reinforcing request–promise patterns.

5.2.5   Event 5: The Undesired Guest

We have already discussed the difference in perspective between Janice on the one hand, and Joe and Mike on the other. As Janice invites Andy to the meeting and Andy accepts, we see the differences escalate from perspective to action. Besides the difference in opinion, we now see a difference in style: a willingness to take action behind the backs of one's colleagues. Since the goal of the initiative is to institutionalize reuse—a form of knowledge sharing—Janice's withholding of information at this point is particularly ironic, a possible indication of "not walking the walk."

The breaking of trust at this point in the story will be a factor in the mixed success that follows. It sets in motion a dynamic, depicted in the system diagram in Figure 5-23, in which individual agendas work against the espoused goals of the team. The pattern starts off with a lack of alignment in the objectives of the team members. Some members may then fear that the team will not approve of certain actions they wish to take. If they nonetheless desire to remain on the team, they will take such actions covertly (Janice's invitation to Andy). This leads to events and consequences that were not foreseen in the team's plans (Andy's attendance), and as a result the plans originally developed by the team (Joe and Mike's memo) become less and less relevant or applicable. If these developments are not acknowledged, the diminishing relevance of the espoused plans will be compensated by ad hoc measures, which can undermine the assumptions on which the team's very formation was based.

The self-reinforcing aspect of this pattern is illustrated in Figure 5-23 by the snowball rolling downhill (a device we borrow from [Seng90]). The self-reinforcement comes from continuing silence about the members' divergent goals. Since the diversity is not expressed, there is no opportunity to manage it through, for example, continual realignment.

In our scenario, part of the problem is that the goals of the team have not yet been clearly articulated. The effort is, after all, still in an initial exploratory stage. Our analysis shows, then, how important it is to articulate stakeholder goals early in the planning process, and to reassess them continually.

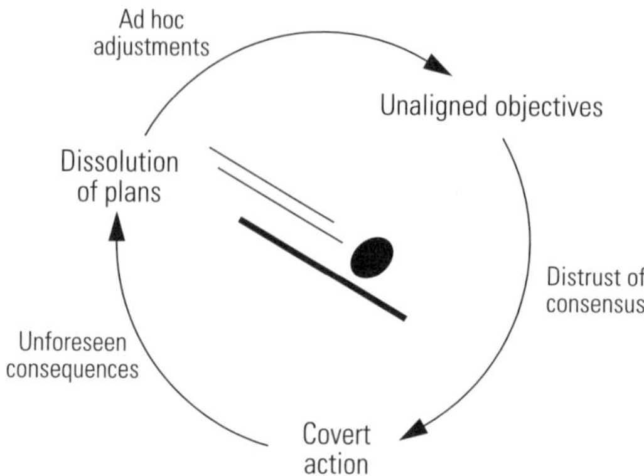

Figure 5-23   Vicious cycle stemming from unaligned objectives.

5.2.6   Event 6: Janice Urges a Big-Picture Approach

Janice's focus on the big picture is an escalation of the issues discussed in the commentaries on events 2 and 3. It is interesting to see that despite the success of the initial reuse pilot project, the positions of the team members have not converged. In fact, the small success can have the opposite effect, reinforcing the divergent beliefs of each team member. With their underlying beliefs now confirmed, each member views the next logical step according to his or her original agenda. Success, then, can widen a rift rather than close it.

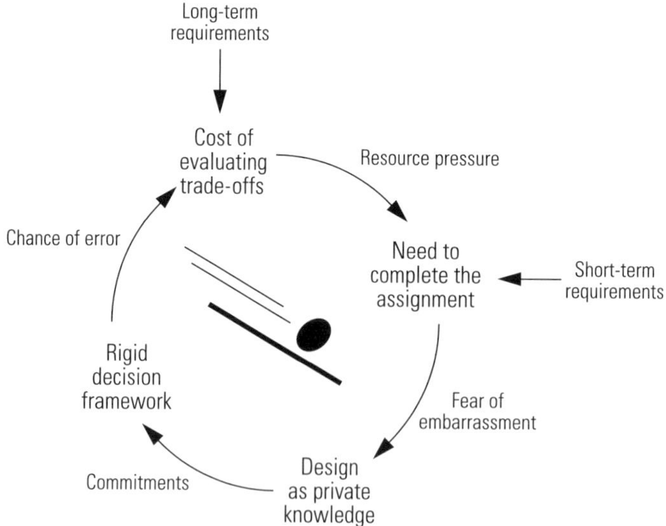

Figure 5-24   Resource pressures reinforce resistance.

REFLECTION ON RESISTANCE:
"REUSE REQUIRES TOO MANY RESOURCES"

The connection of this event with reuse as knowledge sharing is worth taking seriously. Argyris writes of the way issues and positions become "undiscussable" in an organization because the participants wish above all to avoid embarrassment—their own as well as others'. When this dynamic occurs in software development, it reveals patterns that work against reuse.

Let us again consider the scenario in which a reuse advocate (e.g., Janice, Joe, or Mike) urges colleagues to package their products for reuse. In addition to the response that "This is not necessary" (discussed in an earlier interlude), another common response is "There are not enough resources." Such responses usually contain an element of truth, but also contain hidden meanings, which make them resistant to dialogue.

Diverting scarce resources can increase development pressure, leading to products that are less, rather than more, reusable. The developer is, in effect, saying "If I have to spend time packaging my product for other developers' consumption, I cannot spend that time designing it for maximal value to the customer." This argument pits the interest of other developers against that of the customer—probably a shortsighted view, since the customer will benefit from cost-effective maintenance of the software. It is a skillful response, though: by shifting attention to a supposed conflict between two other parties, the developer removes himself from the spotlight.

This pattern serves to conceal two types of information: (1) trade-offs between immediate customer satisfaction and long-term reusability, and (2) design decisions intended to maximize customer satisfaction within the constraints of a project's schedule, budget, staffing profile, development environment, and so on. The truth in the developer's response is that resources are limited and, therefore, compromises are probably necessary. The falsehood in his response is that numerous policy decisions are not subjected to resource constraint arguments. They are viewed as necessary priorities. The allocation of different tasks is a value-based decision, disguised as a decision driven entirely by resource constraints.

The resistance, seen in Figure 5-24, is airtight: with every privately made decision, the framework of design commitments and constraints becomes more restrictive, narrowing the range of choices for future issues. This in turn raises the stakes when a decision turns out to be wrong: although there is a need to reevaluate the decision, the cost of reversing all dependent decisions has risen dramatically, and so has the potential for embarrassment. All participants, then, have a stake in maintaining the "undiscussables."

The system diagram in Figure 5-25 describes this dynamic and shows how it interacts with the pattern discussed in the commentary on event 5. The reinforcement of beliefs that success brings causes each member to believe more strongly in his or her original agenda. As long as people keep their differences visible and make a conscious attempt to find common ground, there is potential for coordinated action. But if the differences become too wide or positions become held too strongly for compromise, the unproductive pattern discussed in Section 5.2.5 can take over.

The unproductive cycle is in its least stable state when plans start to dissolve. That instability provides an opportunity for systematic (rather than ad hoc) adjustment, which if taken can lead back into the productive cycle.

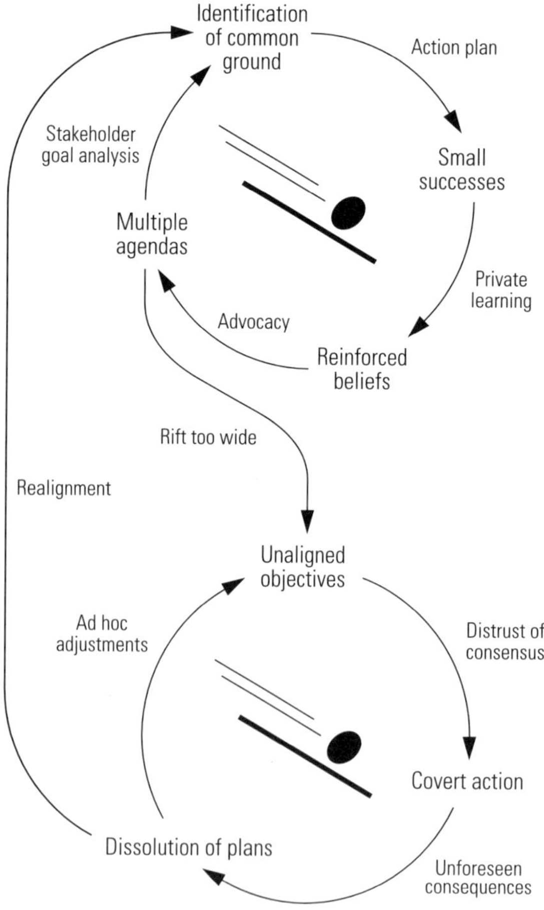

Figure 5-25   Small successes reinforce divergent beliefs.

Finally, the potential for instability in the productive cycle can be reduced if private learning is replaced by team learning. This is shown in Figure 5-26: when the perspectives of all members of the team are applied together to draw lessons from a successful project, beliefs may be modified instead of reinforced. By collectively drawing conclusions from a common experience, the team can become more cohesive and the agendas more, rather than less, aligned.

5.2.7   Event 7: Joe and June Feel Used

Joe and June's response is another symptom of the differences in vision discussed above. The fact that the team continues to move forward reflects the recognition that, despite these different agendas, the two "camps" depend on each other. Joe and June need Janice to represent them to management—or they think they do.

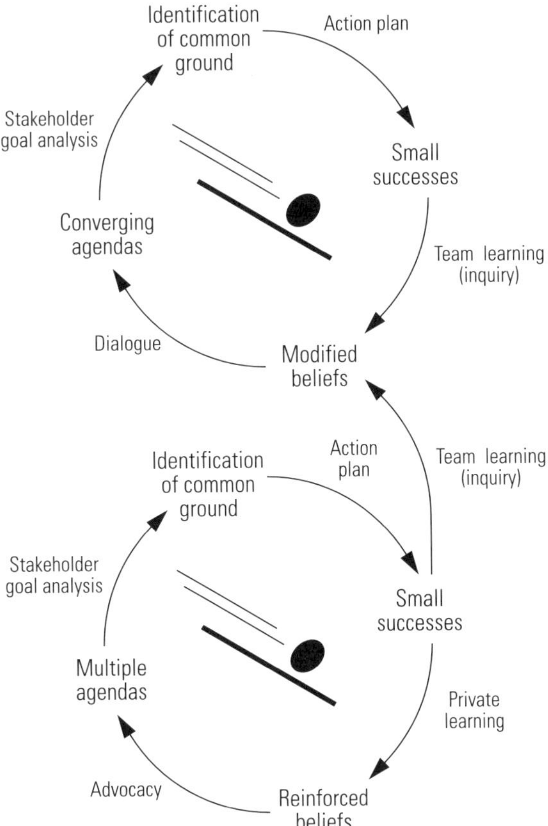

Figure 5-26   Team learning replaces private learning.

At the same time, they wonder whether she is a "loose cannon" given to overambitious declarations which they, as the engineers, will have to make good on. They are worried that her real goals in this initiative have more to do with empire building than with improving the company's business processes. If so, are they simply her pawns? Or are they overestimating Janice's power, and her hunger for power? Janice, in turn, needs Joe and June to give her credibility among the organization's engineers. We do not see any sign, however, that Joe and June will use this leverage to temper Janice's vision with their own.

We see in this event how the undiscussables become food for speculation about motives. The speculation reinforces feelings of disempowerment, which in turn fuel unspoken resentments, which raise the stakes and make the issues that much more difficult to discuss, as diagrammed in Figure 5-27.

5.2.8   Event 8: Joe's Project Manager Feels Bypassed

The ambiguities discussed above in relation to Jim's no-show have now escalated to the point of potentially damaging the reuse initiative. As the initiative expands, the buy-in of project managers will become more and more crucial. But Jim has never explicitly bought in, nor has he explicitly rejected the initiative.

All we can say about Jim's position in relation to the initiative is that it remains ambiguous, both to us, as outside observers, and to the reuse team—perhaps even to Jim himself. His concerns about meeting project milestones and having resources taken away from his project are fully understandable. He witnessed such problems even during the initial experiment. But is it also the case that he simply feels left out of the process—that he is not viewed as a stakeholder in the reuse initiative? Janice's method of keeping Jim nominally in the loop by sending him periodic

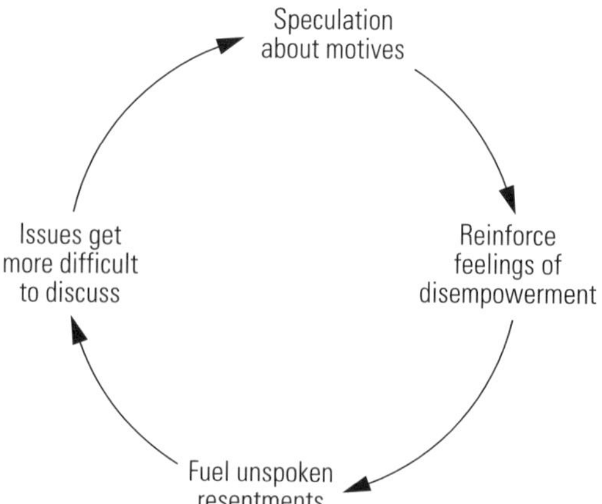

Figure 5-27   Undiscussables fuel a vicious cycle.

e-mail may be backfiring, giving Jim the sense that Joe and Mike are now reporting as much to Janice as to him.

The reuse team is probably speculating a great deal about the reasons behind Jim's no-show. Such disconnects can escalate quickly and reveal that all was not well before. Clearly Janice or Joe would help the project a great deal by using the Ladder of Inquiry here to directly find out about Jim's reasoning for his behavior. Given Jim's focus on his projects and his impatience with anything else, it is the team's responsibility to check more frequently and more thoroughly with him about where he stands vis-à-vis this project.

A laissez-faire attitude may be adequate in this case, and active support may not be required. However, it is also a case in which the reuse team should have been rigorous about stakeholder analysis in order to identify who can hurt the effort if a stakeholder's needs (stated or unstated) go unmet. Luckily, Jim is just getting nervous and perhaps flexing his muscles so far. He has not pulled Joe or Mike off the project... yet.

5.2.9   Event 9: Nothing But Good Software Engineering

A lot of attention has been paid to quantifying the return on investment in software reuse [Gaff89, Crui91, Barn91, Reif91, Gris95]. The reason is clear: investment in reuse competes against investment in direct value-producing efforts. If reuse is seen as a means of process improvement rather than as a direct value-producing endeavor, the burden of proving ROI will lie heavily on the advocates of reuse. The competition between the two forms of investment is summarized in the system diagram in Figure 5-28.

Janice was right in expecting management to challenge the team with this issue, but she did not foresee all the related arguments. ROI arguments are vulnerable for several reasons. First, there are not a lot of data to support them, because there has not been long-term comparative measurement of processes with and without reuse. This is partly because reuse as a recognized discipline is still fairly new, and also because researchers are still trying to decide what the appropriate measurements should be.

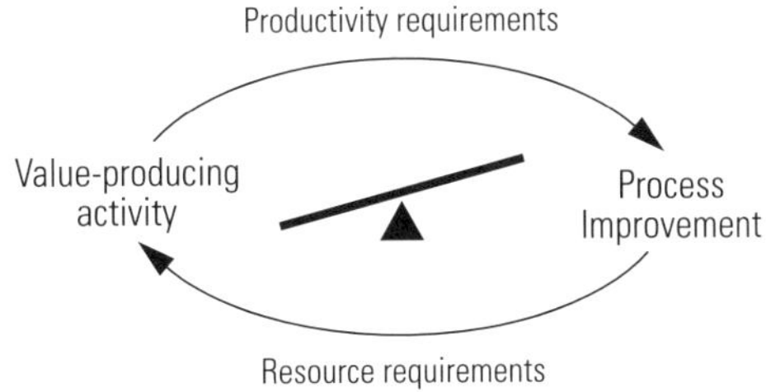

Figure 5-28   Competition between application and infrastructure investment.

Second, ROI arguments are always speculative, in any endeavor. The listener knows full well that the best "spin" and the most optimistic interpretation are being put on the available data. This knowledge, however, remains undiscussable because the ostensible purpose of the ROI presentation is to provide solid, credible predictions. Thus, if the listener is not predisposed to invest in the venture, ROI arguments are unlikely to convince him.

Janice also did not foresee the argument that reuse is "nothing but" good software engineering. Coming from management, this argument is remarkably similar to the software engineer's response discussed earlier: "We already do this." Both responses demonstrate the trap of regarding reuse as a technology that must be promoted and transferred, rather than technology transfer in reverse (as discussed in Chapter 3). The more one argues the issue in terms of conventional technology investment and transfer, the weaker one's position becomes, because the thing one is promoting is so intangible. To quote Gertrude Stein, a noted literary change agent, "There is no 'there' there."

When a presenter is caught flat-footed, it is a sign that the belief systems of the listeners were not adequately considered in developing the presentation. In our scenario, careful thought about the LoB manager's belief system might have revealed the need to present reuse as a measure that directly creates value (as opposed to indirectly, by improving processes), and to present it as technology transfer in reverse rather than as something new to be foisted on software developers.

5.2.10   Event 10: Didn't OO Already Solve Our Reuse Problems?

Managers who have been sold on object-oriented technology are often confused by the promotion of reuse as something distinct from OO. Less technically savvy managers may have bought into OO as the "silver bullet" that was supposed to transform software development from a craft into an engineering discipline [Cox90]. To such a manager, the appearance of reuse as "the next latest thing" may seem like technological bait and switch: "We know we told you that OO was going to solve your problems, but now we're here to tell you that what you really need is reuse."

Managers who understand something about OO may have assumed that objects (as opposed to other types of software component) are intrinsically reusable, since they have well-defined interfaces. This position has been put forward by technical advocates of OO, and it should not be regarded as an expression of technical ignorance. Arguing to the contrary—explaining why even a well-encapsulated object is not necessarily reusable—requires subtle software design considerations that are not easily communicated to management [Berl90]. Arguing that even reusable objects may not actually be reused involves broader considerations such as those discussed in the OO literature [Gris95].

In the OO community itself there is skepticism about reuse as something different from, or value added to, OO [John95]. Belief mapping and the Ladder of Inquiry can be effective tools in defusing this clash of communities and self-interest by shifting the focus onto the technical and empirical facts: how and when software is reused. Conveying the point to management can be more difficult, though, because the detailed technical facts cannot be brought to bear.

Here the grander view held by Janice and her ilk can be effective in winning management over. The idea that reuse is more than constructing reusable components, the notion of reuse as knowledge creation and sharing, the view that reuse is technology transfer in reverse—these concepts are potentially meaningful to people who think in terms of business models. The challenge is to formulate the argument in those terms, starting from the models a manager already uses to understand his or her job.

5.2.11   Event 11: Clueless About Domain Analysis

Pitching domain analysis to a management audience is a challenge. If the problem in selling reuse is that there is no "there" there (other than OO, which "we already do"), then consider how lost managers will become when the talk turns to modeling commonality and variability in a domain. Is it reasonable to expect management to understand these concepts? A manager may never have suffered through trying to bend a rigid software interface. He may never have been forced to reinvent the wheel because the last one built was the wrong size. Few managers have ever experienced the harsh realities of software development: for example, learning that the new whiz-bang component one has just built is totally at odds with the design assumptions of a fellow developer. Can such people, even if quite intelligent, really see the significance of domain modeling, and the distinction between reuse and OO?

The problem is not that the listeners are unintelligent. It is that their experience is different from the software developer's. The reuse advocacy team, as the petitioner in this process, cannot expect management to come out and meet them on the turf of technobabble. Failure to meet management on their conceptual terrain may be enough to disqualify the presentation from the start, in some managers' eyes.

The LIBRA scenario technique is one way to bridge this gap. The concrete role-to-role interactions and decisions are common experiences that everyone in the organization can relate to. By keeping the scenarios fictional, the emotional temperature can be kept down, at the same time allowing each participant to see herself in the story.

5.2.12   Event 12: Why Not Contract R&D?

The query about funding the reuse initiative through a contract should serve as a warning sign to the presenters. It suggests half-hearted commitment on the part of management: "We will support the effort as long as it does not cost us anything." This can be a form of resistance similar to the proof-of-ROI cycle discussed above. At worst (as happens in our scenario) it can lead to efforts undertaken without sufficient resources, and without a commitment by management to follow through in the long term. This is a setup for failure.

Alternatively, the contract R&D proposal might indicate a sincere desire to minimize the cost of the initiative, without implying a lack of real support. But such a position reveals a misunderstanding of the initiative. Contract R&D could certainly support the development of method and tool prototypes, and even their pilot application. But technology development and evaluation is not the goal of this initiative (although it may occur along the way). The goal, rather, is to change the way business is performed. Contract R&D by its very nature cannot effect such change: its course is, in the final analysis, driven by the contract rather than by the needs of the performing organization.

Because the suggestion is, on the surface, so innocuous—who could argue with an approach that allows the initiative to happen and at the same time reduces cost?—it can be difficult to confront. To argue against it can be construed as weakness in the proposal, a lack of confidence that the initiative could be sold to an outside customer. Responding to the suggestion requires that it first be interpreted correctly, either as stalling tactic or as misunderstanding. In the former case, contract R&D is not the issue at all; the presenting team must try to find the real reason for resistance, and then decide whether they can address it. In the case of misunderstanding, it is important to stress the need to change the business model through technology transfer in reverse.

5.2.13 Event 13: The Pilot

The undiscussed issues and ambiguous motives that we read between the lines of the presentation now converge in the outcome, the decision to fund a pilot domain analysis. The allocation of funds for a pilot can be viewed as an attempt to test the waters before making a major commitment (a form of learning), or as a setup for failure (a way of maintaining the status quo). The latter interpretation is supported by the observation that management made no longer term commitment, even contingent on the pilot's success. Specific success criteria were not identified as part of the funding decision. This suggests that the pilot was not viewed by management as a step toward a strategic goal.

The small level of funding may also indicate a misconception about such efforts, namely, that they are "linear and continuous," in the sense that if you provide a fraction of the requested funding, you will get that fraction of the results. In reality there is a quantum relationship between investment and results: a certain critical amount of effort must occur for there to be any useful results at all. Making this point can be dangerous for the reuse team, since it can be construed as a sign of weakness in the proposal. Turning down a reduced level of funding can be viewed as a sign of business immaturity or rigid idealism, or as a defensive measure to avoid having to put one's ideas to the test.

All this is the stuff of belief models, and in our scenario most of it remains unarticulated—a fact that does not bode well for the continued success of the effort.

REFLECTION ON RESISTANCE:
SURFACING THE HIDDEN REALITY

The team tried to anticipate concerns and objections in their planning. In the actual presentation, however, they encountered problems for which they had no plans. These came from several areas. In dealing with objections and concerns, it becomes a challenge to distinguish "good faith" concerns from resistance. At first, it is most appropriate to take the issues at face value and seek clarification, address them with more/better evidence, or communicate additional information at a future time. However, when the same response persists repeatedly despite reasonable attempts to directly address the concerns, the responses may be construed as resistance.

Some resistance can be quite overt, stemming from basic differences of opinion about the effectiveness of an approach. More typically, resistance is covert, involving some objection or concern that a person does not want to state directly; this form of resistance is quite difficult to identify and deal with. Such resistance is an indirect expression of a harsh reality. Harsh reality is a strongly motivating problem that influences thinking and behavior and does not easily go away. Articulating a harsh reality takes skill and trust; most people don't advertise their harsh realities readily. Rather, what usually happens is that the harsh reality is expressed in some indirect form. This keeps it private and makes the behavior that *is* visible quite difficult to interpret and respond to appropriately.

Covert resistance is manifested in many forms, such as active objection, changing the subject, attacking the method, silence, or even half-hearted agreement. The team in our scenario cannot yet tell if it is meeting resistance to reuse in general, or resistance to any activity that does not immediately produce revenue, or resistance to anything new. They do not know...yet.

Using belief mapping and the Ladder of Inquiry, they might have been able to close the gap between the expressed objections and the real concerns of the management. What actually happened is that the real concerns (harsh realities) were undiscussable, so the objections and the responses took place only in the realm of what is discussable—the stated objections. This may be even more true when the managers are together in a group, as opposed to smaller meetings with the team members. In our scenario, the stated concerns take a few forms: asserting that we already do this ("There is no problem"), the technology argument ("But OO will handle all this"), just plain confusion, and the suggestion that "We want it if we can get it for nothing." As stated above, these are not necessarily resistance—unless they persist.

The team could have used belief mapping and the Ladder of Inquiry to (1) figure out whether these responses were in fact resistance, and (2) if they were resistance, draw out more direct expressions of the harsh realities.

5.2.14 Event 14: Janice Goes for the Glitz

Janice's increasingly rhetorical style shows the pros and cons of missionary zeal. Without such enthusiasm and commitment, it is unlikely that an initiative can overcome an organization's natural resistance to change. But when converting people to the cause becomes a driving force in its own right, the original purpose of the effort can be lost. The reuse initiative then becomes a technology initiative, subject to the conventions of technology transfer and, in this case, to the notion of "technology push" rather than pull. Priority then goes to demonstrations and other marketing devices; these give investors the impression of progress, but they can divert attention from the real work to be done. The system diagram in Figure 5-29 shows how this process becomes self-reinforcing.

Flashy demonstrations tend to confirm and increase management expectations, thus adding to the pressure to keep the executives happy with more demos. At the same time, the lack of attention being paid to the difficult but unglamorous issues prevents the initiative from having any substantive effect on the organization. This absence of obvious benefits tends to aggravate management skepticism, which also creates more pressure for flashy demos.

5.2.15 Event 15: Joe, Mike, and June Take Shortcuts with Domain Analysis

The belief that "reuse is just good software engineering" has a more specialized counterpart, the belief that "domain analysis is just identifying what is common to a

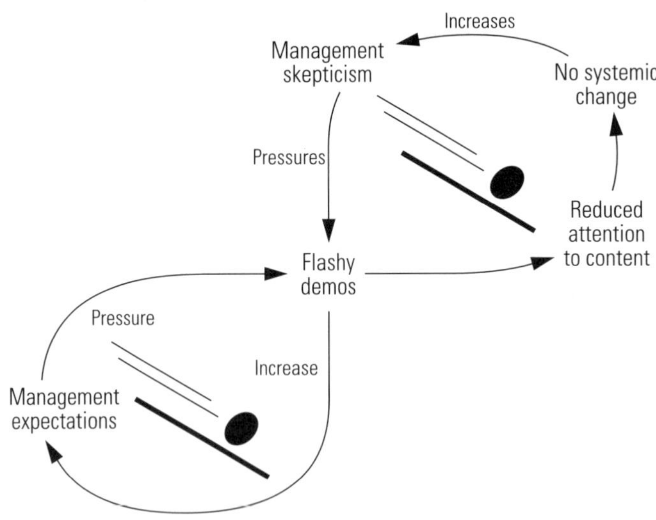

Figure 5-29   Self-reinforcing "demo-ware" cycle.

set of systems." All you have to do is gather some people who know the systems well, and have them articulate what's common and, by implication, what is variable.

Those who have tried it know that successful domain modeling is difficult because of such questions as the following:

- Which systems do we examine?

- Whose vocabulary do we use?

- How do we represent common functions?

- How do we represent variability?

- How do we avoid bias toward particular systems?

- How much detail do we provide?

- Who do we envision using the results?

- How do we envision the results being used?

From the point of view of the engineer in the trenches, such questions can have the ring of methodology-speak. They would say that so-called technologists who don't earn their living building systems raise such issues to justify their employment. They create problems where there aren't any.

We therefore find Joe, Mike, and June taking shortcuts around these questions. This is not necessarily a sign of ignorance on their part. We have encountered this type of impatience within the reuse community itself, including some of its most prominent members.

The problem is that the motivation for considering such questions has not been made clear. In our scenario, since Janice introduced the others to the domain analysis method, it was incumbent on her to motivate its steps. Otherwise, given the limited resources of a small pilot project, and the pressure to deliver tangible results to a doubting management, any steps that seem superfluous will invite being bypassed.

It is easier for Joe, Mike, and June to take shortcuts because their vision has still not been reconciled with Janice's. Faced with an apparently superfluous step, they can dismiss it as a symptom of Janice's grand vision to which they do not subscribe. Modifying the method can be a way for the engineers to reassert some authority, to regain a feeling of influence over the process, which up to this point has been dominated by Janice's agenda.

These shortcuts may succeed at making the technical team feel better, but ultimately compromise the technical work. What the team members still have not done is openly state and address the conflict. As pointed out previously, they could use the Ladder of Inquiry and belief mapping tools to do this. At this point in the scenario, we see how their continued failure to address these feelings in a direct, social interaction will begin to negatively influence the technical content of the work itself. These self-protective actions will make the real issues (i.e., differing goals and agendas) even more difficult to discuss in the future.

5.2.16   Event 16: One Stakeholder Project Pulls Out

The pullout of one of the two participating projects reveals a weakness of short-term reuse pilots: a client project has an interest in the pilot only insofar as it can employ the results within the project's time frame. When there are only two such clients, the pilot is placed under enormous pressure to deliver usable results. This, in turn, can lead to premature decisions in the design of assets that are meant to be reusable in many future projects.

The lesson in this is that reuse is not a short-term endeavor. If a pilot is started as a way of mitigating investment risk and as a vehicle for learning, then the short-term nature of the pilot must itself be recognized as a risk, which can be mitigated by placing the pilot in the context of a longer term plan that builds on the lessons of the pilot. There is also a simple lesson in numbers: if you need two pilot projects, you had better line up three or four in case one or two drop out.

There is a deeper issue as well. While some of the problems in Act Two were a result of viewing reuse as process improvement rather than value creation, here we see the opposite. The reuse pilot is expected to produce assets of provable value and to do so in a short time frame. The problem is an overly restricted concept of "value," which is still seen to reside in consumable products rather than in applicable knowledge. The organization has not assimilated the idea that systematic learning produces value. As a result, the reuse pilot is viewed as a form of technology evaluation, reuse being one technology alongside many others, and when it fails to deliver as promised, attention can shift to the "next latest thing," as seen in Figure 5-30.

5.2.17   Event 17: Other Project Managers Decline to Adopt the Domain Model

The failure of the pilot domain analysis to scale up is an outcome of the unresolved issues we have observed: unreconciled visions, incomplete stakeholder analysis, and lack of attention to domain scoping and pilot project goals. The team failed to define a business model that would address the concerns of potential client

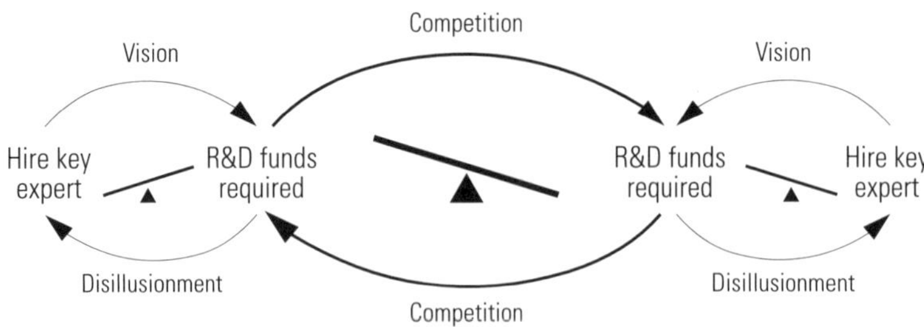

Figure 5-30   The technology investment seesaw.

projects, such as ownership of the reusable assets, responsibility for maintenance, and warranty of the assets' performance within well-defined contexts.

The importance of these issues is most easily seen in retrospect when attempts to scale up fail. Even among proponents of domain analysis, little attention tends to be given to the early phases in which stakeholder goals and alternative domain boundaries are considered. If we refer again to the knowledge creation grid, we can see that the focus of effort in domain analysis is still on the progression from implicit to explicit knowledge. The progression from private to shared knowledge—in this case, from relatively private (small pilot team) to more widely shared (multiple projects)—is assumed to be a natural consequence of articulating the knowledge explicitly, as long as it is articulated well via good domain modeling.

But the greatest difficulties in institutionalizing reuse lie on this private-to-shared axis. Even Janice did not see the extent of this. She recognized that the reuse initiative was about cultural change, but she failed to see the depth of the required change: that it involves embracing not just the idea of reuse and a general model of reuse processes, but also the knowledge, assumptions, conventions, expectations, and commitments that are expressed in a domain model. Until the domain model itself is shared and embraced, the cultural shift has not occurred.

We see again, then, the danger of starting a pilot project without establishing buy-in from key stakeholders to encourage shared ownership of the results and scale-up to other client projects. To do this in a sustainable way requires significant organization-wide planning. This is evident from the diagram in Figure 5-31, which shows the inevitable tension between local project interests and common organization-wide benefits.

This learning cycle is the core dynamic within all software reuse. The tension between codifying and stabilizing knowledge for reuse in a variety of contexts, and evolving and adapting that knowledge for specific application needs does not disappear with the appearance (or even the endorsement) of a domain model. The projects themselves occur in a dynamic customer environment. Reuse and evolution are two sides of the same coin. To attempt one while ignoring the other is to ensure failure.

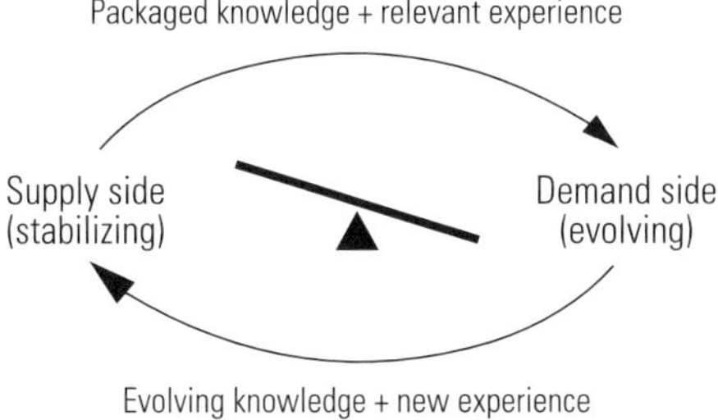

Figure 5-31   The learning cycle underlying asset supply and demand.

REFLECTION ON RESISTANCE: "REUSE IS TOO HARD"

The problem of shared domain models, which we have seen to lie behind the difficulties in scaling up, appears in everyday practice between software developers. Consider the following very common interaction: one developer has created a component he believes to be reusable in a variety of contexts. He hears of a colleague whose current task could make good use of such a component; so he informs the colleague of the component's existence.

The colleague attempts to use the component and discovers the hard way (after spending significant time trying to use it) that it does not fit into the design scheme—the network of assumptions, conventions, and commitments—upon which his application is based. This scheme cannot easily be changed because it involves the use of several other existing components and a code generator, all of which conform to the same design assumptions. As a result, the second developer eventually decides that he cannot reuse the first developer's component. He feels that he has wasted precious time trying to do so, and this reinforces his tacit belief that reusing other people's software (except well-established commercial products) is not effective.

From this example we draw the following lessons:

- Failure to articulate architectural or design assumptions can lead to reuse failure. (Knowledge must progress from implicit to explicit.)
- Failure to *negotiate* architectural and design assumptions can lead to reuse failure. (Knowledge must progress from private to shared.)
- Failed attempts at reuse reinforce skepticism. (Retreat back to private knowledge, or at best, implicit shared knowledge.)

5.2.18   Event 18: LoB Manager Fails to Champion Asset Base

The LoB manager declines to exert any influence on the projects under him to adopt (or try to adopt) the asset base. This confirms the indications during the presentation, in Act Two, that his support for the initiative is lukewarm. Since the pilot domain analysis was not placed in the context of a longer term plan, it is simple to let its results drop out of the limelight now. There is no perceived need to evaluate the reasons for nonadoption, to see whether the asset base or the underlying domain model can be adapted to meet the needs of other projects, or to draw lessons about the pilot project itself: its level of funding, scope, method, staffing, and so on.

To the LoB manager, the experience falls under the category of failed technology experiments. The monetary loss is not too serious because the level of funding was kept down, precisely because of this risk. The larger issues—what the experience means for the organization's business processes and software development competency—are not paramount for the LoB manager because he never fully understood what the initiative was about. His apparent fickleness is just a consequence of the gap in belief models, which the presentation did not succeed in bridging.

The organization's paradigm has not shifted from producing products to producing value through knowledge and learning. In a world in which this shift was truly embraced, we would expect the LoB manager to have a different view of his job than just, "Where shall I invest the money?" Rather, he would be a manager of learning and would champion a process to capture learning for better future investments. He would do this even if he still chose not to champion the asset base to other projects.

Until such a time, however, the team will have to settle for their own learning: they failed to bridge the belief gap. In retrospect, perhaps anticipating this consequence, the team might have used the Ladder of Inquiry and belief mapping in more frequent, individual, informal conversations with the LoB manager.

5.2.19   Event 19: Corporate Top-Down Initiative Launched

The appearance of the "gladiators"—a corporate SWAT team whose mission is to bring reuse to the LoB—is the next swing of the technology seesaw (see Figure 5-30) that occurs in the absence of long-term commitment.

The good news is that reuse is (apparently) being taken seriously at the top levels of the company. The bad news is that the SWAT team, too, is likely to view reuse as the next latest technology, to be disseminated through conventional technology transfer mechanisms (promotion, training, incentives). If so, it is reasonable to expect a replay of much of the pilot domain analysis scenario, perhaps on a larger scale.

Perhaps, however, the members of the SWAT team understand the idea of reuse as technology transfer in reverse, the principle of knowledge creation as value creation, and the view of evolutionary domain modeling as a form of team learning. If so, when they enter the scene they may take some time to consider the lessons of the scenario we have just witnessed; they may work with the local team to identify the disconnects that account for the pilot's less-than-resounding success; they may even take those lessons with them on their subsequent stops along the company's software development map.

If the SWAT team does promote the concepts and tools of LIBRA, their efforts may, over time, engender new learning-oriented, reuse-supportive patterns of interaction within the organization. Chapter 6 offers examples of some patterns of interaction that are characteristic of learning-oriented reuse.

NEW CONVERSATIONS

Having gone through the scenario exercise, our reuse advocates resume their dialogue, reflecting on what they have learned.

Paula: That was fun, and enlightening. I wouldn't have thought that constructing a fictional story would generate much insight.

Jack: The scenario approach has several advantages. It allows you to talk about the "undiscussables" indirectly. Because it is fictional, it can express concerns that would otherwise be threatening to the speaker, or to someone spoken of. And because the story is developed by a team, no one viewpoint will dominate.

Paula: What I liked about it was the brainstorming aspect. The characters and events turned out to be blends of the team members' experiences. By pooling our insights, we avoided what I was most afraid of: thinly disguised renditions of actual people and events. That almost certainly would have been counterproductive.

Hans: Did you notice how the analysis allowed us to capture the fine-grained dynamics of the reuse process? I was thinking: "Yes, that is what really happens person-to-person when people try to reuse. Those are the interactions that will make or break a reuse effort." And the system diagrams speak more loudly than all the process descriptions I've ever read. I see them and I say: "Uh huh, yeah, I've been there."

Cassandra: But in the final analysis, it is all just diagnostic. Suppose we develop a scenario and then analyze it. We arrive at fresh insights into what we do wrong. How does that help us do things better? Does all this new insight help us implement reuse?

Jack: I think it does. It shows how the conversations themselves are the conduit for sharing knowledge. If you hold certain types of conversation, knowledge sharing will not occur. It shows us the conversations that have to be changed.

Cassandra: But changed how? What kinds of conversation will allow knowledge sharing to occur?

Paula: I think the scenario analysis implies how. Consider the key events that we focused on. Each of them involved one or more players with his or her own agenda, his or her own values, his or her own beliefs about what works and what doesn't, formed over time through his or her own experience. None of this is articulated, so the players at best talk past each other. At worst, they dig in their heels and face off:

- The engineers (Joe, Mike, and June) did not fully appreciate the impact of the chosen domain scope on the potential for scale-up and winning consensus.
- Janice, the technologist, and Andy, the marketer, did not fully appreciate the complexity of the trade-offs that must be considered in arriving at a common domain model.
- Andy, in particular, did not have the technical background necessary to understand the harsh realties that Joe, June, and Mike faced.
- Ross did not understand domain modeling, and he did not see how reuse was anything out of the ordinary.

Rudy: So the players all had different belief systems, they pursued their own agendas, meant different things by the same words, were never really aligned in their objectives, and thus failed to accomplish what seemed to be a common goal. Does that happen often in the so-called real world that I'm about to enter?

(The rest of the group laughs.)

Jack: The question is what they could have done differently. I think the answer is this: they could have had a different type of interaction. Suppose we call these new interactions *reuseful conversations*. Paula, you've started thinking about reuse in these terms. What can you tell us about reuseful conversations?

6.1 PAULA REFLECTS

What makes a conversation reuseful? The distinguishing characteristic is the replacement of *advocacy* with *inquiry* when belief systems come into conflict. When the conflict occurs, you try to understand why it is occurring, rather than trying to make it go away by persuading the other party of your position.

Figure 6-1   If the essence of reuse is in sharing problem-solving knowledge, the essential barrier is the conflict of mental models.

This approach assumes, of course, that a conflict or divergence between belief systems is recognized—not always an easy thing to do in the heat of a task that has to be completed. Once acknowledged, the divergence in beliefs must be treated as the starting point for inquiry:

- What can this other person possibly have in mind?
- How is the other person's view of the world different from mine?
- What, in the other's experience, led to this way of looking at things, and can I appreciate its validity?
- What challenge does this pose to my own model of the world?

6.2 NEW CONVERSATIONS THROUGH INQUIRY

Let's consider what kinds of conversation the scenario might include if the players were tuned to identifying models in conflict, and treated such events as starting points for inquiry and learning.

Figure 6-2   The road to reuse lies in identifying model conflicts and learning from them.

Event 1. Jim (the project manager) tells Janice (the technologist) that the reuse proposal is probably a nonstarter. Suppose Janice asks Jim why this is. Jim might respond with some war stories about previous failed productivity initiatives. Or he might enumerate the programmatic obstacles to developing common components.

As the conversation moved toward specifics, Jim and Janice would be able to consider the current situation, how it is similar to or different from past experiences, and whether there might (or might not) be an opportunity for reuse now.

If Jim's beliefs are founded on general cynicism—for example, "people just won't do it"—the two might pursue the reasons for this. Instead of challenging the validity of such a belief, Janice could encourage Jim to articulate it further, and try to identify why "people just won't do it." This could lead to new insights into the cultural and social aspects of the organization, including the reward system and unspoken assumptions about employees' roles and responsibilities.

Event 2. Janice's vision of organization-wide reuse is more ambitious than the original ideas of the engineers, Joe and Mike. As we showed in the scenario analysis, the knowledge creation grid sheds light on both the validity and the limitations of each position. Janice is most concerned with progress from *private to shared* knowledge. The engineers are most concerned with progress from *tacit to explicit* knowledge. As the conversation clarifies this difference in concerns, both sides could gain insight into an aspect of the challenge that they did not fully appreciate beforehand.

Many of the subsequent events are similar, so let's skip to the latter part of the scenario:

Event 16. One development project pulls out of the domain analysis pilot, leaving only a single project as a customer for the pilot. A starting point for inquiry would be to contrast the current realities of the departing project (which needs the reusable components now rather than later) with the expectations of all parties when the pilot began. Were the expectations unreasonable? Did the development project's schedule or requirements change? If so, was the change something that could have been foreseen as a common risk? What does this experience imply for the allocation of resources between the supply side (those producing reusable assets) and the demand side (those who could use them if they were available when needed)? There is much to be learned here, and conversations between all parties would allow this to be organizational rather than individual learning.

Event 17. Other projects decline to adopt the domain assets produced by the pilot. The reasons for this resistance suggest topics for inquiry. Project managers were afraid that the pilot assets would not meet their projects' needs—understandably, since they had no say in the design of the assets. Members of the reuse team and members of the projects could now talk about what those needs are. Members of the projects would have to be willing to convey their requirements and constraints (including schedule, reliability requirements, etc.). Members of the reuse team would have to demonstrate sensitivity to the requirements, and reflect back to each project the variation they hear from other projects. By assuming the role of knowledge brokers, where the projects themselves serve as the ultimate source of the knowledge, the reuse team could improve the projects' confidence in the team's ability to provide value and diminish the perception of the pilot as a sandbox demonstration.

6.3 CASSANDRA INTERRUPTS: HARD TECHNICAL DIALOGUE VERSUS SOFT PROCESS TALK

Cassandra: All right, enough! You are showing what can happen when people listen to each other and are open to others' ideas, rather than facing off against each other. All that is well and good, but it is quite general. It seems little more than a problem-solving approach to professional interactions. Are you saying that that's all there is to implementing software reuse?

Paula: No, but it is the starting point. Let's remember that software development *is* a form of modeling. Many—perhaps all—technical barriers to reuse can be viewed as stemming from models in conflict. Some good examples of this are the papers [Berl90, Garl95] that describe how the architectural assumptions underlying a component's implementation can preclude its reuse in certain situations.

Hans: Are you suggesting that this kind of "models-in-conflict" situation is essentially the same thing we observed in the scenario? For example, Janice's big picture in conflict with Joe's pragmatism? The software design "models-in-conflict" seems like a solid technical issue, while Janice and Joe's issue seems a bit "touchy-feely."

Paula: This is a crucial point in LIBRA. Our position is that these conflicts *are* similar in an important way. Conflicting design models are one cause of resistance to reuse, but the scenario illustrates that there are other causes too. Even a conflict of design models is not strictly a technical problem. The nontechnical aspects concern the way in which the developers *respond* to the technical conflict.

Hans: You have a point. Software developers tend to think that there are two ways to design something: their way and the wrong way. Of course, better developers will regularly consider the trade-offs between alternative designs. But only rarely do they respond in a spirit of inquiry to a situation of models-in-conflict—another developer coming to different conclusions. For this reason, I guess I agree with you, Paula. The issues that arise in collaborative software development, where the agendas and models are of a technical nature, are the same as in collaborative planning and management of software development—which we illustrated in the scenario.

Paula: The difference between these settings concerns the type of agenda, model, etcetera. In one case, the agenda might be implementing a particular function to perform as efficiently as possible, while in the other it might be ensuring that the implementers themselves perform efficiently. For the implementers, the models to be negotiated will be models of the function being automated; for planners, the models to be negotiated will be models of the development process itself. The technical and process models inform each other; they are not separable. Inquiry into conflicts about one or the other type of model (technical or process) will inevitably lead to considerations of the other type.

Jack: That is why I believe there is a new, reuse-fostering flavor of conversation, which can be practiced at all levels of a development organization, and between all varieties of job role. Paula and I have developed some prototypes of these new conversations. They provide a roadmap to an alternative outcome to our scenario. For example, they could be used by

Janice and Andy (technology planner and marketer) to discuss the potential for a reuse-based process. They could be used equally well by Joe and Mike (both engineers) to discuss a build-versus-buy decision. These new interactions are the lifeblood of a *reuseful organization*.

6.4 THE REUSEFUL ORGANIZATION

Reuse is technology transfer in reverse: taking what the best software engineers already do, and extending it along both axes of the knowledge creation grid (see Figure 5-21). The two axes of the grid pose two broad challenges:

- Articulating reusable knowledge
- Sharing, negotiating, and refining that knowledge into shared assets

When the interactions between stakeholders do both these things, technology transfer in reverse occurs, and the organization moves closer toward institutionalized reuse. (In fact, it is practicing reuse.) The defining properties of a reuseful organization are as follows:

- It is knowledge creating.
- It learns.
- It converts its learning into knowledge assets.
- It applies those knowledge assets to produce further value.

In other words, a reuseful organization is one that *recycles knowledge*. It is characterized by a cyclical value chain in which existing knowledge (legacy) is built upon to generate new products or services ("assets"), new knowledge is created in that process, the new knowledge is integrated with the previous knowledge (perhaps complementing or displacing it), and is packaged for reuse in future products and services:

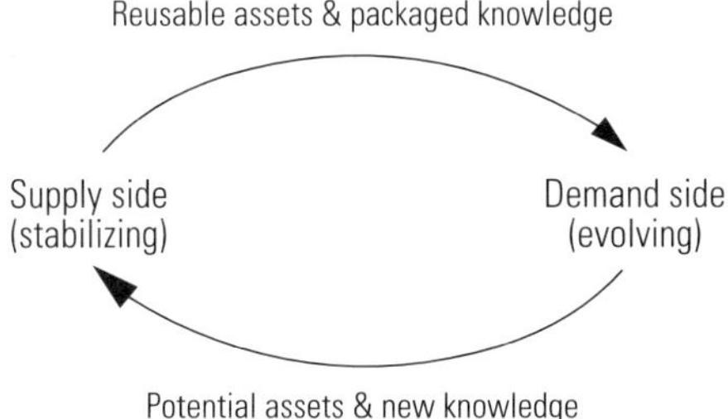

Figure 6-3   The reuseful organization recycles knowledge.

6.5 EXPLORING THE POSSIBILITIES
OF REUSEFUL CONVERSATIONS

The supply-side/demand-side model can serve as a roadmap to the universe of reuseful conversations. A reuseful conversation will typically be concerned with one of the two sides of the model, or with one of the two information flows. Figure 6-4 shows some examples: topics of inquiry are clustered around the part of the model they most closely pertain to.

We are not suggesting that these questions are the starting point for all possible reuseful conversations. They do, however, form a plausible set of periodic inquiries into the knowledge-recycling process. The conversations that we suggested earlier in this chapter as ways to turn around the scenario from Chapter 5 all fall into one or more of these categories, as shown in Figure 6-5. As that correlation shows, the questions can be adjusted to many different contexts. We invite the reader to discover additional situation-based inquiries and the reuseful conversations that can flow out of them.

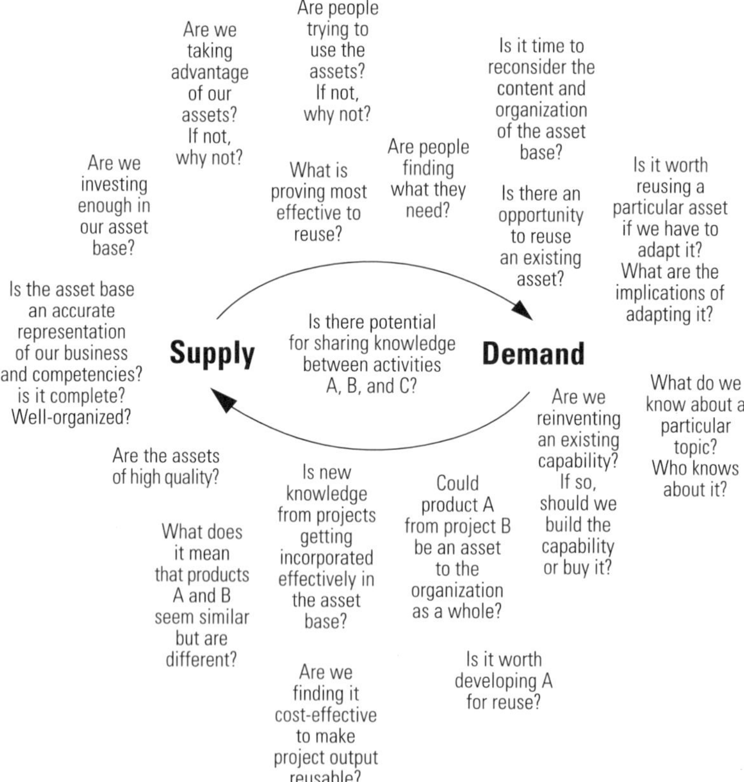

Figure 6-4   Each phase of the knowledge-recycling process invites a set of inquiries.

New Scenario	**New Conversation**
Event 1:	
Jim and Janice consider whether there is an opportunity for reuse. In considering why people might not reuse, they uncover new insights into the cultural and social aspects of the organization	Is there potential for sharing knowledge? Are people trying to reuse? If not, why not?
Event 2:	
Janice explains her concern with the transition from private to shared knowledge. Joe explains the difficulties of making tacit software knowledge explicit.	Could product A be an asset to the organization as a whole? What does it mean that products A and B seem similar but are in reality different?
Event 16:	
The pilot team and the departing project review their expectations and consider what changed and what could have been foreseen.	Are we investing enough in our asset base? Are we taking advantage of our assets? If not, why not?
Event 17:	
The reuse team and members of resisting projects consider the projects' requirements. The reuse team reflects back to each project the variation they hear from other projects.	Are people finding what they need? Is the asset base an accurate representation of the business?

Figure 6-5   Rescripting of the case study can be understood in terms of reuseful conversations.

6.5.1   Where and When?

The suggested topics of inquiry are both *scalable* and *translatable*. They are scalable in the sense that they can occur at widely different levels of an organization: from a team of developers charged with implementing a specific software function, to a corporate team monitoring software competencies and competitiveness.

Take, for example, the inquiry:

Are we taking advantage of our assets? If not, why not?

At the corporate level, the answers to "Why not?" might include some or all of the organizational barriers described in Chapter 5. Within a development team (or between teams), "Why not?" could open a series of technical discussions about design standards and architectural compatibility.

A more exciting development would be a combination of the two levels of discussion, as shown in the following example.

NEW CONVERSATIONS BETWEEN MANAGEMENT AND DEVELOPERS: AN EXAMPLE

1. Upper management decides that development productivity must be improved.
2. Directives flow down the management chain, urging employees to think about reuse and report back with respect to its feasibility.
3. The technical teams converse within and among themselves. They conclude that in principle more systematic reuse is possible, but that there are numerous nontrivial technical obstacles.
4. These conclusions flow up the management chain, but with each step up, the reporter's understanding of (and conviction about) the obstacles diminishes.
5. Upper management, now assured that there is an answer to the productivity problem, but forewarned that there will be some technical challenges, allocates a modest amount of funding for a reuse initiative.
6. These reuse and productivity goals are announced by upper management to the company at large.
7. Havoc breaks out in the ranks of the developers, who see these goals as completely unrealistic.
8. In response to the crisis, conversations are held between the developers and various levels of management. The developers try to explain some of the difficulties. Management tries to translate the implications into dollars and time.
9. The two species start to learn a little of each other's language. While managers are coming to appreciate the technical challenges, the techies are discovering cultural issues within their own teams that are getting in their way.
10. At the same time, more conversations are held within and between the technical teams. They explore the underlying design conventions and their implications for reuse. The newfound cultural insights are applied to these conversations, and the teams find it possible to talk substance much more effectively than before. They begin to have deep respect for each other's technical insights.

In this example, the conversations about "Why aren't we reusing?" occur not only at distinct levels of the organization, but also *between* those levels. This ability to cultivate new channels of information flow gives the conversational model of reuse far greater power than conventional methods such as mandates and pilots.

In addition to being scalable, the reuseful conversations are *translatable,* by which we mean that they apply equally to the negotiation of process models ("How do we build things?") and product models ("What are we building?"), and combinations of the two. Consider, for example, the inquiry:

Is it time to reconsider the content and organization of the asset base?

From a process viewpoint, this question could introduce an inquiry into the need for continued investment in domain analysis. From a technical viewpoint, the question could open a dialogue about mismatches between older and newer design paradigms.

Again, the most exciting development would be an interleaving of the two types of conversation. This might occur, for example, when an organization considers the need, opportunity, costs, and risks of a major legacy migration, say, from mainframes to Internet-based applications.

So, with all that said, let's look at how some of these conversations might play out.

6.6 PATTERNS OF INQUIRY-BASED CONVERSATION

A characteristic of an inquiry-based conversation is that there is *movement over a terrain of understanding*. At the end of the dialogue, at least some of the participants have a changed model of the world. When advocacy dominates, the participants may find themselves stuck in a process of continually repeating fixed positions. To the extent that the conversation moves, it is only to find new ways of refuting an adversary's argument. A good metaphor for this is a game of Ping-Pong in which the players continually hit the ball back at each other, trying to score points (Figure 6-6).

What kinds of movement occur in an inquiry-based conversation? We can identify a few basic patterns out of which such conversations tend to be composed. The simplest pattern is just monotonic *accrual of information*: each contribution to the dialogue adds a certain amount of information to the shared understanding of the participants. This is illustrated schematically in Figure 6-7.

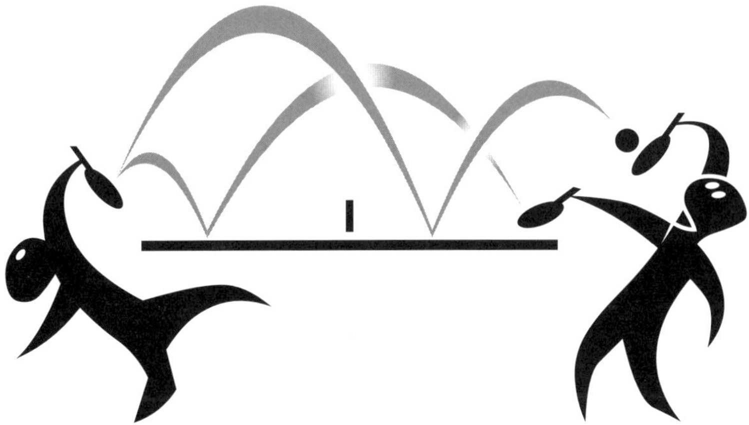

Figure 6-6   The Ping-Pong pattern is one sign of an advocacy-based conversation.

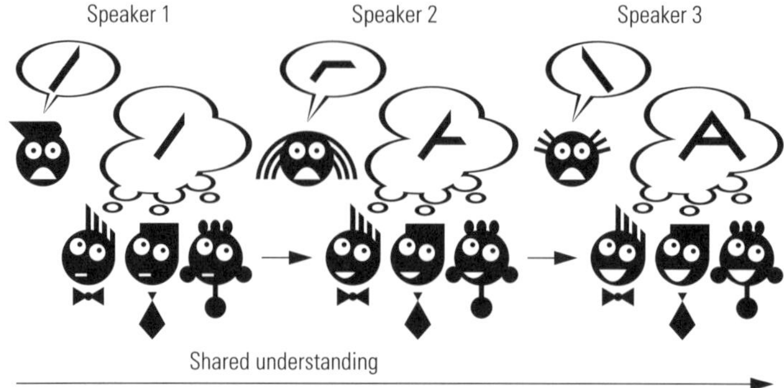

Figure 6-7   The simplest inquiry-based conversation pattern is accrual of information.

Here is an example of a conversation whose main movement is the accrual of information. In this and subsequent examples we make use of several generic roles to identify the participants in the conversation. Some of these roles are self-explanatory, but others may need more explanation. Rather than present all the roles at once, we introduce them as they are used in the examples.

EXAMPLE CONVERSATION: CAN SOFTWARE THAT CAME OUT OF A PARTICULAR PROJECT BE AN ASSET TO THE ORGANIZATION AS A WHOLE?

A software developer presents a new artifact (program, technique, etc.) to a colleague (the Evaluator) whose job is to select reusable software for inclusion in the organization's asset base. The Evaluator's task is to decide whether it should be included—and whether the artifact must be repackaged, or otherwise modified or enhanced, before it can be considered an organizational asset.

Developer: I just developed this incredibly cool capability. Let me demonstrate it for you.

He does so, and supplies the Evaluator with a package of information about the new software.

Evaluator: Impressive. I don't think we have anything else like that in our asset base.

Developer: I'm sure we don't—I looked hard for one before building this.

Evaluator: But it probably fits into—let me see—this category in the asset base, alongside these other assets here.

Developer: I agree, that's where it should probably reside.

(continued)

Each participant has now brought some information to the table: the Developer has brought information about the new component, and the Evaluator has brought information about the asset base. What follows is a question-and-answer process that elicits more such information.

Evaluator: How customized is it to your specific project's needs and constraints?

Developer: There are a couple of project-specific features. I tried to isolate them in modules with a well-defined interface so that other projects could replace them.

Evaluator: Do you have a design narrative to clarify for me which aspects of the software you regard as generic and which are project specific?

Developer: Sure do. I learned the hard way that it's the only way you'll let something into the asset base—and with our new incentive program, I'm pretty motivated to get things in there.

Evaluator: And to have them reused. That's a condition of the incentive program. It might seem as if I'm being picky, but it's in your interest as well as everyone else's.

The Evaluator again contributes some information, after which the question-and-answer process resumes.

Developer: Understood. When you look at the package I gave you, you'll see that I used literate programming techniques to create a nauseatingly complete record of my design decisions and rationales. It actually made development easier for me: I didn't have to hold as much in my head all the time.

Evaluator: And did you use any of the common design patterns that are becoming part of the community knowledge these days?

Developer: Yes, and when I departed from them I explained my decision in gory detail in the design narrative.

Evaluator: It sounds as if we might have a valuable addition to our asset base here. Let me study the material you've given me and get back to you.

An alternative outcome of this dialogue is that the Evaluator sees the potential value but does not believe that the artifact is reusable in its current form. She would then have to decide—along with those responsible for funding the asset base—whether it is worth investing in making the artifact reusable. Still another outcome might be that despite the project-specific implementation, the artifact is useful as an example for other projects needing a similar capability. In this case, the design process could be reused even if the software itself could not.

Figure 6-8   The elicitation pattern combines back-and-forth exchange with growing shared understanding.

In the example just given, we also see a slightly more complex pattern, which occurs when one participant requests clarification of what another participant has said. More generally, a participant may request information clarifying the situation being discussed. This pattern is distinguished from the first in that it explicitly invites interaction between the participants. We can think of it as combining aspects of the Ping-Pong pattern with the accrual pattern. There is a back-and-forth play between participants (consisting of question and answer), but with each exchange there is an increase in the shared understanding (Figure 6-8).

Here is another example of the *elicitation* pattern.

EXAMPLE CONVERSATION: REUSE AN EXISTING ASSET?

While building a system, a developer is faced with a functional requirement that she suspects has been encountered before. She converses with a colleague—the Broker—who she thinks may know of a suitable asset.

The Broker is a person who directs others to the reusable assets they need. The role may be viewed as part of the traditional librarian function. In this setting, however, the destination is not necessarily a "place" in a repository. It may also be the names of people who can provide useful knowledge about a type of task.

(continued)

> **Developer:** I need a component that performs the following function [she describes it] and it is subject to the following constraints...
>
> **Broker:** Here is a component that is probably the best match.

What follows is a conversation about the "3Cs": concept, context, and content [Lato90]. The concept is the function that the component is described as implementing. The Developer and the Broker compare this to the functional requirement that needs to be met:

> **Developer:** From the description, this component looks similar to what I need, but I'm not sure it's an exact fit.
>
> **Broker:** That may be because of the terminology the creator of this component used. Let's look more closely at the description.

A close examination of the component's documentation indicates that it might fit the bill, but the Developer is still wary. The second "C"—context—is addressed as a way of gaining more insight.

> **Developer:** What sorts of context did the developer of this component intend it to be used in?
>
> **Broker:** I wish he had provided that information, but all we have is some experience reports of previous users of the asset.
>
> **Developer:** Let's look at them, maybe they will give me a feel for what the asset is good for.

They examine the experience reports. These include reports of usage similar to what the Developer is intending, but apparently problems were encountered when the component was used this way.

> **Developer:** It looks like they were able to use the component, but it wasn't simply a matter of plug and play.
>
> **Broker:** No, but they did develop workarounds to the problems— maybe you could reuse those too.
>
> **Developer:** I would want to see how they implemented the workarounds. Performance is a key success factor for the system I'm building. I want to make sure they didn't insert code that will slow the system down too much.
>
> **Broker:** Luckily they included the content of the workarounds with the experience report. Take a look at it and let me know what you want to do.

(continued)

EXAMPLE CONVERSATION:
REUSE AN EXISTING ASSET? (continued)

The Developer examines the content—that is, the implementation—of the workaround, which from her point of view is part of the asset she is considering for reuse. It looks satisfactory from a performance standpoint, but the implementation will clearly use a lot of memory.

Developer: I will have to talk to the systems engineers, and maybe even the customer, about the memory implications. I'd like to reuse this component—it would save me a lot of development time—but I will need to get their approval. It might mean compromising on some other requirements.

Broker: Let me know.

The conversation then triggers several additional conversations between the Developer and her system engineering colleagues as well as with the customer. Various alternatives are considered, including relaxing some of the system memory requirements, and the possibility of modifying the found component or modifying the current design so that there is more memory available. In the end, the developer decides that it is worth modifying her design to enable her to reuse the component, and this decision becomes part of the design record for the system. The broker makes a note of this experience because it may indicate a recurrent need for a variant of the component.

A still more complex pattern illustrates the process of *progressive refinement* of group understanding. This pattern occurs when one participant makes a suggestion, another participant points out a problem with the suggestion, and the suggestion is then refined to accommodate the critique. As shown in Figure 6-9, this is an

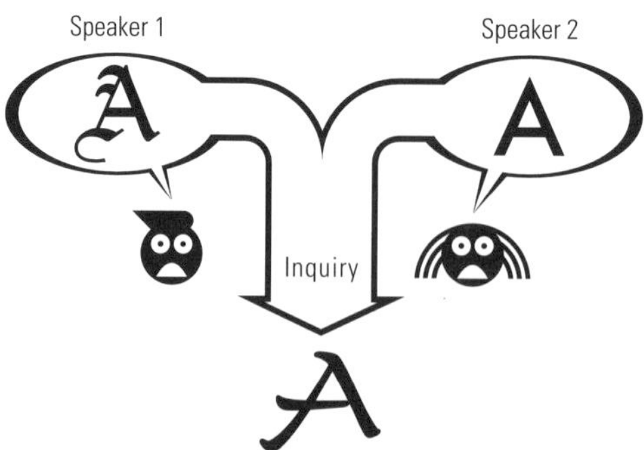

Figure 6-9   Shared understanding is refined through a pattern of hypothesis and critique.

example of the philosophical pattern of thesis/antithesis/synthesis, in which an apparent contradiction or conflict in views is resolved through a new formulation. The progressive refinement pattern represents the process of descending the Ladder of Inquiry; it is a sign of significant movement in group understanding.

EXAMPLE CONVERSATION: IS THERE POTENTIAL FOR REUSE BETWEEN CERTAIN ACTIVITIES?

This dialogue occurs between the Promoter and several developers. It represents the first step toward recognizing knowledge as an organizational asset.

The Promoter is someone who looks for reuse opportunities and communicates them to the people who can act on them. He may promote reuse on either the supply side (encouraging development of reusable assets) or the demand side (encouraging the reuse of such assets).

This conversation introduces three variants of the Developer role, each of which represents a certain attitude or orientation toward software development and, in particular, reuse. The Skeptic expresses doubts, the Practitioner draws on recent tasks for insight, and the Veteran talks from her experience. The roles are not meant as rigid categories. They are situated roles, which represent distinct stances or relations to the current topic of conversation. A Skeptic in one conversation may be a Practitioner in another.

Promoter: From the descriptions I've heard of your projects, it sounds to me as if you develop many similar capabilities. I wonder whether some economies could be obtained by pooling ideas and resources?

Skeptic: We've recognized this for quite some time. The problem is that each project has its own unique constraints and requirements, and it would take some serious thought to come up with a way of sharing capabilities.

Practitioner: Of course, we already do that at the level of common subroutine libraries and off-the-shelf packages. All the line of business projects use the same graphical user interface toolkit unless a particular customer objects vociferously. But the real economies would come from sharing application capabilities.

Veteran: The problem is that when a project gets turned on, it is under intense time and budget pressure right from the start—we always bid jobs as optimistically as possible. No one ever has the time to do the thinking that the Skeptic is talking about.

Promoter: But you all agree that in principle it would be a good thing?

(continued)

EXAMPLE CONVERSATION: IS THERE POTENTIAL FOR REUSE BETWEEN CERTAIN ACTIVITIES? (continued)

In response to the mixed receptiveness to his first proposal, the Promoter has qualified it somewhat.

Skeptic: A funny thing about software is that good things in principle turn out quite often to be not so good in reality. There are so many layers of interrelated issues that one cannot see in advance.

Practitioner: But I think we would all agree that it is worth considering: there is at least potential.

Veteran: But where could we get the resources even to consider it?

Promoter: You need to be paid to reflect, for a change. A lot could come out of it.

After first weakening his proposal (adding "in principle") the Promoter has made a new and stronger suggestion.

A variant of this pattern occurs when a question is posed by one participant, and another participant responds by pointing out a problem with the question. For example, it might be difficult to obtain an answer to the question as posed. In response to the critique, the question is reformulated.

EXAMPLE CONVERSATION: ARE WE REINVENTING THIS CAPABILITY?

A developer is assigned a task that she suspects may have been done before. She discusses this possibility with a colleague responsible for getting assets reused—the Broker.

Developer: This development item strikes me as something that other people must have done already. I wonder if there is anything available for me to use.

The Developer characterizes the development item in terms of the "3Cs"—primarily the concept (the first "C") which is a description of the purpose or function of the item.

(continued)

> **Broker:** There is a lot of work being done in that area. You might be able to find a commercially available product, or maybe even shareware, that does what you need.
>
> The Broker has acknowledged the Developer's concern, and made a suggestion.
>
> **Developer:** I know that this field is moving rapidly: last year I probably would have had to develop it myself, but I suspect by now there are a lot of implementations. The problem is, how do I find out what is available?
>
> The Developer acknowledges the Broker's information, and refines her statement of the problem accordingly.
>
> **Broker:** Our asset base has links into the World Wide Web. For this type of item you might look at the shareware repositories listed here.... You might also post a request for information on the following news groups.... I also recommend contacting a couple of companies, QWE, Inc. and RTY, Inc., and there are some recent books by Briar, Patchen, and Thorn that talk about this type of technology and might mention specific software packages. Also, give Patrick MacMullen over in Space Systems a call. He might be able to give you a dump on what's out there and what really works.
>
> The Broker has offered a refined response to the refined problem statement.
>
> **Developer:** I'll follow up on those leads.

Still another variation of the refinement pattern occurs when a problem statement is progressively refined. A participant presents a problem; another participant suggests a possible solution, but this does not completely address the situation, so the problem is reformulated.

A more complex variant of the progressive refinement pattern involves *resolution of multiple conflicting viewpoints*. In this pattern, the shared understanding is a growing realization of just how many disparate points of view there are concerning a given issue. At some point, a critical level of inconsistency is perceived, and there is an effort to resolve the views, resulting in a new, synthesized understanding (Figure 6-10, page 128).

EXAMPLE CONVERSATION: ARE WE INVESTING ENOUGH IN OUR REUSABLE-ASSET BASE?

This dialogue is initiated by a Promoter, who poses questions about the current state of the organization's reusable software assets. In response, several distinct viewpoints are offered.

Two new roles are introduced in this conversation. The Strategist takes the long view, the Analyst looks at the underlying causes, and the Technologist looks to the future. Again, these are situated roles: they reflect each participant's relationship to the topic being discussed (and to the other participants), and do not necessarily correspond to specific job functions or positions.

> **Promoter:** Do we have all the assets we want? Are they of sufficient quality? Are they flexible enough to support our projects? Are they known to developers, project managers, others? Are they ossifying through lack of use? Through lack of maintenance?

> **Strategist:** If we really want to share knowledge between projects, we need a richer asset base.

> **Veteran:** My experience using these assets has been mixed. I no longer assume that all their relevant features and constraints have been documented.

> **Analyst:** There are implicit architectural and design assumptions that reflect the historical source of the assets. I have run into conflicts between these assumptions and those of the contractors with whose software we have to interface.

> **Practitioner:** I might have used some of these assets on my last project if I had known about them.

> **Technologist:** These assets no longer reflect current design practice. The field has advanced rapidly and our support of the assets has lagged.

This example illustrates a diversity of viewpoints concerning the quality of the organization's reusable asset base. Some think the assets may still be useful, others believe that they are hopelessly out of date. When the conversation shifts to looking at the assets themselves (i.e., the topic changes from process to product), the diversity actually corresponds to the different software problem-solving models used by developers of the assets. This is illustrated in the following conversation.

EXAMPLE CONVERSATION: WHAT DOES IT MEAN THAT ASSETS FOO AND BAR SEEM SIMILAR BUT ARE DIFFERENT?

This dialogue illustrates an attempt to discover the significant features that distinguish, at some level of detail, assets that from a more abstract point of view are similar.

Another two roles are introduced in this example. The Classifier is responsible for organizing assets so they can be easily located by potential reusers, and for deciding where in the classification a particular asset belongs. Like the role of Broker, this may be viewed as part of the traditional librarian function.

The Negotiator's task is to mediate between models-in-conflict (more precisely, between the proponents of such models). In particular, the Negotiator might be called on to mediate between proponents of an existing classification system and of a revised one.

Classifier: I've just been handed asset FOO by the Evaluator for inclusion in our asset base, but I'm not sure what to do with it. It seems to be another version of asset BAR, but I don't fully understand their differences.

Negotiator: Are you sure they are different?

Classifier: The documentation suggests that the assets behave differently. The problem is that the differences I see concern very low-level properties. They seem like implementation accidents—choices that the implementers made for convenience, perhaps. But if I just place them both in the same bin, without providing any guidance on how to choose between them, I know I will get some angry reusers who have chosen the wrong one.

Negotiator: If you are correct in predicting that there is a right one and a wrong one for different contexts, then the differences must be significant.

Classifier: Yes, I'm sure they are, but I'm not sure that the developers themselves recognized the significance. They certainly haven't expressed it in their documentation.

Negotiator: Then we will have to get with them and jointly try to understand the difference.

Classifier: And if it turns out that these were accidental features?

Negotiator: Then we'll have to infer what the significant differences in behavior are going to be, and use those as the distinguishing features in the asset base.

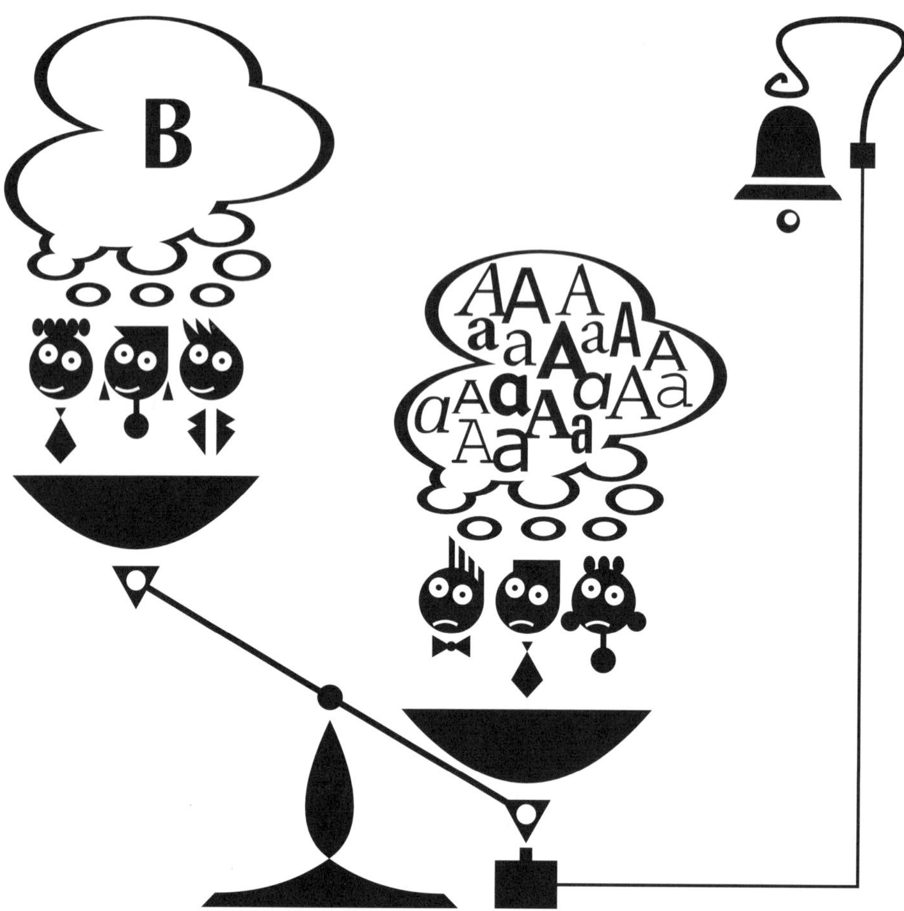

Figure 6-10   Inquiry occurs when the accumulation of diverse viewpoints reaches a critical mass.

6.7 COMPOSING THE PATTERNS: DYNAMICS
OF INQUIRY-BASED CONVERSATIONS

In an inquiry-based conversation, the patterns we have described are chained together in various combinations and orders. The particular pattern of composition accounts for a conversation's rhythm, its ebb and flow from tension to resolution, engagement to relaxation. The simplest composition pattern is a *succession of queries and answers* in which information is gradually accrued. Each query might be directed at a new source of information.

EXAMPLE CONVERSATION:
WHO KNOWS ABOUT A PARTICULAR TOPIC?
(OR: WHAT DO WE KNOW ABOUT THIS TOPIC?)

A Developer is faced with a task in an unfamiliar area, or a problem he is not sure how to solve. The dialogue is a chain of references to people or assets representing expertise or experience in the unfamiliar area.

> **Developer:** I need to know what we have done in this area. I have to build a component in this domain and I have never done that before. Where can I obtain insight into the do's and don'ts? In particular, I've encountered the following problem. . . . Has anyone encountered this before, and if so what did people do and what did they learn?

> **Broker:** There is a portion of our asset base that contains systems of the type you are working on. You could use those as a model, or look at the experience reports to see what the main issues are. I also know that Developer 2 has encountered similar problems—why don't you contact her?

Each resource to which the Developer is referred may in turn refer him to other resources (people or assets). In an asset base this may take the form of a series of hyperlinks, which the Developer can traverse until he finds the information he needs. Alternatively (or complementing this), a succession of contacts with people resources may occur:

Developer 1 [to Developer 2]:   I heard from Broker 1 that you've encountered the same problem I'm having. What can you tell me to help me expedite the task?

Developer 2 here assumes the role of another Broker:

Developer 2 as a Broker: What I encountered was a little different from what you're describing. I suppose Broker 1 referred you to me because of my work on the XYZ system. I can tell you about that, but I think Developer 3 has experience more in line with what you need.

> **Developer 1:** Tell me about your experience anyway—it might give me some context in which to understand my own problem even if it doesn't directly apply. I'll also contact Developer 3 as you suggest and see what she has to say.

Just as information accrual steps can be composed into a conversation, so can problem refinement steps, as shown in the following example.

EXAMPLE CONVERSATION: SHOULD WE
BUILD CAPABILITY FOO OR BUY IT?

A Developer has followed up references from a Broker to locate people with expertise in implementing a particular type of function. She has concluded that there are several similar components available off the shelf. However, the issue of context (the second of the three "Cs") now looms.

Yet another variant of the Developer role occurs in this conversation. The Adapter is a developer whose responsibility is to tailor an existing asset to a new use. The Adapter is the quintessential reuser of an asset that cannot simply be plugged into its new context without modification.

The conversation also includes an Investor, who provides the funds for development of a reusable asset base.

Developer: My concern is that I'm developing in a workstation environment, and a lot of the commercially available components are for the personal computer market.

Broker: Are you committed to a workstation environment?

Developer: It would be a major decision to change that. We would have to consider whether there would be sufficient cost savings from using an off-the-shelf product. But it does make me wonder whether a personal computer would be a more appropriate platform. It might allow us to take advantage of a lot of outside work.

Broker: Developing this type of component can easily become a work sink—there are a lot of bells and whistles that you might decide you need, and it may end up being a larger development job than you've planned for.

Developer: It reminds me of our BAR component: when we started developing that, three years ago, there was nothing comparable around—at least nothing publicized. By the time we had invested two years' worth of effort it was still in the form of an evolving prototype, but there were a bunch of commercially available products that did similar things, and better. I don't want to make that mistake again.

Broker: Sometimes it can't be helped—you need the capability when you need it. But it is worth making that decision carefully. However you decide, be sure to document the decision and the rationale for it, and put that information in our corporate knowledge base. That way, even if the decision turns out to be wrong, at least others will be able to learn from it.

(continued)

> **Adapter:** Even if there isn't anything available now, try to design your system so that you can throw out your own implementation and plug in an off-the-shelf version if one eventually shows up. That way you'll be able to take advantage of it when it appears, and you won't be playing catch-up with your homegrown implementation.
>
> **Investor:** In some circles it's heresy to talk about throwing something out after we've invested so many dollars in it. But it would be wrong to view that as a waste, in this kind of situation. I see it as a set of coordinated decisions that balance short-term and long-term needs.
>
> This dialogue applies also to situations in which the available software is an asset of the organization, rather than a commercial product. There is one major difference: since commercial products are invested in heavily and evolve quickly, they present a significant threat to outpace any homegrown development. Internally supported assets may or may not present a similar "threat." In both cases, however, the decision must be made on the basis of trade-offs such as those considered in the dialogue.

Refining the group's understanding of a problem is different from simply dwelling on it with no movement. One sign of an advocacy-based conversation is the repetition of the same point, over and over—for example, the same answer to some question or suggestion. Sometimes this is necessary: for example, the dialogue up to that point may not in fact have adequately addressed the problem. If that is the case, however, there is some understanding to be gained about why the problem remains: Did others misunderstand what the problem is? Did the solutions being discussed prove to be dead ends? Are people simply avoiding the issue? In all these cases, there is an opportunity for productive inquiry. Rather than simple repe-

Figure 6-11   A conversation in which inquiry prevails can have the rhythm of teamwork in a ballgame.

**EXAMPLE CONVERSATION: ARE WE TAKING ADVANTAGE
OF OUR REUSABLE ASSETS?**

This is a dialogue between stakeholders responsible for an organization's competitiveness—we will call them the Strategists—and those involved with software development and reuse.

Strategist 1: Competition is getting stiffer. Company FOO, Inc. has carved out a market niche as the experts in PC-based 3D animated Web moles. The whole world knows them for that and goes to them for it. If we don't define ourselves in a similarly clear fashion, our market share is going to plummet over the next year.

Strategist 2: If you look at our products over the last two years, you can see some distinguishing characteristics. There are certain things that we do better than FOO, Inc.—always have; we have the best people for it. But we've never capitalized on that distinction, made it a part of our stated identity.

Strategist 1: So we do have some unique areas of expertise. We need to turn them into corporate assets.

Strategist 2 [to a reuse Broker]: Have you noticed any sustained "best-sellers" in our software repository?

Broker: Certainly. We have an excellent collection of scheduling algorithms, for example; people don't develop their own any more. But I've noticed that there are some equally excellent assets that nobody ever requests. I don't know whether it's because people don't know about them, or are concerned they will be too difficult to reuse. I just know that we do not reuse as much as we could.

Strategist 2 [to Developer 1]: The Broker just told me that we have some excellent generic design assets that nobody ever requests. Don't you folks have a need for them?

Developer 1: I honestly did not know about them.

Developer 2: I did, but frankly my one attempt to use them cost me multiple staff-weeks, and I'm really gun-shy now.

Strategist 2: The Broker told me about that, but he says your comments led to an overhaul of the assets and they are much stronger for it.

Developer 1: We need to do a better job of checking before we build something from scratch.

(continued)

> **Strategist 1:** It's not just a matter of increasing productivity, or even increasing quality. In this competitive climate, it's a question of creating an organizational identity and culture so that the market knows who we are, what we're the best at.
>
> Strategist 1 has repeated his initial point, but it acquires new significance in light of the preceding conversation.
>
> **Developer 2:** I never thought of it that way: I'm always so immersed in the crises of the current project.

tition of a point previously made, there can be *repetition in light of the discussion* since then, as illustrated in the next example.

Another measure of a conversation's level of inquiry is the extent to which each new utterance refers to those made shortly before, as opposed to none at all (the *red-herring* pattern) or those made long before (the *stuck-in-place-and-time* pattern). Again, this is not a hard rule. Reference to a point made much earlier may indicate a new insight or new angle on a problem. However, when new utterances simply fall on the floor rather than being handed off to the next speaker to run with, that is a sign that inquiry is flagging. This suggests another pattern, which we might call the *black hole*, and it is a symptom of advocacy-based conversations.

Conversely, when each new utterance picks up on the last one, the process starts to resemble a basketball or soccer team passing the ball from one player to another as they progress to the goal. Each player moves the ball to a new place, or perhaps puts a different spin on it. Here is an example of the *move-the-ball* pattern.

**EXAMPLE CONVERSATION: IS IT WORTH REUSING
A PARTICULAR ASSET IF WE HAVE TO ADAPT IT
(OR ADAPT OUR DESIGN TO ACCOMMODATE IT)?**

It is a fortunate developer who finds exactly what he needs in an existing product, in a form that fits perfectly with the rest of the system being built. In many—perhaps most—cases, some compromise and/or adaptation must occur. The question initiating this dialogue indicates two ways for adaptation to occur. The reusable asset itself may be adapted, producing either a variant or an enhanced version of the asset (if a consensus can be reached among all stakeholders in the asset). It is equally likely that the context into which the asset will be placed—the relevant system design decisions—will be adapted to accommodate reuse of the asset.

(continued)

**EXAMPLE CONVERSATION: IS IT WORTH REUSING
A PARTICULAR ASSET IF WE HAVE TO ADAPT IT
(OR ADAPT OUR DESIGN TO ACCOMMODATE IT)? (continued)**

The dialogue is initiated by the Developers responsible for making such design decisions. It may also involve other roles. The Investor's concern is to amortize previous investment in reusable assets. The Broker helps the Developers access the information they need to make a sound decision. The reuse Promoter is concerned with maintaining a coherent development approach throughout the organization and preventing spurious variation among products.

Veteran: It's hard to estimate what it's going to cost to adapt this asset for our needs. In my experience there are always little "gotchas" that you can never predict until you cut the code—especially since none of us is familiar with the asset's implementation.

The Veteran has raised the issue of the third "C"—content. Because our ability to specify a component's behavior is limited, there is always the possibility that the "black box" description of a component (its concept) omits crucial—often assumed—information.

Investor: All we can do is factor that risk in as a cost element, and make our best judgment.

Practitioner: We can also look at previous experience reusing this asset.

Investor: And use our previous experience developing this asset to help estimate what it will cost to redevelop a similar capability.

Veteran: Do we have all that information?

Broker: Some of it, at least. The asset base administrator and the reuse Promoter are becoming more hard-nosed about requiring it when anything is added to our asset base.

Veteran: The problem with considering previous uses of the asset is that they may not have been subject to the same constraints as this project. I can only repeat that we should be very careful. If it were an exact fit I wouldn't have any problem, but once we start talking about modifying a component that someone else has produced—or retracting some of our own design decisions—I start to get worried. I've been burned too many times.

(continued)

> **Practitioner:** I agree, but we should at least make an informed decision. If we decide not to reuse it, we should be able to justify that decision.
>
> **Promoter:** Even a negative decision on your part will be a contribution, if you provide a solid rationale. It will give me more insight into what makes an asset truly reusable. It might help me make more intelligent investment recommendations.
>
> **Veteran:** Let's develop a table of pros and cons, and cost estimates for both approaches. An expected cost saving is a "pro," and every risk is a "con." Then we'll use that old faithful technique, engineering judgment, to decide which way to go.
>
> **Practitioner:** As we proceed we'll keep track of whether our predictions have proved accurate, and we'll add that information to the design record.
>
> **Promoter:** If your experience proves quite different from past projects, I'll have to figure out why and then modify our classification schema to reflect the difference.

The soccer metaphor needs to be extended to take account of another pattern, which is that sometimes the ball has to be replaced. The participants in a conversation may need to stop, reassess where they are going, and redirect their inquiry to be more productive. Here is an example of the *change-the-ball* pattern:

Figure 6-12   Sometimes the team needs to replace the ball.

EXAMPLE CONVERSATION: IS IT WORTH DEVELOPING A PARTICULAR CAPABILITY FOR REUSE?

In the course of a project, a capability slated to be developed is perceived to be of potential value to other projects. A similar conversation could occur during development of a reusable asset base, when choices have to be made about which assets to develop.

The many participants in this conversation bounce ideas back and forth, but midway through the dialogue there is a shift of direction.

The roles might be interpreted as follows: the Investor is project manager, the Skeptic is a software engineer working on the project, and the Promoter and the Negotiator are representatives of the organization's software engineering process group.

Promoter: You know, there are other projects that could use this asset if you make its interface general.

Skeptic: We don't need that generality for this project, and it will cost us to achieve it.

Negotiator: I can provide some idea of the level of generality required to meet the needs of the other projects.

Investor: Would they be willing to chip in some funds?

Promoter: They might, if they had a say in how the asset was developed.

Negotiator: We're talking about a continuing domain engineering activity here. I would be careful about doing this under the aegis of one project.

Skeptic: I have a tight schedule commitment. If we are talking about convening a domain analysis team to specify the requirements, I don't have much confidence about being able to meet my commitment.

Negotiator: Then perhaps I was wrong. . . .

The shift in direction occurs here.

Negotiator: Maybe I can give you an overall idea of what other projects need, and you can just see what you can do.

Investor: With the understanding that the project commitment comes first, given that we're paying for it.

Skeptic: So the design/cost trade-offs will be left to me? I'm comfortable with that if you are.

(continued)

> **Negotiator:** Perhaps we could be involved in the design review. That way you would gain the benefit of insights from other projects, without being constrained in a way that would jeopardize your current commitments.
>
> **Investor:** It's a good idea: input from the outside generally keeps us all honest anyway!
>
> This is not the only possible outcome. If the schedule commitments were looser, a multiproject effort might be feasible. There might be an asset base maintenance activity already in place to respond to newly discovered needs and opportunities. Or the project pressures might be so great that any attention to other projects' needs is out of the question. The dialogue allows these paths to be explored in the spirit of inquiry.

The change-the-ball pattern as a conversational dynamic meets up with the reuse content of the dialogue when the issue is the continued viability of the current software models. Here is an example of such a conversation.

> ### EXAMPLE CONVERSATION: IS IT TIME TO RECONSIDER THE STRUCTURE AND CONTENT OF THE REUSABLE ASSET BASE?
>
> Some threshold of classification exceptions has been reached in the incorporation of new components into the asset base. Exceptions occur when assets do not fit neatly into the taxonomy of the asset base, or when they violate the architectural assumptions of the asset base. This example concerns exceptions caused by evolution from a centralized to a distributed application architecture, but the architectural issue could be anything.
>
> This final example introduces another role, that of the Contrarian. This is the person who likes to point out what's wrong with things as they are. While sometimes difficult to interact with, this role occupant can be useful and important in a learning organization.
>
> **Contrarian:** The centralized processing architecture that your asset base assumes is completely out of date. The old systems are being replaced one by one with distributed workstation networks. Soon there won't be any use at all for this asset base if you don't seriously rethink its contents.
>
> **Negotiator:** Many of the assets are compatible with the newer distributed architectures.
>
> **Contrarian:** Yes, but how does a potential reuser ascertain that?
>
> *(continued)*

EXAMPLE CONVERSATION: IS IT TIME TO RECONSIDER THE STRUCTURE AND CONTENT OF THE REUSABLE ASSET BASE? (continued)

Classifier (to the Broker):   Have you found that demand for these assets is decreasing?

Broker: Yes, and I'm continually being asked whether the assets are compatible with a distributed architecture.

Classifier: I've tried to include variants that have come from the newer projects. The asset taxonomy is becoming hopelessly complex because they do not really fit with the old way of doing things.

Contrarian: We need to revisit the domain model, in a major way.

Negotiator: That will cost, as you know.

Broker: But we're rapidly slipping back to a situation of not having an active asset base. Do we really need to go through all that again?

Negotiator: If there is consensus among us, we'll have to approach the Knowledge Investor and tell him the news.

An alternative outcome might be this: the Negotiator is able to convince the Contrarian and the Classifier that the exceptions are not as unmanageable as had been feared. Instead of radically revising the domain model, then, the participants would revise the way they interrelate assets of the new and old architectures.

6.8   SUSTAINING A NETWORK OF REUSEFUL CONVERSATIONS

The discussion in this chapter up to this point has focused on patterns of individual conversations guided by inquiry. While individual conversations probably will not make a significant change in a software shop, a *network of conversations*, sustained over a significant period, may do so. The network need not be organization-wide. A key principle of LIBRA is that change can start locally, bottom-up. What critical mass of new conversations is required for the network to have real impact? How is the critical mass achieved and sustained?

A key to cultivating the attitude of inquiry is understanding that knowledge creation and codification are not universal panaceas, to be applied with equal benefit in all situations. We want to look for leverage points, strategic opportunities where motivation is high and the factors leading to resistance are weaker. The need for inquiry can then be more authentically understood by reuse proponents, not simply as a technique for indirect persuasion, but as a practical data-gathering activity that will help us know whether reuse is truly a viable response.

Two models can help us reason about knowledge in an organization, and aid us in identifying and understanding reuse leverage points. One is the knowledge creation grid, which was introduced as Figure 5-21. The other is the knowledge evolution life cycle, described below.

6.8.1   Moving through the Knowledge Creation Grid

The knowledge creation grid, repeated here as Figure 6-13, can be used to identify and evaluate knowledge creation opportunities.

Suppose a company has developed a track record for successful implementation of hospital information management systems. With respect to a specific area of knowledge within this line of business (e.g., the design of the patient information database) the question could be asked: "Who knows how to do this?" or, phrased another way, "How is it that the organization knows how to do this?" Each quadrant of the grid corresponds to a different reply to this question:

- **Quadrant A (private/tacit).** The knowledge resides in the heads of a few key expert or veteran developers.

- **Quadrant B (private/explicit).** The knowledge has been codified in documents or software tools, but these artifacts or tools themselves still live in individuals' desk drawers or personal directories. Anyone else who wants to use them, still needs to know who the experts are and then go speak with them.

- **Quadrant C (public/tacit).** The knowledge of "how to do it" lives in the social network—in the culture—of a development group. (Such groups are typically small because this kind of knowledge creation, being nonsystematic, does not scale up well to large groups.) When a job of this sort needs to get done, it is accomplished through a complex, largely informal series of communications, handoffs, conversations, and messages among the members of

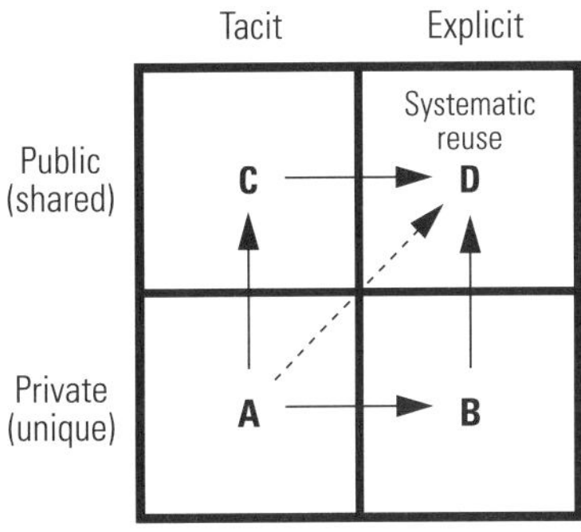

Figure 6-13   The knowledge creation grid.

the team. No one of them has the whole picture, and the whole picture is not written down anywhere.

This is the kind of knowledge that proves most ephemeral, when, for example, a software system is acquired and one or two experts follow along, but the sustaining social network that really kept it running is destroyed.

- **Quadrant D (public/explicit).** The knowledge has been codified in some kind of enterprise infrastructure. This is the state of affairs desired by most reuse advocates: for example, a company-wide library of reusable software makes the knowledge both public and explicit. Similarly, a corporate intranet can support a distributed form of knowledge repository. Search engines could allow anyone in the organization to access knowledge across the enterprise.

  One reason such corporate-wide repository efforts have had limited success may lie in a failure of reuse technologists to see the links between this quadrant and the others in the grid. For a large company with many lines of business and divisions, a corporate-wide repository may be the wrong level at which to direct efforts. The kind of information that makes it into such a repository may be information perceived as domain independent (e.g., general utility libraries have been set up in most large software-intensive companies). The information most critical to capture, however, may be much more local to different groups: the private explicit knowledge codified in individuals' tools, or the public tacit how-to knowledge that grows in close-knit informal group interactions.

Returning to the question of how a network of reuseful conversations develops, we can ask how an organization moves toward the upper right-hand quadrant of the grid. It is difficult to shift knowledge in one step from private/tacit (quadrant A) to public/explicit (quadrant D). Such a step really involves two important bridging activities, and each has its own set of motivators and points of resistance.

Excluding this direct, diagonal path, we can consider four distinct knowledge-creating shifts in the grid:

- **A $\rightarrow$ B (from private/tacit to private/explicit).** This shift takes place when individuals codify their own knowledge in more tangible form: writing it down, implementing it as a software tool, maintaining an informal library of code that they can reuse on multiple projects. Repeated shifts of this type are the basis for how experts or "gurus" develop their skills in particular areas. This kind of knowledge typically leaves with an engineer when he or she moves out of an organization.

- **A $\rightarrow$ C (from private/tacit to public/tacit).** This shift takes place when team interactions are fostered within a group. The knowledge may be transferred in hallway conversations or scribbled on napkins in the cafeteria, but it can still be a powerful source of a group's productivity. Managers who understand the dynamics of this shift can do a lot to foster it. On the other hand, these dynamics can be sabotaged by beliefs like "if people are standing around talking, they can't be getting work done."

- **B → D (from private/explicit to public/explicit).** This shift takes place when incentives are created for individuals to migrate their private reusable solutions and tools into some common infrastructure. For example, when a corporate reuse library is set up it might be assumed that contributed assets must be created from scratch. But in many cases, there will be prototype assets scattered throughout the organization that have never been moved from private to public status. Understanding this dynamic can help those who are initiating reuse efforts to tune incentives and qualification criteria.

  For example, one common pattern of failure in reuse libraries is that people will readily place their own components in the library. But they will not use other people's components, nor will they make efforts to see that their own components are used by other people. These patterns can be measured and addressed more readily if it is understood that the library is being used as an intervention to move knowledge from private/explicit to public/explicit.

- **C → D (from public/tacit to public/explicit).** This shift occurs when knowledge that is held informally in the network of interactions is codified. This dynamic combines the organizational learning disciplines Senge refers to as *team learning* and *mental models* [Seng90]. The process of converting shared but unarticulated knowledge to something repeatable, transferable beyond the group, or amenable to automated support, requires that people work together in teams to learn and codify their learning, not just to get the job done. (Or rather, to get a different kind of job done: the learning job.)

  Domain modeling, treated as an activity that involves full participation of the domain practitioners (which ideally involves both the developers and the users of software systems in the domain), is a process designed to facilitate this shift.

These four separate shifts form two distinct paths toward optimal knowledge sharing in organizations. The greatest flexibility exists when the current state of the knowledge is both private and tacit. In such a situation, the model suggests that an incremental strategy makes good sense. You can encourage public sharing of tacit knowledge in an informal setting, deferring the pressure to codify the knowledge explicitly until later in the process. Alternatively, you can encourage codification (letting a thousand flowers bloom) before enforcing standards and sharing the resulting knowledge assets.

6.8.2   The Knowledge Evolution Life Cycle

The knowledge creation grid is useful for understanding how knowledge migrates from private and tacit to public and explicit. However, the grid does not address the strategic competitive value of the software knowledge that is reused. Thus, in isolation, it can be misleading; every organization must identify the areas of software knowledge that are critical to its core business, and those that are ancillary or peripheral. Since systematic reuse requires commitment of resources, it is not really helpful to say that the organization should create knowledge in all areas of software practice, with equal priority, all the time.

A related insight is that organizations do not work efficiently by leaving knowledge at its most public and explicit all the time. For any given area of knowledge there is a *life cycle* [Nona95], illustrated by Figure 6-14. The heliform pattern illustrates the shift over time between *implicit* (or tacit) and *explicit* knowledge. The picture emphasizes Nonaka's idea that knowledge does not remain indefinitely in a fully explicit state. Knowledge is made explicit for particular purposes; then, over

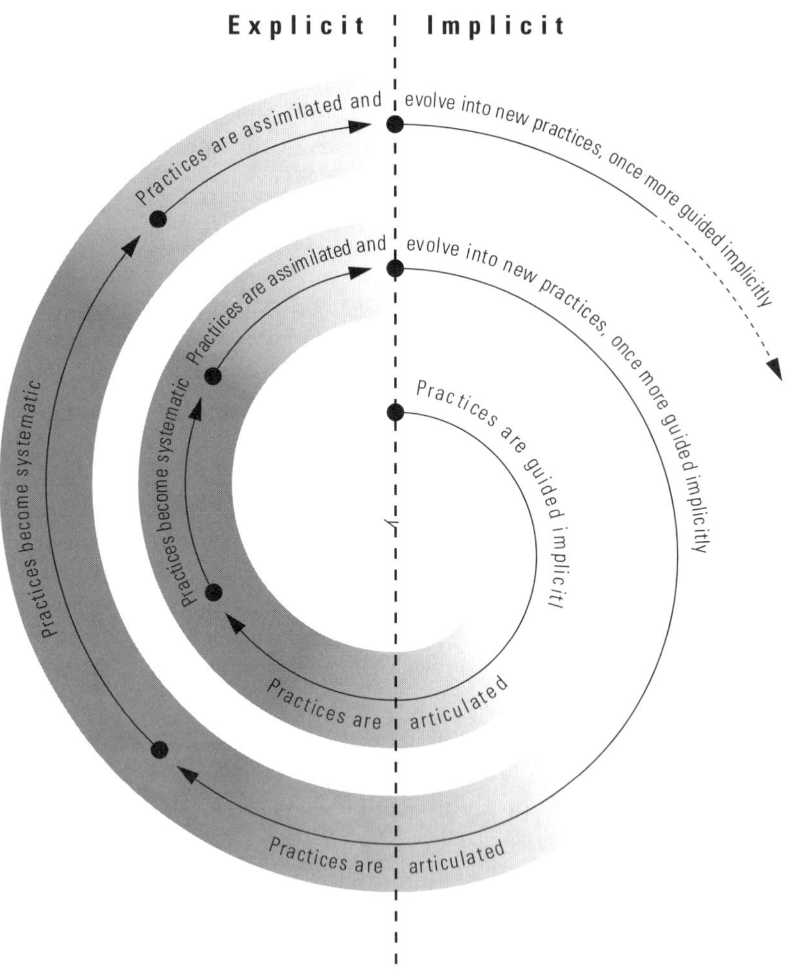

Figure 6-14   The knowledge evolution life cycle.

time, there is a natural tendency for the knowledge to settle back into implicit form. This resubmergence is an indication that the knowledge has become deeply internalized and shared.

Most of the knowledge we employ in any technically intensive task remains implicit. This includes the shared technical culture, the contextual assumptions that free us from defining terms from scratch with each interaction, and the accepted ways of doing things that lead to smoothly running, competent organizations. Some reasons to make knowledge explicit include the following:

- To codify it and make it more systematically reusable

- To transfer it to different groups or individuals

- To reduce dependency on particular experts for maintaining the knowledge

- To validate the knowledge and verify that it is still relevant in a changing business and technical environment

- To be able to reexamine and evolve the knowledge

The last point is key: knowledge needs to become public and explicit before it can be strategically evaluated and changed. It can then gradually be reintegrated into the organization's tacit knowledge base.

By using the knowledge creation grid and the knowledge evolution life cycle in combination, it should be possible to ask the following questions for any domain or area of competency:

- How strategic is this knowledge to our organization? Is it a core competency or a means to an end, a way of getting something else done? Does it contribute to our competitive advantage?

- Where does this knowledge reside in the grid? How public and explicit is it in the current environment?

- What is the current trend within the organization? Are there initiatives in place that are moving the knowledge toward more codified form? Conversely, is a previous codification effort beginning to decay back toward private and implicit forms of the knowledge?

- How desirable is the current state, and any current movement? Is the movement in accord with the current life cycle stage? Is it an appropriate time to initiate a new knowledge creation life cycle for this domain?

By addressing these questions, it is possible to focus efforts and resources on knowledge creation initiatives that will produce the maximum strategic benefit for the organization, or to diagnose problems with efforts that are already under way but are facing significant business obstacles.

CHAPTER 7

PUTTING LIBRA INTO PRACTICE

In the preceding chapters, we presented a view of software reuse as learning and knowledge creation. We illustrated the implications of this view through dialogues, dramatic scenarios, system diagrams, belief models, and inquiry. Chapter 6 presented examples of what "reuseful conversations" might look like when learning and inquiry are incorporated into day-to-day software development.

In this chapter, we present options and guidelines for applying the LIBRA tools: putting LIBRA into practice to facilitate inquiry and sustain systematic learning and reuse.

In the practical application of LIBRA, the content presented earlier in the book can be used as a basis for reflection and discussion, or as templates for groups to create their own materials. The LIBRA tools can be used separately or in combination, and can be incorporated with other approaches to reuse assessment, planning, and adoption, combining bottom-up inquiry with more conventional top-down advocacy. This chapter describes a variety of ways in which LIBRA can be applied and offers guidelines for how to best use LIBRA.

We first explain how LIBRA supports a fluid relationship between assessment and adoption, both of which create a training ground for learning and inquiry. We give two small-scale examples of applying LIBRA within conventional processes: one is within an advocacy-based conversation, and the other is in a traditional assessment and planning activity.

We then discuss options for full-scale LIBRA: developing, adapting, and running dramatic scenarios, and interpreting them with system diagrams, belief maps, and the Ladder of Inquiry. LIBRA scenario sessions can play a useful role at many points in the path from assessment to adoption, as well as in support of sustained reuse. Scenario sessions seamlessly incorporate training and skill development, and can serve as interventions in certain organizational settings.

Shifting from assessment to adoption, the chapter closes with strategies for planning, introducing, and fostering new conversations in day-to-day software development. This includes altering the *who, what,* and *how* of those conversations, and planning which types of conversation, in what sequence, will be most easily incorporated into everyday practice. We provide guidelines for observing and improving the inquiry level of conversations. We discuss a range of tactics for seeding new conversations, from small-scale, informal interactions (similar to those illustrated in Chapter 6), to work teams organized around specific learning goals, to forums on a larger scale where inquiry is integrated into a broader organizational change process.

7.1 THE LIBRA CYCLE—FROM ASSESSMENT TO ADOPTION

The path from assessment to adoption takes a software shop from a state in which reuse is dormant, contested, or ad hoc to a vibrant network of interactions in which reuse is a key issue in the everyday business of software development. Conventional technology transfer or process improvement strategies often sequentially *assess* (i.e., evaluate) a given technology's potential and then *adopt* only after high-level selling, approval, investment, and piloting. In LIBRA, **the very activities of collaborative self-assessment are already a step in the process of adoption.** Similarly, sustainable adoption includes on-going assessment. The two processes mesh with each other, sustained by inquiry and knowledge-creating conversations, as shown in Figure 7-1.

Heisenberg tells us, "You cannot measure something without affecting what is being measured." The act of assessment is never entirely neutral in its effect on the system being assessed. Assessment that does not take this dynamic into account may inadvertently increase the barriers to adoption. LIBRA *assessment* is a kind of Trojan horse that helps to initiate and prepare the ground for later *adoption*.

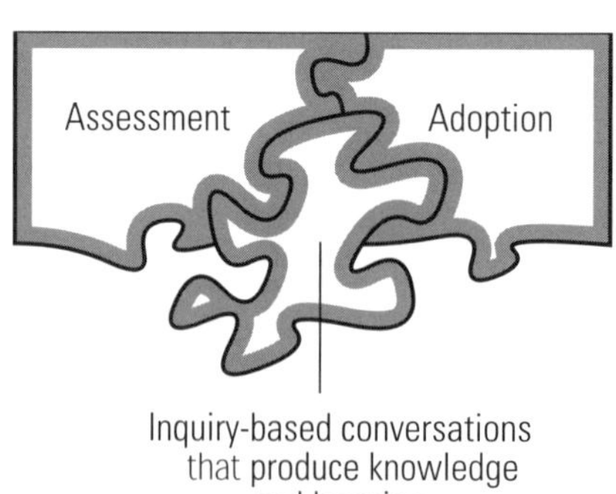

Figure 7-1 Assessment, adoption, and inquiry.

7.1.1   Where and How LIBRA Can Be Applied

The interdependence between assessment and adoption marks a break with the convention of sequential selling, planning, and implementing. It opens the door to intervening in the organization's way of working.

This intervention can take many forms. The paragraphs below provide a roadmap for LIBRA application, identifying particular points on the path between assessment and adoption. LIBRA can be applied at all these points, with different outcomes and benefits. The subsequent sections of this chapter explore these different points of application:

- **Reuse proponent reflection and training.** In its simplest application, LIBRA can be used by reuse proponents to reflect on their own beliefs, history, and attitudes, ways in which they can be more effective, and ways in which they may have been standing in their own way. The scenario and analysis in Chapter 5 provide a focus for this type of directed reading.

- **Advocacy interactions.** At the next level, reuse proponents can use LIBRA techniques as a way of evaluating and guiding informal interactions where advocacy would have been the more familiar approach. Typical examples are a conversation with a manager to propose a reuse project and a conversation with software engineers about their willingness to reuse components.

  In such interactions, which are not framed explicitly as training or skill transfer settings, a proponent models inquiry with his own behavior. The "personal reflection" use of LIBRA builds the needed skills.

- **Assessment processes.** Reuse assessment involves a *conversation about reuse* within an organization. There are many forms of general organizational assessment, ranging from climate assessment to the Capability Maturity Model (CMM) audits of the Software Engineering Institute. Many of these techniques address questions that are relevant to reuse adoption.

  LIBRA suggests styles of individual behavior and group facilitation that can be applied in assessment, either explicitly or indirectly. If explicit, the techniques can provide a form of just-in-time training about LIBRA. For example, by using system diagrams or belief maps to talk about reuse opportunities and challenges, a group can move between objective analysis of the organization and self-observation of the interactions occurring in the session.

- **LIBRA Scenario Sessions.** The applications described so far provide a gentle slope toward LIBRA. A more comprehensive approach is to structure an entire LIBRA inquiry session or set of sessions around the reading and possible creation of a dramatic scenario.

  We treat this as the stereotypical LIBRA assessment session. It demonstrates how all the LIBRA tools can be used in tandem, and it reflects, in both structure and intent, the essence of the LIBRA approach. It can be tuned along a variety of dimensions (fictional vs. real scenarios, preexisting vs. participant-generated materials, etc.).

- **Envisioning, planning, and team-building.** As we move farther along the path from assessment toward adoption, the emphasis shifts to envisioning opportunities for reuse, deciding on specific reuse initiatives, and preparing those who will carry them out. The function and contribution of LIBRA shifts significantly in this phase.

   In planning, LIBRA can provide data about past history, current beliefs, stakeholder interests, and organizational culture. This information can help planners identify promising focus areas. Scenarios can be used for envisioning, plan validation, contingency planning, and rehearsal for deployment of plans [Schw91]. LIBRA training sessions can prepare groups for new roles within a reuse initiative.

- **Reuse adoption.** In the adoption phase, business and engineering processes can be adapted or augmented to include LIBRA. The applications range from informal *reuse inquiry moments* within conventional development, to *reuse inquiry teams* that focus on learning and knowledge creation. Larger scale *reuse inquiry forums* apply the same techniques to long-term questions about the organization.

7.1.2   Using LIBRA When Resistance Is High

LIBRA can work in situations where other planning or adoption techniques might be rejected. An inquiry-based approach is one of the few viable options when there is high resistance or strong denial about harsh realities. A prior history of strong reuse advocacy may have produced little change, and may even have inhibited change. Advocacy may have led to initiatives that backfired, failed, or were co-opted by other interests.

LIBRA is not magic: it cannot change a situation truly inopportune for reuse. It may, however, allow people to face the reality of such a situation. If the situation is stressful and seemingly hopeless, people may be willing to experiment. They may appreciate the opportunity to let off steam. At the least, in stuck situations where an open request for commitment to reuse is likely to be rejected, LIBRA supports conversations about "why reuse is impossible here."

7.1.3   Integrating LIBRA with Other Approaches

We have described several points on the path from assessment to adoption where LIBRA can provide value. At any of these points, LIBRA can be integrated with other reuse assessment, planning, and adoption methods, including those that use more advocacy than inquiry:

- At the simplest level, LIBRA can improve the quality of interactions. This applies to conversations between reuse proponents and other stakeholders, conversations about planning, and software design conversations.

- LIBRA can be used to gather data in support of other methods.

- Dedicated LIBRA processes and sessions can be introduced as tools in their own right.

The following sections illustrate the use of LIBRA at these three levels. Section 7.2 shows how to use LIBRA techniques in an informal one-on-one conversation. Section 7.3 shows how to use belief maps within a larger reuse planning process. Sections 7.4 and 7.5 provide guidelines for more extensive application of LIBRA: scenario sessions for assessment and new conversations for sustained reuse.

7.2 APPLYING LIBRA IN REUSE ADVOCACY INTERACTIONS

Reuse advocates find themselves trying to champion reuse to a software engineer, a midlevel manager, or a CEO who may be enthused or cynical about the prospects. They encounter a mixture of beliefs, past experience, and stakeholder interests. LIBRA offers the reuse proponent a flexible set of tools to prepare for, participate in, and evaluate the success of such interactions. The example dialogues, dramatic scenarios, system diagrams, and belief maps codify some of the experience of the reuse field and can help in preparing for a conversation.

Inquiry techniques can also be used during the conversations. Since the conversations are usually informal, there is no overt signaling that a formal technique is being applied. But system diagrams, belief maps, and the Ladder of Inquiry translate into a style of questioning that meets people where they are, opening possibilities for change.

The proponent should use each interaction to gather data and assess receptivity and resistance. The interaction should not increase resistance and should ideally increase the receptivity of other participants. The best way to ensure this is to maintain respect for the interests, experience, and beliefs of others, even when these are inconvenient to the broader agenda of reuse.

7.2.1 An Example Interaction: Strategies for Sustaining Inquiry

The interaction that follows exhibits a variety of inquiry strategies. It is typical of interactions in which a reuse advocate would likely become defensive and challenge the espoused beliefs of a colleague. Inquiry enables the reuse proponent to obtain more data; it may also affect the mood of the interaction in a positive way.

The script that follows offers alternative strategies at particular points, then proceeds via the dialogue down the path of one of the strategies. The strategies can be thought of as fine-grained patterns of LIBRA use. They illustrate an improvisational style that assumes that the reuse proponent has thoroughly internalized LIBRA. Some strategies illustrate belief mapping: accepting a colleague's belief as a description of the world, exploring the scope of where and how that description is grounded, and getting the colleague to articulate how the belief differs from those of others. Other strategies involve tracing beliefs back to evidence and assumptions—applying the Ladder of Inquiry. In pushing backward from beliefs to assumed causes, or forward to anticipated consequences, the conversation begins to trace out a system diagram. The script itself is a tool for reflection and training.

EXTENDED EXAMPLE OF SUSTAINED INQUIRY ABOUT REUSE BELIEFS

- **Eliciting a direct expression of the belief**

  "So tell me what you really think about whether this reuse plan would work."

  "Management doesn't really believe in reuse. They say they do but that's just hot air. They are really only interested in their project bottom line."

[**Observation:** Inquiry thrives in conditions of perceived interest and rapport. A person must feel that an inquirer is interested in what he or she has to say, and that there is basic trust. It can help to have the conversation on neutral turf or in a space that feels "backstage" in some sense.]

- **Getting to authentic belief**

  "I'm willing to explore the reality of what you're talking about. But first I want to be sure you really sincerely believe what you've said. I mean, it's quite fashionable to bash management for being short-sighted, but sometimes when push comes to shove we're just letting off steam."

  "No, I'm not just letting off steam. In my time I've seen a dozen bright ideas come floating down from the R&D group. Or the group manager comes back from a weekend seminar and suddenly everything's going to be clean-room, or structured walkthroughs, or this month's quick fix to the world's technology problems. The furor lasts a month or two or three, long enough for everyone to get behind on their project schedules, which means pulling late nights for a few weeks just to get caught up and recover from Brilliant Management Plan #57.

  "Look, I know you reuse folks mean well and have good intentions. I know that, rationally speaking, you look at all the wasted rework and I agree it's just stupid. But I also know that management is only half hearing what you're saying. They're going to listen to the good news—cost savings—and conveniently not listen to the bad news—investment

  (continued)

---

up front; they'll sign on to a company-wide initiative, get everyone either frustrated or cautiously hopeful; then, when the hard work starts, they'll get distracted. The next financial crunch or near-missed milestone comes and it's just forgotten. I've seen this too many times."

- **Getting belief acknowledged as belief.** The goal is to contrast the belief with a differing belief in some relationship (even if at first the comparison is dismissive in tone). This can be done in a variety of ways:

  Scoping the range. "Do you think this is true of all the management in this company? Are you really talking about one manager in particular? Or, is there one manager who seems to you like an exception to this?"

  Comparing to other contexts. "Do you think that it's this way in every software company, or just this one, or just the short-sighted ones?"

  Scoping in terms of time. "Has it always been this way? Do you foresee conditions changing in the future?" Or: "Did you always believe this?"

- **Linking beliefs to other beliefs and data.** This helps to reify or objectify the belief as a speech act. As the linked belief becomes an object of scrutiny, it may be held more lightly or reevaluated in light of the evidence.

  Tracing back to evidence or examples. "Can you tell me about a specific experience you had that helped convince you that this is the state of things?"

  Tracing the root cause. "Why do you think it's so hard for management to see what needs to be done?"

  Following beliefs to consequences. "Let's assume that what you say is true. I mean, it sounds like a pretty hardheaded look at the real world to me. But let me ask you, just because this is true, why does that automatically mean that it would be impossible for reuse to get adopted to some level here in the company?"

[**Observation**: The phrasing above begins to hint at argumentation. In starting to challenge the colleague, the inquirer has begun to cajole and persuade a bit. Better would be: "If this is true, can you tell me how that prevents reuse from getting adopted here?"]

"Because if management doesn't back it, it ain't gonna happen. Even the reuse experts say that."

"Haven't there been some technology initiatives that get adopted because of acceptance at the grassroots level? Didn't they finally bring in direct Internet access because the engineers nearly rioted, after fighting it for months and months because they said everyone would waste time surfing the Web? So, if engineers wanted reuse to happen, couldn't they be the ones to pressure management instead of the other way around?"

(continued)

EXTENDED EXAMPLE OF SUSTAINED INQUIRY
ABOUT REUSE BELIEFS (continued)

- **Following beliefs to implicit assumptions**

"In effect, aren't you saying that when it comes to reuse, management's word is law, so when it doesn't fly it's their fault? Yet in other areas we readily acknowledge that management is helpless to really make it happen and just might not know it yet. So you're saying: management has control of things. Do you believe that?"

[**Caution**: The preceding two or three interchanges begin to use argumentation contrary to the spirit of inquiry—e.g., reductio ad absurdum. Inquiry patterns are not the same as debating techniques!]

- **Getting the speaker to self-identify as a representative of a belief community**

"Do you think that most engineers in this division/company feel the same way you do about this? What do you think is the basis for people seeing it this way? Have you all lived through the same empty revolutions too many times?"

- **Identifying different belief communities**

"Are there people in this division that might not feel the way you do about this issue?"

"Well, sure, I guess there would be. For example, some of the newbies, fresh in from college, who've never worked in an industry environment before. They're likely to get caught up in the wave of enthusiasm and really believe management's rhetoric—at least the first time or two around. Eventually the hard facts catch up with them. Then there are the corporate crusaders, who really think we can turn the company around. They're smart people, for the most part. They look at the current business world and know what we need to do to compete successfully. They're probably right about what they say we should do; they're just deluded about what management is actually going to do about it.

"Finally, I guess I'd have to say management themselves don't believe what I say is true. I mean, some of them might be very matter of fact about the disparity between their ambitious programs and the reality of what happens. Maybe they do it deliberately, just to get us pumped up and motivated for awhile and feeling like the company is really moving somewhere. But the sad thing is, I think most of them sincerely believe the grand vision when they send the memos around. I think they have a combination of delusions of grandeur, fits of optimism, lack of awareness of how cynical and dispirited people have become, and temporary amnesia about the last time they got religion."

(continued)

> - **Distinguishing belief, value, and self-interest**
>
>   "I hear what you're saying about how it is. But tell me, are you happy with that? Do you think that's the way it should be?"
>
>   "Of course not—it should be pretty obvious I think this is a dumb way to run a company. I'd respect them more if they stuck to their guns."
>
>   "And is that because of what's good for the company, or because of how it affects you personally?"
>
>   "Hey, I'd be happy to see them take reuse more seriously even if it hurt my position. Right now, I'm actually pretty secure because there is always going to be too much of this driver software to get written, even if they hired another two or three guys like me. But if they wanted to, they could turn me loose for maybe half a year and I could parameterize the whole thing. And then, who knows? Maybe they'd be happy to get rid of me! Well, by then maybe I'd be happy to move on to something else. In any case, if they were smart enough to ask me to do that I wouldn't stonewall or stall; I think it's the right idea and I'd back them all the way. I'd be happy to see the company do the right thing. I just have too many years of bitter experience that tell me it won't happen. Here's the real irony: that's one of the things that makes me feel this is a dead-end job; management's just not smart enough to do it right. If they did, and they made me expendable—well, I might just start feeling like this was a company worth working for!"

Principles Illustrated.   The goal of inquiry is to gather data about what people believe. In the conversation illustrated above, there is a *shift from discussion of content implicitly framed by beliefs to discussing the beliefs themselves as content.* A few common principles are applied:

- Inquiring to obtain more information from the speaker.

- Validating the authenticity of the person's experience and reporting of it.

- Not espousing your own belief in an argumentative way.

- Acknowledging wherever harsh realities are being confronted.

  This is necessary for the interaction to be authentic rather than a case of people talking past each other. The reuse proponent should not label these beliefs as resistance or denial. The engineer espousing the beliefs may herself feel that the advocate is in denial about the harsh realities.

- Tolerating the expression of belief in whatever form the speaker chooses.

  It would not be helpful to say: "Instead of stating this as a flat statement of fact, I'd find it easier to listen if you could acknowledge this as just your opinion." "It's just my opinion, except that I'm right," would be one understandable response. Inquiry can only be demonstrated, not coerced.

Once a belief has been articulated, authenticated, and acknowledged as belief, it is easier to get the speaker to articulate the basis or rationale for the belief. This leads to greater tolerance for diverse beliefs and openness to challenge by contrasting evidence. As we uncover experiences that provide the basis for a belief, we may find that our understanding of the facts may not be shared: the same facts may be used by different people as a basis for contrasting beliefs. Conversely, the same belief held by two people may have different justifications.

A final and potentially powerful question might be the following:

"What evidence would you need to induce you to believe differently from what you now believe?"

A possible answer to the question might be

"For me to believe that management is serious about reuse, I would need to see a title and position created and backed by Personnel. I would need to see a charge number associated with every project for documenting lessons learned and encapsulating and submitting potential reusable assets created as a spin-off of the project. The cost for that charge number would have to come from a corporate 'learning' fund and not off the project bottom line."

The goal is not necessarily to have beliefs shift during the interaction. Rather, it is to get individuals to envision a possible world where a different belief might hold, and to empower people to see that *they can make choices about their own beliefs.*

7.3 A MORE SYSTEMATIC BELIEF-MAPPING EXERCISE

Belief communities can cross both organizational units and knowledge communities. For example, of those involved with introducing OO into an organization, some may believe that OO will solve the reuse problem; others may be skeptical although (or perhaps because!) they are knowledgeable about OO. Some of the most avid advocates of OO as a reuse panacea may not be members of the OO knowledge community.

In this exercise, we draw relationships between belief communities, knowledge communities, and organizational units. The exercise is adapted from the Systems Envisioning Workshop at the 1997 conference on Object-Oriented Programming Systems, Languages, and Applications (OOPSLA).

You can use the exercise in two ways: first, to elicit data that help to predict receptivity and resistance; second, to identify the communities of belief that need to be represented in reuse planning.

1. Participants are given a theme, topic, or straw man statement to react to.
   This could be: "Do you believe systematic reuse could succeed in this organization? Why or why not?" The question should elicit beliefs about software development, reuse, people's willingness to reuse, or the organization.

2. Participants write answers on separate note cards, with one distinct belief per note card. This process usually should be limited to 5–10 minutes. People can write new belief cards as the discussion unfolds, or you can constrain production of new cards so that the first set accurately represents the initial response.

3. Participants are first encouraged to write down *their own beliefs.* (For example: "This company will not adopt systematic reuse because we are driven by the desire to please each customer above all else.") Those who see multiple reasons for the likely failure of reuse can write each as a separate statement. Those who feel some ambivalence can write down both positive and negative evidence.

4. Participants are then asked to write down beliefs *they believe are typical* of others whose opinions could affect an initiative. This part of the exercise can generate some of the richest data and the greatest energy. It is helpful to frame the statements with an attribution of the belief holder (e.g.: "Engineers believe that managers will always say they want reuse but will never devote any real resources."). Such attributed beliefs can reveal much about the organizational climate, the history of past efforts, and the way reuse is understood (as process improvement? good component engineering?).

5. Participants read their cards aloud and hand them to an appointed scribe or facilitator, who posts them on a shared public surface like a wall. The cards are posted provisionally according to a simple layout scheme (e.g., a quadrant layout with "Our Beliefs/ Others' Beliefs" along one axis, and "Resistance/ Receptivity" on the other). Participants hear each belief as it is posted. For continuity, try to follow the last belief read with one as close to it as possible.

6. At this point, you can create a gallery in which participants can look at other people's cards. Try to identify clusters of beliefs (those most likely to co-occur for a single stakeholder) and poles of beliefs, and map the belief clusters or poles to communities within the organization.

7. Next we have interpretation, discussion, and validation: Which polarities represent boundaries between distinct communities? Which capture key issues or points of dissent within a community? Validate the data by asking: Are the significant beliefs of this community up on the wall? Work from remembered arguments or controversies that generated energy for the community in the past. Can these conflicts be located in the beliefs captured on the board?

Results and Evaluation of Effectiveness   This exercise can be highly motivating to the participants. It makes discussable issues that might otherwise lurk in the back of participants' minds. When these issues are brought into the process rather than excluded, people feel more ownership, engagement, and sense of reality. If not carefully facilitated, the exercise can degenerate into "us against them"; but if done well, it allows people to put themselves in other people's shoes.

7.4 FULL-SCALE LIBRA ASSESSMENT: SCRIPTING, RUNNING, AND INTERPRETING SCENARIOS

LIBRA sessions are an opportunity for an organization to assess its receptivity to reuse. There are three main elements in this process:

1. Develop or modify the scenarios.
2. Conduct readings and walk-throughs.
3. Discuss key scenario events and decision points using the other LIBRA tools.

Dramatic scenarios are an unusual format for data gathering in a technical environment. The scenario process is effective for three salient reasons: the focus on *dramatic* moments, the use of *fictional* content, and the *highly structured* format. Effective use of scenarios involves choices concerning emotional temperature (hot vs. cool), degree of engagement with the material, and the relative directness of the subject matter.

7.4.1 Hot Versus Cool

What makes a conversation tend toward hot or cool? Physicist David Bohm draws attention to the degree of interest or engagement that participants have in the topic of conversation [Bohm90]. The interaction of these two factors is illustrated in Figure 7-2.

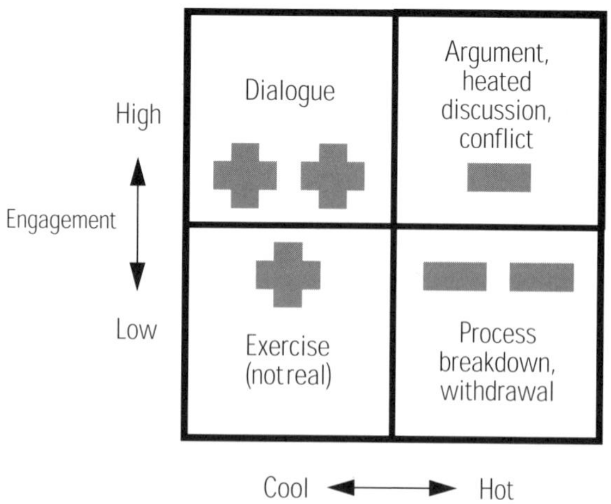

Figure 7-2   Relationships between engagement and quality of discourse.

As the diagram illustrates, it is no challenge to stay cool about a topic in which one is not particularly interested. This quadrant (low engagement/cool discourse) is best exemplified by a group of bored students dozing in a classroom. The problem comes as our engagement increases. Without inquiry, the heat of the discourse tends to increase with the degree of engagement (moving along the diagonal to the high engagement/heated discourse quadrant). If things get bad enough and the process breaks down, the heat remains but the engagement wanes (low engagement/heated discourse). Process breakdowns ensue over smaller and smaller issues. One or more parties may completely withdraw from the interaction.

The challenge is how to get to the upper left quadrant (high engagement/cool discourse). How do we reason together about things that matter a great deal to us? Two paths lead to this state. Moving directly from argument to dialogue means overcoming a large differential and usually requires outside facilitators or conflict resolution consultants. If you are trying to manage your own meetings and develop your skills incrementally, a safer path is a gradual shift from low engagement to high engagement, keeping the discourse cool throughout the process.

7.4.2   Direct Versus Indirect

Chris Argyris, an authority on organizational learning, has identified a classic double bind [Argy91]:

- Professional knowledge workers have strong defenses against learning from their own experience.

- These defenses cannot be easily challenged because they are *self-sealing:* direct confrontation about the defensiveness activates the very defensive patterns that are being questioned.

How can this double bind be avoided? Argyris suggests a productive kind of indirectness. A CEO writes a script for a staff meeting he intends to hold; he includes dialogue for the obstacles he expects to face and his own internal thoughts during the interchange. Then, instead of holding the meeting described in the script, he holds a meeting at which the participants reflect on the script itself. This level of indirectness, also called *distancing,* allows reflection that is not otherwise possible.

7.4.3   Dramatic Scenarios Are Engaging, Indirect, and Cool

Normally, as subject matter becomes less directly relevant, people are less engaged and interested. Dramatic scenarios are designed to increase engagement. Theater's appeal stems from our ability to become absorbed in an unfamiliar situation that resonates with our own experience. However, often when people become more engaged they grow more heated. In situations of conflict or tension, this can escalate until difficult but important topics have become undiscussable. Use of a fictional story means that the material only indirectly describes participants' work processes and environment. This indirectness, along with structured facilitation of the scenario session, helps keep the quality of discourse cool.

You can use dramatic scenarios to take your group to a state of high engagement and cool interaction, and then, once the spirit of inquiry can be maintained, gradually shift attention to the real organization's issues. You can reflect on scenarios at many levels: the hypothetical or fictional story, your real organization, and the stakeholders in the temporary community formed by the session itself.

7.4.4   Caveats: Resistance to Scenarios

Full-scale LIBRA may itself create resistance in "hard" engineering environments. We do not advocate overtly applying scenarios, belief maps, or other non-technical tools when this is likely to raise additional barriers. A key LIBRA principle is that assessment should not increase resistance. On the other hand, we have been surprised by the willingness of people who are comfortable about aims, focus, and safety to try such techniques.

Conversely, when there is already high receptivity to reuse, the indirect scenario technique may appear too cautious. In such cases a direct assessment of the real situation in the organization may be appropriate.

It is easy, however, to be overly optimistic about the level of directness. If such assumptions prove wrong and a process breaks down, it may be difficult to back off to a more indirect approach. Relations between participants could be on shaky ground, and the credibility of the process could be lost. Erring on the side of caution makes sense because a scenario session can easily be shifted toward greater directness.

7.4.5   Developing and Modifying Scenarios

As in developing software, modifying and extending an existing scenario is usually preferable to starting from scratch. If the scenario in Chapter 5 or another existing scenario reveals the key issues for your organization, take advantage of it and proceed to discussing the issues as quickly as possible, using the other LIBRA tools. Consider constructing your own scenario under the following conditions:

- Your organization has issues not addressed in Chapter 5, or the characters are not real or pertinent enough to be credible.

- You and others are totally on board with LIBRA and want to learn as much about it as possible.

- You want to bring a few people together to strengthen their understanding and commitment to LIBRA, and you think the group authoring process can achieve that.

If one or more of these conditions obtains partially, you may want to modify or extend an existing scenario. For example, cut out the OO incident, or add management's imposition of a new software life cycle model or incorporation of code management or process flow tools. Change June's character to be easier to convert, and have her come back charged up from going to a reuse conference. Have Ross replaced or move on for some unrelated reason, and leave the position open. Introduce a third project that heard about the pilot and is totally on board. Include more specific technical and product application information.

A scenario can be composed by one person or by a group. If it is authored by a group, members can work alone or together; they can prepare material in advance of a meeting or develop it at the meeting; they can offer round-robin critique and commentary on each other's work. As an opportunity to practice inquiry, at least some group work is helpful. It is true that group writing takes considerable skill and may demand greater commitment to inquiry and collaboration than the participants currently have. Authorship is not everyone's strength and may be an obstacle for some strong and important stakeholders. The risk of an individually authored scenario, however, is that others may not buy in, even if they get a chance to review.

7.4.5.1   Anatomy of a Scenario.   The raw materials of a scenario are character profiles and scene descriptions. The sidebar entitled *Anatomy of a Character Profile* lists the information that should be included for each character. For example, in Chapter 5, Joe brings in June because she is a "dyed-in-the wool software engineer" whose "skepticism" is known. Therefore, having her support will lend credibility. The description in Act One, Scene 3 makes the point that "June works on a different project." The character description covers her expectations of others (skeptical about managers) and what constitutes goodness in her job ("get the job done, whatever it takes" and "a fast workstation, decent compiler, and a closed door").

Similarly, Jim's character description prepares us for his behavior. He is customer oriented; he is concerned only about his project. He expects project managers to burn themselves out, and he expects to have to fight for resources. This helps to explain why he commits to attending the meeting in Scene Three of Act One but then does not come.

You can treat the organization itself as a character by describing the overall business environment, and the organization *spine*—the part the organization plays in the drama. Characters may be in conflict with organizational goals, climate, and beliefs as much as with each other.

The sidebar entitled *Anatomy of a Scene Description* lists the information you should include for each scene. You might organize the scenes into acts to give the story shape and a recognizable *throughline* or plot.

<table>
<tr><td valign="top">

ANATOMY OF A CHARACTER PROFILE

For each character, the profile should include the following:

Name, age, job title, or position

Salient beliefs, including:

- What is expected of me in my role(s)?
- What resources do I need to meet those expectations?
- What do I expect of other players?
- What is "goodness" in my job (pleases/satisfies me)?
- What is "badness" in my job?

Resources available to me (technical or other) to meet my objectives?

My situation: anything else about the job context relevant to how this character will perform; in particular, any potential sources of "dramatic conflict"

The character **spine:** a concise statement of what this character is "all about" in the drama (not necessarily the same as the official job role!)

</td><td valign="top">

ANATOMY OF A SCENE OUTLINE

For each scene, provide the following information:

What is the "objective" (theater and film directors call this the **throughline**) of the scene?

What characters play a role in this scene?

What is each character's main objective (overt or tacit?)

What conflict or challenge motivates the scene?

What are the major interactions?

How is the conflict or challenge resolved?

</td></tr>
</table>

7.4.5.2 *Exercise: Develop a Scenario Outline.* As you define the characters and scenes, consider the following:

- The *goal* is to reveal key behaviors, beliefs, and possibilities relevant to reuse.

- The story should *dramatize the characters' different reactions* to and interpretations of the events in accordance with their character descriptions.

- The story should encourage *intelligent interpretation* of the scenario by the participants.

- The characters and situation should *strike a note of reality and significance* for participants.

With these in mind, iterate between character profiles, scene descriptions, and a list of key issues, considerations, or objections that the scenario should illustrate.

CHARACTER DESCRIPTIONS.   Sketch out two or three characters. One or more will probably be based at least loosely on real people. This can be done by one person and reviewed by others over e-mail or in person. Each person can take a character and exchange. Group writing can occur separately with immediate exchange. A tape recorder can be used to capture the flavor of characters in oral individual speech or group brainstorm. This is a good way to obtain quotes, make the composing more humorous and spontaneous, and work with people who are not skilled writers. After initial material that covers all or most of the questions has been generated, it is best for one person to edit the descriptions to be concise and consistent for easy reading by participants.

SCENE DESCRIPTIONS AND THROUGHLINES.   Start by considering overall beginning and end points. Also determine roughly the number of acts and number of scenes per act. One person should begin the outline at this level. Either alone or in a meeting, with or without a tape recorder, an early scene or two should be titled, characters chosen, and critical choice points identified. The choice points should reveal something about one or more of the issues on the issues list (to be discussed next). They may also show the need for additional characters or slight changes to original character profiles (above).

LIST OF KEY ISSUES.   This works best as a brainstorm, facilitated on a board or flipchart, or gathered individually via e-mail or memos. The issues should reveal (1) the organization's stance regarding systematic reuse and (2) arguments and considerations that surface some not-yet-voiced beliefs.

For example, in Chapter 5, events 9, 10, and 12 are constructed to draw out typical reuse issues: return on investment, object orientation, problems with contract R&D funding, and failure to distinguish reuse innovation from other technical innovation. As with characters, you need a handful of issues for a start; others may emerge as the character and scene descriptions unfold. In the end, the issues pertinent to the organization must be at least touched upon. Key issues that will provide data for reuse assessment must be included.

7.4.6   Reading and Running Scenarios

The next step is reading and running the scenario in a group session. We recommend holding sessions in 2-hour blocks. Two 2-hour blocks are the minimum for working with the scenario in Chapter 5. You can read through the scenario individually or as a group, identify new key events as discussion points, develop dialogue for key events, and even role-play a portion of the scenario.

7.4.6.1   *Reflecting on Key Events.*   A LIBRA scenario draws attention to key events, which are critical choice points in reuse adoption. The choice points are

numbered and labeled as key moments in which reuse stakeholders choose behaviors that improve or compromise reuse adoption.

Homing in on the key events allows participants to reveal and reflect on their own preferences and perceptions. This generates the information we call *assessment* about the relative *receptivity* and *resistance* to reuse in the organization.

A scenario can be constructed with particular key events in mind. However, key events represent an intermediate interpretation that can be adapted for each reading of a scenario. Even when you are using a predefined scenario, you can identify the key events that are most significant to your group. Key events should relate back to the issues identified during scenario development (or adaptation). Seeing which of these events strike a chord with a particular group is one way to elicit data about the organization's living concerns.

Each key event can be used as the focus for a facilitated inquiry conversation. For each key event, questions could include the following:

- What are the key issues faced by the characters?
- What key themes are emerging?
- Was an opportunity lost here?

To take the discussion farther, your group can develop more detailed dialogue, or it can explore alternative choices. In a later phase, the other LIBRA tools can be brought to bear on the dynamics of each key event.

7.4.6.2 *Connecting Key Events.* Look for relationships between key events. For example:

- **Backward threads.** What premonitions or clues in the scenario foreshadowed the issues in this event?

- **Forward threads.** What are the repercussions or consequences of this event later in the scenario?

- **Mirroring and echoing.** What other events in this or other scenarios reflect the same issues in different settings? Are these the effect of relationships between the characters? (For example, managers receiving pressure from above tend to deflect that pressure down onto subordinates; companies tend to replicate their relations with suppliers in their supplier role to their customers.) This kind of resonance in the events is called *mirroring*. It is an organizational pattern that helps to sustain certain behaviors. If there is no clear causal connection between similar events, we call the relation *echoing*. Even more than mirroring, echoing between events can reveal patterns of organizational culture.

7.4.6.3 Hot Versus Cool.   Consider placing all the scenes of the scenario on the coolness/indirectness grid (Figure 7-2). Place each scene number somewhere in the four quadrants. Then decide how quickly you want the group to challenge itself, keeping in mind the risk of losing the mood of inquiry.

Talking *about* the scenario keeps the dialogue cooler than quoting from or running a scene. At one extreme (coolness), you just read the scenario and discuss prepared questions. You may then draw a system diagram, or analyze one. You may develop a belief map of one character after a key event.

A middle-of-the-road approach is to read through or role-play two or three scenes. Select scene(s) with the right level of coolness and directness for your group. For example, you can read Scene Three of Act One with a group of engineers to elicit their feelings about marketing people's involvement. If OO is a hotly contested topic, you can role-play the OO scene, embellishing or tailoring it to your environment.

Alternate read-through/performance and interpretation to keep the temperature down. Make each time segment longer if you want participants to get more emotionally involved before stepping back to analyze. One way to combine coolness with heat is to have some participants act out a scene, while others observe and draw a system diagram to illustrate what is happening. You can have one observer per character develop a belief map while the scene is enacted.

If you perform entire acts or the whole scenario, it is best to have plans for stopping and discussing, or even quitting, if the situation generates "too much heat and not enough light." If the scenario inspires only grand positioning or defense of past mistakes or going down technical rat-holes (too cool), nothing useful is accomplished. If topics are broached that cannot meaningfully be maintained in the spirit of inquiry (too hot), the session will backfire. People may leave the room, stop listening, blame others, or at best just turn the session into a time waster.

In all cases, consider (1) the known strength of opinions of the participants, (2) easing carefully into hotter and more direct issues, (3) using scene selection and enactment to test the temperature of the issue, and (4) when to back off—if your plan calls for enacting a sticky scene that you decide not to try after all.

7.4.6.4 A Ladder of Directness.   Imagine a "Ladder of Directness" with pure confrontation at the top and discussion of purely hypothetical situations at the bottom. This ladder reflects the following principles:

- Theory or abstract discussion is cooler than narration of a scenario, which is cooler than dramatization.

- People resist abstract presentations (the AMEGO or "And My Eyes Glazed Over" phenomenon). They almost always say that they prefer concrete examples. But if the examples touch on sensitive issues, increased engagement and heated discussion may interfere with reflection and listening.

- Working with predefined materials is cooler than having people generate their own material.

- Working with hypothetical material is generally cooler than using examples or real case studies.

- Working with examples from other organizational settings is generally cooler than selecting examples from the organization conducting the inquiry.

- The more distanced the elicitation technique, the cooler and more easily facilitated will be the interactions, but the more expertise will be required to interpret the data derived from the exercise.

- Conversely, the more direct the elicitation technique, the hotter and potentially risky will be the interactions, and the greater will be the required facilitation expertise. However, interpretation of the data may be easier, with less translation required.

- Humor can cool down hot topics and make them more discussable.

7.4.6.5   Caveat.   Despite the symmetry of these principles, the ladder metaphor is only a convenience and may be misleading. It is not always true that interactions are automatically cooled through indirectness. Dramatization, even of hypothetical case studies, can lead to emotionally charged interactions. It can evoke responses at a symbolic and nonverbal level that may be difficult to anticipate or control. There is always a risk in facilitating such interactions, and the task should not be attempted lightly.

Unskilled facilitation of a hot exercise could result in overheating and poorly resolved conflict; or it could result in apparently sound results that provide inaccurate or masked data. *Unskilled interpretation* of a cool exercise could result in significant distortions of the data. Most important, such situations could evoke strong personal reactions difficult to predict in advance. Before trying the hotter and more direct approaches, make sure you understand and respect the risks and have access to facilitation expertise.

7.4.7   Interpreting and Analyzing Scenarios

This section describes how to conduct structured conversations that balance interpretation, analysis, and application of the scenario. Some of the choices are illustrated in Figure 7-3.

Start by trying the scenario in Chapter 5 with a small group of reuse-friendly people and minimal facilitation. Consider the interpretation and analysis in Chapter 5 as guidance about the key learning points.

7.4.7.1   A Four-Part Rhythm of Analysis.   Separately and in combination, system diagrams, belief maps, and the Ladder of Inquiry have both cooling and heating, and direct and indirect applications. The tools can be applied in any order and can play off each other in a variety of ways (e.g., belief maps explain system di-

	Cool/indirect	◄ - - - - - - - - - -	- - - - - - - - - - ►	Engaged/direct
Developing	As is Plotline/narration	Modify	Extend	New Scene dialogue
Running	Read alone	Oral read-through	Selected role play	Perform
Interpreting	Unstructured No facilitation, no assigned reader No documentation No skill-building	Semi-structured Members rotate as lead Selective documentation Low emphasis on skill-building	Semi-structured Partial facilitation Outside coaching by facilitator Someone documents Skill-building of key importance	Highly structured Outside, expert facilitation Possible training of members also External role for documentor Skill-building equal goal to reuse readiness
Resulting knowledge	Okay to remain implicit and private	Shift to more public, even if still implicit	Remain private and explicit	Public and explicit

Figure 7-3   Portfolio of choices for developing, running, and interpreting dramatic scenarios.

agrams, system diagrams show shifts in beliefs). We suggest a four-phase rhythm to the analysis of a scenario. The phases correspond to the three LIBRA tools—system diagrams, belief models, the Ladder of Inquiry—followed by a deliberate move from fiction to the real organizational situation. Then there is an intentional shift *back* to discussion of the scenario, cycling through the tools again. This four-part rhythm should be applied to groups of one to three scenes and groups of one to three critical moments. Then the cycle should start over with variation. Cycles should typically take 30–60 minutes.

The cycle is an idealized session structure, which in actual practice is likely to be freer ranging. Use it only as a framework. We first describe the cycle in more detail, and then provide an example.

1. BEGIN WITH THE MOST VISIBLE: BEHAVIOR PATTERNS IN SYSTEM DIAGRAMS. Begin with clearly observable behaviors and a visual representation of them, such as the request–promise cycle in Figure 5-22 (repeated as Figure 7-4 below). Responding to an already-made picture is cooler; creating the picture is hotter. The picture allows you to describe behavior objectively without agreeing, disagreeing, or taking positions on the right or wrong. It does not (yet) delve into *why* a person behaved as noted. It may, however, describe the visible consequences of the behavior.

For example, including Andy in the meeting must have an impact on Joe. The scenario does not tell us what it was. But considering Joe's character, we could surmise what it might be. Similarly, there is a pattern to Janice's overemphasis on demos in the face of resistance. Skillful use of the LIBRA tools begins by *describing* behaviors and their *impact* with a system diagram.

2. LOOK BENEATH THE VISIBLE: BELIEF MAPPING.   The second step is to use belief maps to delve beneath the behaviors to their motivation. Understanding the beliefs behind the behavior is a key step in recognizing the different realities of different stakeholders. When the beliefs are seen, heard, and correlated with behaviors, some shifts of belief may occur.

Particularly when beliefs are in conflict, as in events 14 and 15 in Chapter 5, tracing the sources of belief can help you break into the self-sealing loops described in the system diagrams. For example, Janice's approach to the pilot is described as a "push"; Joe, Mike, and June are uncomfortable with such an approach. Their response, rather than to recognize a conflict of beliefs about how effective change happens, is "taking shortcuts with the domain analysis method." They react in response to Janice's "pushy" actions. The beliefs remain unacknowledged and undiscussed.

The beliefs being mapped must be named *out loud* or *seen in tangible form*, making discussable what was undiscussable. You can do this by writing lists of beliefs and actions on a board, developing a description of the characters' internal dialogues, or eliciting via cards or self-sticking notes some beliefs that account for the observed behavior. (Try adapting the exercise given in Section 7.3.)

The tangibility of the sound and sight of beliefs is both heating and cooling. The tone of the conversation should be one of appreciating different realities. The Ladder of Inquiry provides guidance for maintaining that tone.

CHARACTER BELIEF MAPS

At this stage, try enriching the original character profiles and organization profile:

- For each character, create a belief map that describes fundamental beliefs out of which the individual approaches situations. Distinguish between *open* beliefs, which are known to the character, and discussable, *hidden* beliefs, which are known but are not discussable, and *invisible* beliefs, which are not even recognized by the character as beliefs. An invisible belief may indicate denial about a harsh reality, or it may be so embedded in the character's worldview that it is not seen as belief.

- List some of the belief issues faced by characters in the scenario. Include conflicts in belief among characters, and tension between characters' beliefs and the situations in which they find themselves. Consider whether the scenario has shaken or shifted the core beliefs of any characters.

- Revisit the organization considered as a character to determine some of the institutional beliefs revealed in the scenario. The belief pattern of the organization emerges through the belief profiles of the characters in interaction. What beliefs do the characters share as a basis for action? What are the things that everyone knows but no one can actually say in meetings? (For example, "Our competitors are eating us for lunch.") What beliefs or mental models are so ingrained in the characters that they don't recognize them as shared beliefs or bases for action?

3. CLIMB UP AND DOWN THE LADDER TO FOSTER DISCOVERY.   Use the Ladder of Inquiry to maintain a mood of discovery about what the characters are doing and why. You can also use it, as in Chapter 5, to suggest how a character might have behaved differently. This exercise clearly illustrates the consequences of not using a tool like the ladder to clarify expectations and recognize biases. When you use the ladder, heat and directness increase, but the tool itself serves to contain and focus the increased emotion.

Apply the Ladder of Inquiry when participants disagree or do not understand each other's points. In each interaction, you should ask, "What are we learning about our own perceptions and beliefs about reuse readiness here?" In the initial small practice group, you should also ask, "What options for using this approach will best fit our situation? Who should be involved?"

4. APPLY THE SCENARIO BY ANALOGY TO YOUR SITUATION.   The sequence ends with a direct question about "us." Shift away from the scenario and characters, toward the organization and individuals in the room. For example:

- Remember the XYZ project. Does that feel like what happened when senior management brought in life cycle management?

- Who does Janice remind you of?

- Have you ever behaved like anyone in the scenario?

- Let's do a system diagram of what happens when we ask for more funding.

- Last week's presentation did not go well because the LoB manager got defensive. Let's develop a belief map about what might have been motivating him and how we might approach him now.

- Is this applicable to us? How? How not?

7.4.7.2 Key Transitions: Getting on Yourselves, Getting Off Yourselves.
The four-phase cycle prepares you for direct scrutiny of current organizational realities, and then deliberately introduces a step backward from these. This provides an opportunity to evaluate people's ability to engage, cool versus heat, and directness of focus. A key point of assessment will always be:

"Can we talk about ourselves? Does the group use the scenario and the tools to *not* talk about us?"

Conversely,

"Can we get off ourselves once we fully shine the light on us?"

The ability to get on to yourselves and then get off in some kind of rhythm, however rough or difficult, is a key and clear measure of the capacity for inquiry. When the skill for these movements is there, it is best to state this explicitly and reinforce its importance for sustaining reuseful conversations. Use the assessment sessions to move increasingly quickly toward "us" and away from "us."

If your group's skill for these moves is weak, different tacks may be needed. You can try a less structured conversation to allow people to vent before directing attention to the scenario. Be extravigilant about use of the tools, shorter sessions, or skilled facilitation. Continually diagnose the group's capacity to move through the four phases, especially into the fourth, and then back to the cooler, more objective description of phase 1.

7.4.7.3 Combining the Tools: An Example. This example illustrates some moves among the tools using events 4 and 5 in Act One of the scenario. Imagine this to be the second hour of a 2-hour session, the first hour having consisted of open, unstructured discussion of events 1–3. That discussion was clear, useful, and positive, but did not explicitly use any LIBRA tools besides the scenario itself. The group consists of six people, and the chairperson acts as facilitator.

GETTING STARTED.   In the scenario, three new people are invited to "broaden the base" by devising an experiment to "pitch to management for increased support." Two of them show up—June and Andy. Jim does not come. The facilitator might direct attention to June's character description and review why Joe "is not happy" about Andy's presence. Details about Jim's first interaction with Janice might be reviewed in light of his accepting the invitation, thinking there is no harm in pursuing the idea,

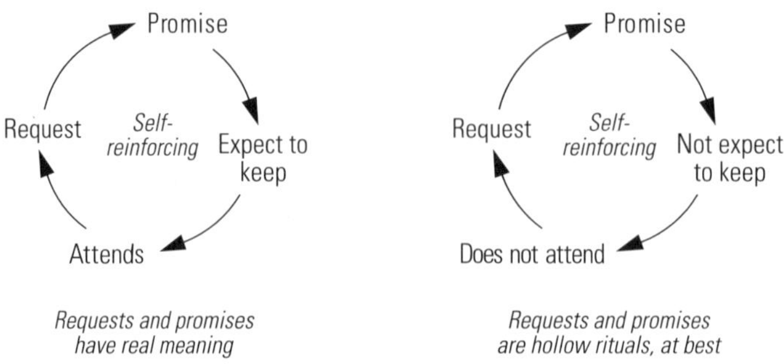

Figure 7-4   Self-reinforcing request–promise patterns.

and then not showing up. The stage is set for presenting the system diagram about self-reinforcing request–promise patterns, as shown in Figure 7-4.

USE SYSTEM DIAGRAMS.   Talk through the steps of each diagram and compare them. Ask participants to apply this to Jim and to others' expectations of him. Possible questions include the following:

- What would Janice's reaction to this pattern be? Joe's?

- Which of the characters are most/least likely to do the same kind of thing?

- Are you surprised by Jim's behavior?

- Do you think this is typical of Jim's behavior?

- As you—what are you telling yourself about this?

- What do you suppose was said in the meeting about Jim's absence?

APPLY THE LADDER OF INQUIRY.   After working through some of these possibilities, move to the Ladder of Inquiry to dig a bit deeper. The facilitator can support moves down the ladder but not up. Use the ladder to investigate why each character did and said what the scenario reveals. Imagine the characters themselves doing this. For example, as in Chapter 5, Joe might use the ladder to disclose his own reasoning and elicit from Jim why he does or does not think the project is important. For Janice, moving up the ladder might prompt her to say: "I guess Jim doesn't put his money where his mouth is," or even to defend him- "Perhaps Jim had something come up. I know he's feeling a lot of pressure about the XYZ project." In either case, she moves up the ladder to belief or conclusion. Moving down the ladder, she might say: "Now it is becoming clearer that Jim sees our work as a 'nonstarter.' I wonder why? Could this be about timing, or his opinion of one of us? Could we take a few minutes to see if we can understand Jim's motivation? This behavior is typical, but also not typical. Then let's see what we can do to find out more directly from him where he is. In fact, maybe when we come out with a proposal, he'll be more on board. At least that will give us a way to test his interest."

THE NEXT STEP: A ROLE-PLAY.   The conversations have moved the session to hotter but still indirect territory. The next move might be to role play, acting out some of what was discussed using the ladder. Keep the dramatization short at this point; just bring stronger emotion into the room. Good candidates might be:

- Discussion of why Jim did not show up; what each player thinks about why and what this means.

- Joe explaining why he invited June; Janice explaining why she invited Andy.

- Discussion of possible experiments, with Joe expressing unhappiness about Andy. Have him—within character—react to some of what Andy says.

To prepare the role-play, write some more dialogue on the experiment that is being proposed and how Andy conducts himself. The improvised role-play can then focus on Joe's reaction.

CREATE ANOTHER SYSTEM DIAGRAM.   With the first three tools having taken perhaps 40 minutes, a next move might be to create the system diagram in Figure 5-23 on unaligned objectives. This will reduce some of the heat of the role-play, but will also deepen the collective reflection, since the group itself creates the diagram.

Introduce the exercise by saying something like what is in Chapter 5: "Inviting Andy escalates the different perspectives into action. This may have consequences for the effectiveness of the project. As the group membership broadens, the espoused goals of the team come into conflict with individual concerns. When these differences are not discussed, events exacerbate them and drive them even deeper, and a self-reinforcing cycle takes hold. Let's develop a system diagram to show this."

MAP THE BELIEFS.   The system diagram about unaligned objectives is a good setup for mapping the beliefs of one or two characters. Ask each participant to pick a person and review that individual's character description and previous actions in the scenario. Ask them to develop a map of the character's beliefs about reuse and the pilot project. For Janice, the map might look like this:

> "Janice is a change maker. She has a lofty vision and thinks reuse should be organization-wide. She positions herself to have the support of management. She believes in involving additional folks quickly, and apparently values this broadening more than deepening her relationship with her core partners. Janice probably has a grand plan that she has not fully articulated yet. She may feel this is as much as the engineers can handle at this point. She thinks she knows better what will really succeed, and justifies her under-the-table tactics because she thinks it will benefit the engineers in the end. She puts the task over the relationship. She needs to be the driver. Her style is push rather than pull."

This can be done in a list or paragraph, on a board or flipchart. It can include what Janice says to herself about her beliefs and actions and what others tell themselves about Janice.

A belief map surfaces stereotypes, automatic assumptions, and unedited reasoning. Being more explicit makes it possible to test the beliefs and possibly change them. Use the Ladder of Inquiry to state the belief and then ask for facts and data to support or disconfirm it. For example: "I have an inference about your belief about the usefulness of software testing, and I want to check it with you."

APPLY THE SCENARIO TO "US AND OUR SITUATION."   At this point, the conversation should move quickly to your organization. Consider the system diagram in Figure 5-27 as an invitation to discuss and thereby break the self-sealing cycle. For example:

- Directly ask about the resource pressure pattern: "Do we have this belief pattern here? Does it keep us from speaking up?"

- Direct a second set of questions to a specific person or project: "John, what about when . . . ?" Or the facilitator can tell about an example that she thinks applies.

- Have participants use the ladder and belief maps to interpret these behaviors.

- Reinforce the idea that undiscussables stay that way only if everyone tacitly agrees to keep them undiscussable.

Continue to ask for and document information about "us and our situation":

- What do we learn about the past effectiveness of our actions regarding reuse? Which belief patterns may be vicious cycles and self-sealing?

- Does this give us any insights about our level of success in reuse? What changes in belief and behavior might help us go forward?

Consider posting these two questions visually and documenting the answers. The written statements say: "Here's what we see when we look into the mirror of these two questions."

EXAMPLE SUMMARY AND REVIEW.   Each step in the process has moved between cooling and heating, indirectness and directness. If you can proceed more quickly than this example illustrates, do so. Each move from behavior (system diagrams) to beliefs (ladder and belief maps) to concretizing beliefs and behavior (role-plays) influences the quality of open, honest self-reflection at the end of the discussion sequence.

The facilitator must ascertain which of these qualities already exist without such a planned, structured approach, and which do not. For those that do not, the tools will help you to obtain rich, reliable data about reuse readiness, while also increasing that readiness through inquiry.

7.4.7.4   *Leadership and Facilitation.*   Should you bring in an expert facilitator? This depends on how hot and direct you expect the sessions to be.

Cool, indirect approaches, described by the left-hand column of Figure 7-3, test the waters with modest goals of movement from implicit to explicit knowledge and modest goals of inquiry. Such sessions can be chaired or moderated by a group member. The required skills are listed in the sidebar entitled *Required Facilitator Qualities: Cool, Indirect Sessions.*

As sessions seek the qualities described in the right-hand column of Figure 7-3 (high directness, high heat, lofty goals for making reuse knowledge public and explicit), skilled facilitation from outside the stakeholder group is recommended. The needed skills are listed in the sidebar entitled *Required Facilitator Qualities: Heated, Direct Sessions.*

REQUIRED FACILITATOR QUALITIES—COOL, INDIRECT SESSIONS

Exhibits listening and openness

Has knowledge of individuals' personal styles

Has knowledge of the issues pressing in the organization

Is comfortable with time management of the discussion

Has thorough understanding of the scenario

Can articulate observations about inquiry versus advocacy behavior

Already has the respect of participants

Is willing to make mistakes in leading and to acknowledge them

Is comfortable objectively stating or writing summary of key outcomes

---

REQUIRED FACILITATOR QUALITIES—HEATED, DIRECT SESSIONS

Experience in facilitating technically oriented discussions among technical people

Capable of balancing high engagement with high documentation

Excellent at setting tone appropriate to sustained inquiry

Able to weave just-in-time bits of learning about inquiry with coaching individuals publicly about inquiry behavior

Intuitive sense of timing about when to move toward applying the scenario to the organization and when to deepen involvement in the scenario details

Low investment as a stakeholder in the key issues and relationships

Knowledgeable about reuse adoption, but not too opinionated

Able to articulate and lead based on the key principles of LIBRA

For sessions in the middle of the continuum, the following examples provide guidance about facilitation leadership and style. Suppose the sessions are divided into two 2-hour sessions in which a key focus of the first 30 minutes will be Jim's reactions and Janice's bringing in of Andy. The key questions might be: "How could they reach commitment?" and "Who should be involved early in a reuse initiative?"

The session might begin in an unstructured manner without read-through or role-play or use of any tools. The facilitator may restate the events of the first three scenes or ask others to do so. The facilitator then waits to see what unfolds in discussion, introducing the two questions stated above if and when needed.

Such leadership can be provided by anyone in the group. It can rotate so that someone else takes a similar tack for the second session of 2 hours. Someone might document outcomes or generalizations that emerge from the two questions. Participants can agree to practice and take brief time-outs to reflect on the level of inquiry.

Since this a cool and indirect approach, the resultant skill learning and assessment data will be modest. Movement along the knowledge creation grid (Figure 6-13) might leave knowledge private but more documented or make the knowledge more public but not necessarily well documented.

A more ambitious session would deal with events 10–12 in which the presentation to the brass meets resistance. The facilitator can run a role-play and stop partway through to ask questions or change role players. He can ask participants to take time out and write a belief map of a key character. He may then shift to asking how the situation reflects participants' own situation.

Candidate questions include:

- How is this like us?

- How is this different from us?

- Does Ross remind you of anybody in our organization?

- Could this really happen here?

- What would you do if you were Joe?

- What should Janice do?

- What do you think would have happened if…?

- Suppose Mike had…, then what do you think would have happened?

As the questions increase in directness and heat, the directive firmness of the facilitator declares "I'm in control here" by taking the lead in asking. This provides a cooling effect. Facilitation at this moderate level requires some ability to shift among the LIBRA tools.

The middle columns of Figure 7-3 describe situations calling for creative decisions about how to share leadership, obtain partial facilitation for more difficult sessions, or compensate for undeveloped leadership skill with creative use of the LIBRA tools.

7.4.7.5 Documentation.   Be sure to document the assessment in some form. Documentation influences the quality of the conversation in both positive and negative ways. As you move farther to the right in Figure 7-3, you should consider having a role dedicated to documentation (even an outside role, and possibly even different from that of the facilitator). At points of discussion in which participants work with their own belief maps and translation to their organization, detailed documentation and even careful restatement of what has been said can be helpful, even if it slows the conversation down.

Too much emphasis on documentation can prompt participants to view the answers recorded as the primary purpose of the session. Documentation may compromise the light touch required for maintaining the spirit of inquiry. The result might be less candor, hence poor data. However, sometimes it is not possible to pursue an inquiry without some form of documentation. Documentation objectifies what is being said—like collectively making a canvas of words or pictures. This can help to cool opinion and emotion, allowing difficult discussion to continue and deepen.

Balance must be struck between capturing the content of the assessment and maintaining the spirit of inquiry. Without adequate trust, the information documented has minimal validity. Without tangible information as an outcome, the conversation may not have a lasting impact.

7.4.7.6   A Final Word About Assessment and Its Relation to Adoption.   We have described options for creating, guiding, and sustaining reuse assessment through scenarios. Unlike an external audit, inventory, or structured questionnaire, a LIBRA assessment is a self-assessment. It is *interpretative:* the goal is to assess reuse readiness in terms of receptivity and resistance to the philosophy and practical realities of software reuse.

An artifact or conclusion must emerge as a product of these carefully orchestrated conversations. You are interviewing yourselves. You are the candidates; you are also the evaluators, asking and answering the questions "What did our conversations tell us about our receptivity and resistance to reuse?" and "What do the conversations tell us about our readiness?" The conclusion is not a yes or no proposition; nor is it a rating. Rather, the assessment phase tells you where in the organization reuse inquiry will take hold most readily.

7.5 ADOPTION: PLANNING AND CONDUCTING NEW CONVERSATIONS

Introducing and sustaining reuseful conversations requires knowing what they look like when they occur (Chapter 6) and strategizing to determine how they can best occur and flourish. This means shifting the key variables that influence the process: (1) WHAT content to discuss, (2) WHO to involve, and (3) HOW to conduct the discussions. Figure 7-5 illustrates these elements.

Changing only one of these elements can offer a smoother introduction, but the chances of snapping back to previous patterns may increase. Changing all three elements—the who, what, and how—can increase interest and win at least temporary willing suspension of resistance.

7.5.1 WHAT to Discuss

New conversations should be introduced intentionally in small clusters—that is, more than one at a time and less than all at once. Try beginning with WHAT, asking: "Which conversations should be fostered in what order?" Then:

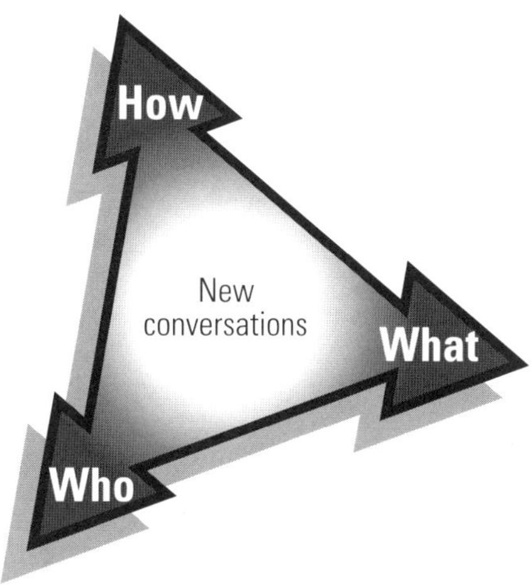

Figure 7-5   Key elements of new conversations.

- "Where in our daily development work are conversations most like the ones illustrated in Chapter 6 already occurring?"

- "Where in *my* daily development work am I conducting conversations that resemble any of those in Chapter 6?"

As a small group, brainstorm the answers to these questions. Review your assessment in this light.

For example, the group may have rejected event 1 (Jim's panning of the opportunity as a "nonstarter") as not typical of your workplace. Regarding event 16, the group's reaction may have been: "That's the risk you take. Timelines and requirements are always imperfect. Even projects committed to the pilot cannot put the opportunity to reuse above their deadlines." Good starting points might then be questions like: "Is there potential for sharing knowledge between activities A, B, and C?" and "Is this an opportunity to reuse an existing asset?" Some questions may not work as starter questions because the assessment indicates weak commitment to reuse. Examples include "Is it worth reusing a particular asset if we have to adapt it? What are the implications of adapting it?" and "Are we investing enough in our asset base?"

More generally, questions that assume the existence of an asset base will not work best as starter questions. For example:

- "Is it time to reconsider the content and organization of the asset base?"

- "Is the asset base an accurate representation of our business and competencies? Is it complete? Well organized?"

Questions about broader use and buy-versus-build are safe starter questions for almost any organization:

- "Could product A from project B be an asset to the organization as a whole?"

- "Are we reinventing an existing capability? If so, should we build the capability or buy it?"

These are good starters because:

- They are familiar questions, probably being asked already in ad hoc ways.

- They can meaningfully be discussed across levels and job functions without the new knowledge roles identified in Chapter 6.

- They do not assume that a reuse initiative is already underway.

Assessment might reveal a strong desire to reuse existing assets, but frustration over how to communicate reusability, or lack of interest among other developers. Questions that are then good starters include "What is proving most effective to reuse?" and "What does it mean that products A and B seem similar but are different?"

Similarly, if group members are versed in knowledge management or the assessment exhibits a strong desire to share oral or tacit knowledge, you can start with questions like:

"What do we know about a particular topic?"

"Who knows about it?"

"Is new knowledge from projects getting incorporated effectively in the asset base?"

The cost or effort of reuse may require observation, measurement, and project tracking. Answering these questions via research and reporting (not just meetings) and discussing the results may be useful for people who are sympathetic to reuse but need to hear the business case. Conversations might develop around specific situations as well as generalizations. For example: "Is it worth developing A for reuse?" "Are we finding it cost-effective to make project output reusable?" The answers might be just yes or no, or they might lead to guidelines for selecting potential assets for reuse.

In choosing starter conversations, ask yourself whether the topic has the following properties:

- Prompts individuals to speak more openly about reuse issues

- Inspires more light than heat

- Leads to additional questions about reuse

- Can be quickly shown to have practical applications

- Appears to be more about smart business and technical content and less about reuse itself

- Will attract more and more people as willing participants

- Addresses in a refreshing way difficult and important questions the organization has been struggling with

- Is relevant enough to hold people's attention, but not so critical that inquiry will be jeopardized

When in doubt about a good place to begin, have the group list criteria for topics. Build on the list above, or create your own.

7.5.2   WHO Should Be Involved

Drawing on a range of individuals with different stakes in the issues can help in discovering new possibilities for reuse. This does not mean being "nice" or "inclusive" for reasons of political interest. It means gathering individuals who have a relationship to the process, product, problem, or opportunity—the WHAT—of the conversation.

To quote Marv Weisbord, innovator in the area of large-group conversations for organizational change [Weis92]:

> If you always do what you always did
> With the same people you always did it,
> You always get what you always got.

Use the following criteria to select participants in new conversations:

- **Diverse views.** Gather as diverse a set of stakeholders as possible around a given topic. This is an important element of *future search conferences* [Weis95]. A search conference for an organization might draw together employees, customers, competitors, members of the surrounding local community, and representatives of regulatory agencies. Such a diverse cast of characters would not be appropriate for a typical decision-making meeting, but diversity in general provides opportunities for learning.

- **Structural relations.** Most meetings in an organization are interactions either between peers or between people one hierarchical level apart (e.g., managers with their direct reports), or events like annual meetings, where the CEO lectures to everyone. Direct communication between people more than one level apart can threaten the authority structure (e.g., occasions for micromanagement on the part of high-level managers, or sidestepping the chain of command on the part of lower-level employees). However, a meeting that involves three or more structural levels, or both managerial and technical personnel, or both technical and marketing staff, could create significant opportunities for learning.

- **Handoff relations.** Identify people along the workflow pipeline. The farther apart people are, the less likely that they have had direct contact through project work. This is particularly true when pipelines cross organizational boundaries such as vendors, suppliers, and customers.

- **Lateral relations.** Identify people who perform analogous roles on different projects. For example, bring together people who have done regression testing on different projects to discover common needs, tools, and sharable artifacts such as test data.

    If there are established forums for this kind of interchange, there may be a positive climate for reuse. There may also be structures in place that provide this type of communication without face-to-face meetings, such as online discussion groups, company e-mail, and informal networks of information exchange.

- **Who is not there.** Consider the potential impact of who is *not* participating. For example, a meeting with a division manager and front-line supervisors will have a different dynamic depending on whether the project manager at the intervening level is present. The presence or absence of outsiders to the organization will also have a dramatic effect.

Every organization has its own association patterns, people who often talk to each other and people who rarely do. For example, veterans who joined the company during one era may not interact with newcomers. Take these patterns into account when selecting participants.

7.5.3 HOW to Conduct the Conversations

Conversations about reuse can occur spontaneously, without much cajoling or persuading. More than initiating, seeding, or jump-starting new conversations, the key challenge may be sustaining the spirit, skill, and benefits of inquiry. This is the HOW of new conversations.

Common wisdom says that if you get the right people in the room, they will produce good results. Yet, time and again, the experience of meetings is that two heads are much worse than one. Expectations tend to be low, and get lower with experience. The willingness to discuss this is also low. To succeed, you must consider HOW the conversations are conducted. Changing the HOW alone may make a significant difference, without directly and formally changing the WHO and WHAT.

7.5.3.1 Encourage Reuse Inquiry Moments. Reuse inquiry moments (RIMs) can occur at the water cooler or in a hallway conversation, and at unstructured, unplanned meetings during lunch, parties, or car rides. Work-related conversations occur without planned outcomes, invitations, documentation, or deadlines. RIMs can also occur at more formal events such as staff meetings and project reviews.

Imagine that someone other than you has brought up a topic: for example, a question about sharing design criteria for user interfaces between two related but not totally similar products. Suppose the others do not train or practice with LIBRA. What options do you have for joining the conversation in a way that supports inquiry? The sidebar entitled *Cultivating Reuse Inquiry Moments* lists some possible tactics.

CULTIVATING REUSE INQUIRY MOMENTS

State the relationships between others' statements before offering your own opinions.

Draw distinctions between implicit and explicit, pointing out the value of making the implicit more explicit.

Explain that you would like to experiment with a way of tracing supportive reasoning: "I have an inference about what you have said and would like to test it." Then use the Ladder of Inquiry.

Start a conversation about underlying beliefs. Disclose your own.

Tell part of the Chapter 5 scenario as an anecdote.

Say: "I don't know the answer; I'm just asking."

Explain or synthesize viewpoints by drawing a system diagram.

Tell what you have been reading about LIBRA and ask for some time to explain how it is pertinent to the conversation.

Explain the difference between inquiry and advocacy and suggest greater balance.

Point out LIBRA principles already at work in the organization—for example, case analysis and code reviews now in use.

Point out when new shared knowledge takes shape. Use the knowledge creation grid (Figure 5-21) as appropriate.

If the meeting is pressed for time and directed toward action, offer to convene a separate learning conversation about a particular point.

Convene a meeting about the question.

Convene an e-mail conversation about the question.

7.5.3.2   Create Reuse Inquiry Teams.   A more formal and planned approach is to convene a reuse inquiry team (RIT). Small, informal RITs resemble in type and size the scenario assessment groups described in Section 7-4.

RIT conversations differ significantly from the less formal, more spontaneous RIMs. Only people who are interested in the topic will come. You can take time to present models and train. You can set ground rules for experimenting with the conversational process. You can set an agenda and plan ahead so that expectations are shifted from business as usual. Here are some guidelines for structuring and evaluating RITs.

Make sure that the topic of the session is clear. Know who is attending, and set clear beginning and ending times. Obtain commitment to three 90-minute meetings.

RIT SKILLS AND MEASURES

Inquiry is occurring when:

Speakers seek to understand before seeking to be understood.

Individuals elicit each other's thoughts.

A mood of discovery and possibility is stronger than persuading and evaluating.

Comments are brief and move quickly around the group.

Incomplete or half-baked thoughts are stated, encouraged, and elicited.

The conversation is more divergent than convergent.

People use phrases like "I wonder how," "does that mean," "how did you get to that," "does that also mean," and "if that is true then. . . ."

People refrain from using phrases like "why do you think that," "I agree," "I disagree," "that can't be right," "you're missing the point."

Listening is deep and helps speakers to be thoughtful and articulate.

Lateral thinking is more common than vertical thinking—making connections versus stating cases and reaching conclusions.

Individuals disclose their biases.

Errors and dead ends energize people rather than discourage them.

Breakdowns in logic or instances of being stuck are allowed to percolate long enough to lead to breakthroughs rather than ending discomfort by grasping at easy conclusions.

Periodic time-outs are taken as/or if conversation seems to move up the Ladder of Inquiry rather than down.

Time and room for advocacy are made consciously and valued rather than stigmatized.

Discoveries, learning, and remaining open questions are restated and recorded.

Movement is seen across the knowledge creation grid: from implicit to explicit, from private to public, or both.

In meeting number one, clarify expectations and discuss LIBRA principles. Explain the difference between inquiry and advocacy. Establish an expectation that the group will self-correct to maintain inquiry. Introduce the Ladder of Inquiry. Explain that a commitment to three meetings is needed to sustain inquiry.

Select a topic with high, visible impact and relatively low resistance. Do not immediately take on either the most significant issue or the hottest one. Have a clear client or customer for the problem or opportunity. Stick to the problem at hand. Near the end, solicit what was learned and what new knowledge was created. Write this down and distribute it. Review the meeting for what was learned *about* inquiry: What helped sustain it? What impeded it? Close by restating the LIBRA hypothesis: "Sustainable reuse may be more successful with less advocacy and top-down mandate, and more of the type of inquiry we have just engaged in."

In the second and third meetings, introduce belief maps. Explain the importance of standing back from our beliefs in order to suspend, understand, or model them.

A RIT must be able to recognize progress and increase its inquiry skills. At the end of a RIT meeting, review progress in terms of the criteria listed in the sidebar entitled *RIT Skills and Measures.*

More advanced measures of inquiry are found in the five qualities of dialogue, described in Figure 7-6. *Separation* begins by objectifying ideas in a tangible and usually visual form. *Suspension* is required for exploring beliefs. A sense of *simultaneous* speaking and listening may take hold as group members almost read each others' thoughts. Appreciation of *silence* develops out of a sense of wonder in *not* knowing. *Selflessness*, a sense of quieting self-interest to tap into the group's capacity for learning, harvests the full benefit of inquiry and may lead to significant new knowledge.

Separation. Objectify what the group creates so that it is physically separate from individuals making verbal statements, as in music, visual model, picture, or group movement.

Suspension. Temporarily put aside beliefs and assumptions to explore where they come from and how they limit observation, interpretation, and action. Hold opinions (positions) lightly enough to be able to look around and behind them (as in walking around an art object or rotating a three-dimensional computer image).

Simultaneity. Listen as you speak, like members of a musical ensemble playing their parts while listening to each other and to the whole.

Silence. Together, make room for new possibilities.

Selflessness. Empty your expectations and put aside your ego enough to allow new possibilities to present themselves. Care more about what the group discovers than what you want or think.

Figure 7-6   Qualities of dialogue, in increasing order of capability.

These qualities of dialogue are usually not present in spontaneous RIMs. They may or may not show themselves in LIBRA scenario sessions. In three or more sessions, RITs may reach this level through a commitment to inquiry. In reuse inquiry forums (RIFs), described next, there is a greater chance of reaching this level of dialogue.

7.5.3.3   *Hold Larger Scale Conversations: Reuse Inquiry Forums.*   In addition to RIMs and RITs, larger forums for sustaining and deepening reuse should be considered. The setting may be a 2- to 3-day meeting of 50–100 participants where participants are carefully selected, tasks and interactions are meticulously designed, expert facilitation is provided, and highly stylized and documented work products are created. Whatever the format, the core principle is to sustain small- and large-group inquiry.

DOMAIN ENGINEERING.   Domain engineering can be an opportunity for large-scale, sustained inquiry. For example, in Organization Domain Modeling (ODM), descriptive models are created before any attempt to conclude, decide, or prescribe a course of action. A rich, thorough description of stakeholders, exemplars, concepts, features, and their interrelationships provides the basis for specifying and advocating a set of reusable assets. The steps, templates, and intentions of these activities are documented in the ODM Guidebook [ODM96].

LARGE-GROUP PARTICIPATIVE MEETINGS.   Large-group participative meetings, based on democratic, bottom-up involvement of diverse stakeholders, have been applied throughout the world over the past 30 years to social issues like daycare, health issues like AIDS, public policy issues like water rights across geographic boundaries, and government and corporate business unit planning. Called by different names such as *future search*, *search conferences*, and *strategic futures*, such meetings have as their purpose large-group envisioning of a preferred and desirable future [Weis95].

The goal is to achieve common ground among diverse stakeholders without directly processing and resolving conflict. There are no paid experts; participants attend as equals, working together on carefully scripted tasks concerning the external environment, diverse pasts, present realities, and co-created, desired futures. The meetings are designed to engage the imagination, produce clear action, and build commitment via a subtle interplay of imagining and action planning together [Levi99].

Such meetings have become the bread and butter of organizational change experts, who recognize the importance of giving voice to all perspectives, rallying all the available knowledge, and generating a commitment to action, often very quickly. An example within the world of software development is the architectural renewal workshop, in which key stakeholders consider a maturing architecture and how to best renew or replace it.

PRODUCT OR UNIT BUSINESS STRATEGIC PLANNING.   Certain approaches to product or unit business strategic planning are based on inquiry. For example, Arie de Geus, who was head of planning for Royal Dutch Shell in the 1970s, designs simulations to emphasize the planning process as group learning. Shell is also famous for joint scenario development, a playful framework in which senior executives hold their highly informed positions and opinions lightly while exploring a range of possibilities for the future [Schw91].

The higher you go in the organization, and the greater the political and financial stakes, the more difficult it is to—in Chris Argyris's terms—"teach smart people how to learn" [Argy91]. However, the rhetoric of sustainable competitive advantage is increasingly sounding like a call for reuse. Ongoing learning and shared knowledge assets are the new capital of the global economy.

CHAPTER **8**

CONCLUSION

This book has applied ideas about organizational learning and knowledge creation to the field of software reuse. In so doing, we aimed to accomplish several goals:

- Explain some types of organizational change and resistance dynamics that reuse proponents have encountered.
- Provide guidelines for reuse assessment and adoption that can circumvent some of these dynamics.
- Concretize organizational learning theory by showing, via an extended (though hypothetical) case study, the challenges in a particular industry, with its own language, culture, and viewpoint.

We have tried to design the LIBRA approach to be applied by anyone in a software development organization who wants to increase the organization's receptivity to reuse. Central principles of LIBRA include the following: (1) reuse is a form of organizational learning; (2) reuse involves shifts in beliefs and interaction patterns in an organization; (3) inquiry should guide the assessment of these dynamics; and (4) reuse can be fostered by new conversations that take place as part of software development work.

Viewing reuse as a form of organizational learning allows us to reinterpret many difficulties reuse advocates encounter. These difficulties can be seen as the challenges of transforming a software organization into a knowledge-creating organization. This helps us interpret beliefs and dynamics encountered by reuse advocates in a more respectful and more actionable way—as reactions to a change toward more systematic knowledge creation.

This insight suggests different ways of encouraging reuse. Since reuse practice suggests that critical reusable software knowledge is domain specific, the cultivation of organizational learning must occur in specific domains. This is what we have termed *technology transfer in reverse.*

185

8.1 IMPACT ON REUSE ADOPTION
AND ORGANIZATIONAL CHANGE

We have found LIBRA to be useful for reflecting in a structured way on our experience as reuse proponents and practitioners. It shows promise as a predictive or diagnostic model for where and why breakdowns in reuse occur, and as a prescriptive set of techniques for avoiding such breakdowns. LIBRA assessment sessions produce useful data about organizational culture and about beliefs relevant to reuse. Such data might need to be validated in other ways as well.

We believe that LIBRA processes can be effective tools for organizational change. Inquiry sessions can increase engagement and participation, and can help foster interaction patterns essential to sustainable reuse. We have little empirical experience to substantiate this hypothesis. At the very least, well-facilitated inquiry sessions will not increase resistance; ideally they will increase receptivity to reuse. We hope this book encourages further exploration and experimentation along these lines.

8.2 IMPACT ON ORGANIZATIONAL LEARNING
AND KNOWLEDGE MANAGEMENT

Although LIBRA focuses specifically on software reuse, it should be of interest to those who are involved with organizational learning, knowledge management, and knowledge creation in contexts other than software development.

Most treatments of organizational learning—an area in which new books are appearing rapidly—talk in general terms. Because this book treats software reuse as organizational learning applied to the field of software, it addresses concrete organizational learning goals in a specific type of enterprise. It can be seen as an in-depth case study of the application of general principles in a particular, albeit highly influential, industry (if software engineering can be treated as a single industry). Readers have seen a repertoire of system diagrams and related materials specific to software-intensive companies. Our description of barriers encountered in reuse should echo more general issues that arise in organizational learning. Those concerned with technology transfer (TT), or attempting other kinds of organizational and technical change (e.g., reengineering), may see some of the pitfalls of taking too strict a TT approach for changes that are about more than just technology.

We believe that insights from software reuse transfer to more general knowledge management. Knowledge management is not like inventory control of physical components. Creating software has a unique and somewhat subtle relationship to other kinds of knowledge-creating work; software lies somewhere between the tangible products of manufacturing and the evanescent knowledge in people's heads and conversations. Because of this relationship, the software field (and particularly reuse) has generated insights and experiences that could be recast in the broader frame of knowledge management.

We even envision applying "reuseful" thinking to capture and codify knowledge of the organizational learning field itself. Consider, for example, an asset base of organizational learning artifacts (system diagrams, scenarios, and belief maps) for a given community. This would help bridge the gap between the organizational learning and knowledge management communities [Dave97].

Our inclusion of specific models in this book can be viewed as seeding such an asset base for software reuse. Our book can be seen as a collection of patterns similar in spirit to [Gamm95]. The system diagrams, and our claim for their applicability in diverse settings, broaden the notion of design patterns to organizational diagnosis patterns.

8.3   IMPLICATIONS OF LIBRA FOR ORGANIZATIONAL CHANGE AND REDESIGN

This book has focused on challenges of introducing systematic reuse in software development organizations. A recurring theme has been *incremental adoption*: significant movement toward new practices can begin in a modest and local fashion, by gathering small groups of people to talk about reuse and to share knowledge in a spirit of inquiry. We have contrasted this approach with planning approaches that put the main emphasis on large-scale change efforts.

This theme may have given a misleading impression: namely, that we believe this incremental approach can simply replace broader and more comprehensive reuse planning or knowledge management initiatives, or can accomplish the same overall organizational transformations. The usefulness of this book does not depend on the truth of this assumption, or on whether readers or LIBRA participants believe it. In fact, as we said at the beginning of Chapter 7, there is a spectrum of strategies that integrate LIBRA with other approaches.

While writing this book, the authors wrestled with different theories about the relation between small-scale and large-scale change, and between transition and end-state reuse processes. When systematic learning is foreign to current culture, one person in an organization practicing inquiry skills is unlikely to start a chain reaction necessary to create large-scale shifts. On the other hand, not all individuals in an organization need to make the shift simultaneously. The LIBRA notion of new conversations can be related to other work on the required roles and functions in a sustainable knowledge creation network. For example, the STARS Conceptual Framework for Reuse Processes (CFRP) describes interlocking, scalable network patterns that can form stable and sustainable islands of reuse interactions in a surrounding transitional environment [CFRP93]. Such work represents a midpoint between purely incremental and global change strategies.

It is intriguing to speculate about large-scale change being triggered by a critical mass of small-scale interactions. If enough people in a given network (or potential network) make the shift, the network as a whole may begin to function as a reuseful process.

We have constructed LIBRA to be independent of particular positions on the continuum of the small-scale to large-scale belief map. LIBRA, we believe, will prove valuable in large-scale, ambitious change efforts, particularly when forces of resistance are strong; but it is not intended as a comprehensive means for large-scale change. For new organizational forms to be sustainable, however, individuals must change beliefs and practice new disciplines. Such individual change might not be addressed by redesign approaches. Perhaps it cannot be, without inappropriate intrusion of the organization into the province of individual freedom. LIBRA invites exploration of these questions, while maintaining respect for people's right to choose and change their own beliefs as they see fit.

It is important to acknowledge different levels of desired organizational change. Some kinds of change are more easily effected incrementally; some require more global restructuring. You need to determine what change goals are appropriate for your organization at this moment in its history. The required rate of change is also a factor.

In the paragraphs below, we describe some stages of progression along two dimensions: the degree to which knowledge creation is central to the organization, and the pervasiveness of the change required.

- **Inquiry as a style.** LIBRA techniques can be practiced by individuals to cultivate interactions in a spirit of inquiry. In terms of software, this leads to ad hoc or opportunistic reuse.

- **Organizational learning as a competency.** Almost any company can benefit from a more balanced allocation of resources and support of learning and knowledge creation. Total quality circles, certain process reengineering initiatives, and the evolving knowledge management field are responses to this need. In terms of software, this corresponds to a program of systematic reuse.

- **Knowledge creation as strategic.** For certain organizations, knowledge creation is critical or strategic. This can be because (1) cost-effective management of knowledge assets is the only way to achieve competitive advantage, or to satisfy key customer requirements; (2) the knowledge is viewed as a direct product or offering to customers (as with an expertise-based consulting firm); (3) heightened goals for profitability, or the global scale of business processes, create the requirement for a knowledge infrastructure.

- **Knowledge creation as pervasive.** We can imagine a company that systematically and pervasively creates and codifies knowledge as a component of all work tasks and products. In contrast to the strategic level described above, for this type of company knowledge creation is pervasive and ubiquitous, throughout the organization and in all interactions with customers and suppliers.

- **The knowledge-creating company.** As a next step in this vision, we see the emergence of a new, highly dynamic and responsive business model: a shift from a primarily product-, contract-, or service-based business to a *knowledge creating company* [Nona91, Nona95]. In this type of company, knowledge creation is not merely a sustaining mechanism; it has the potential to transform the nature of the business, enabling the company to address entirely new markets with different offerings.

The farther along a company is on the path toward full-scale strategic commitment to knowledge, the more essential the principles of LIBRA will be. To conclude, we come full circle to explain why this is so important for the software field.

8.4   THE KNOWLEDGE-CREATING SOFTWARE ENTERPRISE

For certain types of company, not just the knowledge codified but the *knowledge creation processes and competencies themselves* will provide competitive advantage. Such companies will help their customers integrate knowledge creation into their own business processes. Software development enterprises, in particular, face the challenge of becoming knowledge-creating companies in this sense—and not just for the benefit of the software industry alone.

In this book, we have advanced the notion of software reuse as knowledge creation. We can go further with the following claim: in the future, support for knowledge creation will be an essential component of enterprise software systems. Information technology obviously plays a vital role in the knowledge management infrastructure of any company. New software tools and environments will be needed to allow the integration of knowledge creation in large enterprises in a way that is seamless, pervasive, and scalable. Software systems will increasingly have to integrate a knowledge creation infrastructure into the functional tasks they support.

This will involve more than introducing new tools. It will have a dramatic effect on software system architectures, components, and technologies. It will involve rethinking the very structure of software systems and the patterns of interaction between developers and users.

Traditionally, software systems have automated (and in so doing, tended to rigidify) the work processes of an enterprise. Learning, discovery, and collaborative knowledge creation occur informally, around the edges of supported work processes, but are themselves unsupported by technology. Knowledge-creating companies will need innovative information technology support to integrate business and learning processes. In the knowledge-based company of the future, knowledge will be codified and translated into automated forms such as software progressively, but much more dynamically. This will require software systems of new kinds that directly support knowledge creation functions and integrate these with day-to-day operations.

To create these new kinds of software system, different kinds of software development processes and software enterprises will be needed. Technological systems are themselves products of human organizations. Conway's law tells us that the structure of software systems tends to replicate the structure of the organizations that build them.

Software enterprises will be hard put to meet the challenge of building such systems unless they transform themselves into knowledge-creating enterprises. Software organizations will need to excel at knowledge creation—internally, in their interactions with customers, and in the systems they build. In this new kind of software organization, inquiry will be applied not just in reusing software, but in dialogue with customers and users to shape systems to come. Software organizations will need to become knowledge-creating organizations to create the software that enables *other* companies to become knowledge-creating organizations!

The challenges are considerable. The culture of software organizations and the engineering mind-set bring special forces of resistance to knowledge creation. LIBRA provides tools to help address these challenges. This is a central role, and a central challenge, for software development enterprises in our time.

REFERENCES

[Argy92] Chris Argyris. *On Organizational Learning*. Blackwell, London, 1992.

[Barn91] Bruce Barnes and Terry Bollinger. "Making Reuse Cost-Effective." *IEEE Software*, January 1991.

[Berl90] L. Berlin. "When Objects Collide." *Proceedings of the Conference on Object-Oriented Programming: Systems, Languages, and Applications/European Conference on Object-Oriented Programming (OOPSLA/ECOOP '90)*. ACM Press/ Addison-Wesley Publishing Company, Ottawa, Canada, October 1990.

[Bohm90] D. Bohm. "On Dialogue." David Bohm Seminars, Ojai, CA, 1990.

[CFRP93] Software Technology for Adaptable Reliable Systems (STARS). "STARS Conceptual Framework for Reuse Processes (CFRP)." Volume I: "Definition, Version 3.0." Unisys STARS Technical Report STARS-VC-A018/001/00, Reston, VA, October 1993.

[Cox90] Brad Cox. "Planning the Software Industrial Revolution." *IEEE Software*, November 1990.

[Crui91] R. Cruickshank and J. Gaffney. "The Economics of Software Reuse." Software Productivity Consortium Technical Report SPC-92119-CMC, September 1991.

[Dave97] Thomas Davenport and Laurence Prusak. *Working Knowledge: How Organizations Manage What They Know*. Harvard Business School Press, Cambridge, MA, 1997.

[Gaff89] John Gaffney and Thomas Durek. "Software Reuse—Key to Enhanced Productivity: Some Quantitative Models." *Information and Software Technology*, Vol. 31, 1989. Also Software Productivity Consortium Technical Report SPC-TR-88-015, April 1988.

[Gamm95] Erich Gamma, Richard Helm, Ralph Johnson, and John Vlissides. *Design Patterns: Elements of Reusable Object-Oriented Software*. Addison Wesley, Reading MA, 1995.

[Garl95] David Garlan, Robert Allen, and John Ockerbloom. "Architectural Mismatch: Why Reuse Is So Hard." *IEEE Software*, November 1995.

[Gris95] Martin Griss. "Software Reuse: Objects and Frameworks Are Not Enough." *Object Magazine*, February 1995.

[John95] Ralph Johnson. "Why Don't Reuse People Talk About Reusable Software?" *Proceedings of the Seventh Workshop on Institutionalizing Software Reuse*, St. Charles, IL, August 1995.

[Lato96] Larry Latour and Kevin Wentzel. "WISR '95: Seventh Annual Workshop on Software Reuse Summary and Working Group Reports." *Software Engineering Notes*, January, 1996.

[Levi99] Larry Levine. "The 5S Model of Dialogue and Inquiry." Thinking Together: Group Creativity in Action workshop, Lexington, MA, 1999.

[Nona91] I. Nonaka. "The Knowledge-Creating Company." *Harvard Business Review*, November–December 1986.

[Nona95] I. Nonaka and H. Takeuchi. *The Knowledge-Creating Company, How Japanese Companies Create the Dynamics of Innovation.* Oxford University Press, New York, 1995.

[ODM96] Software Technology for Adaptable Reliable Systems (STARS). *Organization Domain Modeling (ODM) Guidebook, Version 2.0.* Unisys STARS Technical Report STARS-VC-A025/001/00, Reston, VA, June 1996.

[Reif91] Donald Reifer. "The Economics of Software Reuse." *Proceedings of ISPA Thirteenth Annual Conference*, New Orleans, May 1991.

[Sche85] E. Schein. *Organizational Culture and Leadership.* Jossey-Bass Publishers, San Francisco, 1985.

[Sche93] E. Schein. "On Dialogue, Culture, and Organizational Learning." MIT Working Paper, Sloan School of Management, MIT, Cambridge, MA, 1993.

[Schw91] Peter Schwartz. *The Art of the Longview, Planning for the Future in an Uncertain World.* Doubleday/Currency, New York, 1991.

[Seng90] Peter Senge. *The Fifth Discipline.* Doubleday/Currency, New York, 1990.

[Weis92] M. Weisbord. *Discovering Common Ground.* Berrett-Koehler, San Francisco, 1995.

[Weis95] M. Weisbord and S. Janoff. *Future Search.* Berrett-Koehler, San Francisco, 1995.

RECOMMENDED READING

The following publications are recommended for further reading.

[Argy91] Chris Argyris. "Teaching Smart People How to Learn." *Harvard Business Review*, May–June 1991.

[Bloc81] P. Block. *Flawless Consulting: A Guide to Getting Your Expertise Used*. Pfeiffer & Company, San Diego, CA, 1981.

[CARD92] Central Archive for Reusable Defense Software (CARDS). "Acquisition Handbook." Unisys STARS Technical Report STARS-AC-04105/001/00, Reston, VA, October 1992.

[Clur72] Harold Clurman. *On Directing*. Collier Books, Macmillan Publishing Company, New York, 1972.

[DoD92] Department of Defense Software Reuse Initiative. "DoD Software Reuse Vision and Strategy." Center for Software Reuse Operations, Technical Report 1222-04-210/40, Alexandria, VA, July 1992.

[Flor78] F. Flores. "Management and Communication in the Office of the Future." Doctoral dissertation, University of California at Berkeley, 1978.

[Laur93] Brenda Laurel. *Computers as Theatre*. Addison Wesley, Reading, MA, 1993.

[Lato90] Larry Latour, Tom Wheeler, and Bill Frakes. "Descriptive and Predictive Aspects of the 3Cs Model: SETA1 Working Group Summary." *First Symposium on Environments and Tools for Ada*, Redondo Beach, CA, May 1990.

[Levi94] Larry Levine. "Listening with Spirit and the Art of Team Dialogue." *Journal of Organization Change Management (JOCM)*. Vol. 7, No. 1, 1994, pp. 61–73.

[Lind93] C. Linde. "Reflections on Workplace Learning." Working paper, Institute for Research on Learning, Palo Alto, CA, 1993.

[Moor91] Geoffrey Moore. *Crossing the Chasm: Marketing and Selling Technology Products to Mainstream Customers*. Harper Business, New York, 1991.

[Mcde95] R. McDermott. "Designing and Improving Knowledge Work." *Journal for Quality and Participation*, March 1995, pp. 72–77.

[RAG93] Software Productivity Consortium. "Reuse Adoption Guidebook." Software Productivity Consortium Technical Report SPC-92051-CMC, Herndon, VA, November 1993.

[RSM93] Software Technology for Adaptable Reliable Systems (STARS). "Reuse Strategy Model: Planning Aid for Reuse-Based Projects." Boeing STARS Deliverable D613-55159, Seattle, WA, July 1993.

[Scho83] Donald Schon. *The Reflective Practitioner: How Professionals Think in Action.* Basic Books, New York, 1983.

[Seng94] Peter Senge et al. *The Fifth Discipline Fieldbook: Strategies and Tools for Building a Learning Organization.* Doubleday/Currency, New York, 1994.

[Weis87] M. Weisbord. *Productive Workplaces.* Jossey-Bass Publishers, San Francisco, 1987.

[Wino87] T. Winograd and F. Flores. *Understanding Computers and Cognition: A New Foundation for Design.* Addison-Wesley, Reading, MA, 1987.

INDEX

ABOUT THE AUTHORS

Sidney C. Bailin is founder and president of Knowledge Evolution, Inc., a company whose goal is to promote knowledge sharing in software and other complex enterprises. Dr. Bailin's software engineering career has spanned 22 years, and has ranged from development of production real-time communications systems to research and development in information agents. Prior to forming Knowledge Evolution, he was a vice president of Engineering at Computer Technology Associates, where for 12 years he played a leading role in that company's software technology program. He was one of the originators of Object-Oriented Requirements Analysis. Dr. Bailin has been active in the software reuse community for the past 14 years, and is best known in that community for introducing the KAPTUR methodology, which links reuse to rationale capture. His most recent work concerns the use of narrative techniques to explain the reasoning behind engineering and business decisions. Dr. Bailin has published roughly two dozen papers on various aspects of software engineering. He currently sits on the Editorial Board of the Encyclopedia of Software Engineering, where he oversees the topics areas of Software Reuse and Artificial Intelligence in Software, and shares responsibility for entries concerning Requirements Analysis.

Mark A. Simos is co-founder of Synquiry Technologies, Ltd., a Boston area software company developing next-generation technology for agent-based metadata modeling and application composition. Mr. Simos has 20 years of experience as a software engineer, researcher, R&D principal investigator, project manager, and consultant. Prior to his work with Synquiry and as an independent consultant, Mr. Simos was a senior research scientist with Unisys. He has more than 15 years of experience in the reuse field, and has authored numerous articles and technical reports on reuse, semantic modeling techniques, and related organizational development issues. Mr. Simos was principal developer of Organization Domain Modeling (ODM), a leading domain engineering methodology that has been applied in varied government and commercial organizations. Mr. Simos also coauthored several other reuse guidebooks under the auspices of the DARPA STARS Program, including the Conceptual Framework for Reuse Processes (CFRP), the Canvas guide for knowledge acquisition planning, and the LIBRA work expanded in this book. He has consulted on strategic reuse and domain modeling with commercial companies such as Hewlett Packard Company, IBM Global Industries, Andersen Consulting, IDX Systems Corporation, FannieMae, and Origin Software/BAS; government and contractor organizations, including Lockheed Martin, Logicon, Air Force CARDS Program, and U.S. Army CECOM/SED; and educational and non-profit organizations. He is also a songwriter and fiddler.

Larry Levine works with organizations to improve competitive advantage through the planning, design, and implementation of strategic change initiatives. He is the co-creator of Whole System Design (WSD), an approach integrating changes to culture, work processes and systems, and technology at the individual, group, and organizational levels. Mr. Levine has 20 years experience in consultation, product development, and management research. Over the past five years, he has led or collaborated on projects within healthcare, high technology and technology-enabled workplaces, including: New England Memorial Hospital, Hallmark Healthcare, Hewlett-Packard, Siemens-Nixdorf, Rational Software, U.S. DoD, New Brunswick Telephone (CANADA), Shell Chemical, Shell Oil, L. L. Bean, Fidelity Investments, Avery-Dennison, IBM, MITRE, Scott Paper, and EMC. Mr. Levine is coauthor of a number of technical reports about software methodology and productivity. These include Organization Domain Modeling (ODM), a domain engineering guidebook; and CANVAS, a knowledge acquisition methodology. He has also authored works in the area of organizational learning, strategic culture change, business process redesign, and team effectiveness. His current research is about understanding and overcoming obstacles to technology change.

Richard Creps is a senior staff applications software engineer with Lockheed Martin Corporation in Manassas, VA. He has over 23 years of commercial and defense-related research and development experience in software engineering, software reuse, software architecture, software engineering tools and environments, application generators, compilers, computer networks, and information security. In recent years, Mr. Creps has worked on several Defense Advanced Research Projects Agency (DARPA) programs, including Evolutionary Design of Complex Software (EDCS) and Software Technology for Adaptable, Reliable Systems (STARS). Under the STARS program, he led numerous tasks relating to software reuse and domain engineering. One of these tasks was the development of the original LIBRA report on which this book is based. More recently, Mr. Creps applied his reuse and architecture expertise on Project Rainbow, an internal Lockheed Martin R&D initiative to improve interoperability, collaboration, and reuse among Lockheed Martin-developed systems. He is currently the system architect on the Joint Theater Logistics Advanced Concept Technology Demonstration (JTL ACTD) program, an effort to develop an advanced, collaborative military operations and logistics planning capability.